EXPLORING THE CAUCASUS IN THE 21ST CENTURY

Exploring the Caucasus in the 21st Century

Essays on Culture, History and Politics

in a Dynamic Context

Edited by

Françoise Companjen

László Marácz

Lia Versteegh

PALLAS PUBLICATIONS

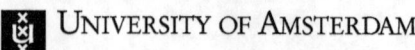

Cover illustration: 'Darial Gorge'. We chose this illustration as a symbol for division and unity in the Caucasus: the mountain range marks a border but the pass has let through many travelers for thousands of years.

Cover design: Neon, design and communications | Sabine Mannel
Lay-out: V-3 Services, Baarn
Map page 9: UvA-Kaartenmakers, Amsterdam

ISBN   978 90 8964 183 0
e-ISBN 978 90 4851 162 4
NUR   686

Table of contents

On the spelling, words and map in this book

The names of people and geographical locations in the Caucasus are spelled in different ways depending on the epoch and nationality of the author. Vocabulary and labels also vary along with the national perspective. In Russian literature, the south Caucasus was referred to as Transcaucasia [Zakavkaz'e]. We simply refer to south and north Caucasus and have described the geographical outline of the region we understand to be the Caucasus in our Introduction. When various names exist for a people we name all: Meskhetian Turks as they are known in the West are also called Muslim Meskhetians in Georgia or Ahiska Turks.

As to the spelling of foreign names, we use the Western style, for example Daghestan → Dagestan; Adyghe → Adyga and Adygeia; Transdniestria → Transnistria.

Foreign words (mostly Russian) such as *krai* and *oblast* (both a term for 'region') or Islamic terms are explained in the text and/or endnotes.

On the map you can find the republics of the Russian Federation in the north Caucasus, such as Kalmykia, Adygeia, Karachai-Cherkessia, Kabardino-Balkaria, Krasnodar *krai*, Stavropol *krai*, Ingushetia, Chechnya and Dagestan. The Pankisi gorge is just over the border with Chechnya in Georgia. A place of conflict is Nagorno-Karabakh in Azerbaijan. South Ossetia and Abkhazia are located between Georgia and the Russian Federation. In relation to the August 2008 war, see the capital of South Ossetia, Tskhinvali, the Roki tunnel close to the Darial Pass. On the Black Sea coast you can find Abkhazia, with, close to the Georgian border, the Kodori valley in north Abkhazia and the Gali region in south Abkhazia close to the Georgian city of Zugdidi. The capital of Abkhazia is Sukhum(i). On the other side of Abkhazia, bordering with Russia on the Black Sea coast, Sochi is mentioned as the city of the Olympic Winter Games in 2014.

Related to the period of 1918-1921 in the south Caucasus, obviously the capitals are important: Tbilisi Georgia, Yerevan Armenia and Baku

Azerbaijan. The cities of Ganja, Azerbaijan's second biggest city (formerly known as Kirovabat), and Sumgait, an industrial city in Azerbaijan on the Caspian coast about 30 km north of the capital Baku, are important. Shusha lies in the disputed region of Nagorno-Karabakh. Stepanakert is the capital of Nagorno-Karabakh.

In connection to the deportations of, for example, the Mezkhetian Turks, the town of Akhaltsikhe in the Georgian province of Samtskhe Javakheti bordering Turkey and Armenia, is relevant.

In connection to the findings of prehistoric bones and skulls, Dmanisi, a village close to Bolnisi, a small town south-west of Tbilisi towards the Armenian border, is important.

Erzinan, Erzurum, Van, Kars, Mount Ararat, all in present day Eastern Turkey, were at one point part of Armenia, the south Caucasus.

The Baku-Tbilisi-Ceyhan pipeline ends on the south coast of Turkey on the Mediterranean, close to the bend where Turkey and Syria share borders.

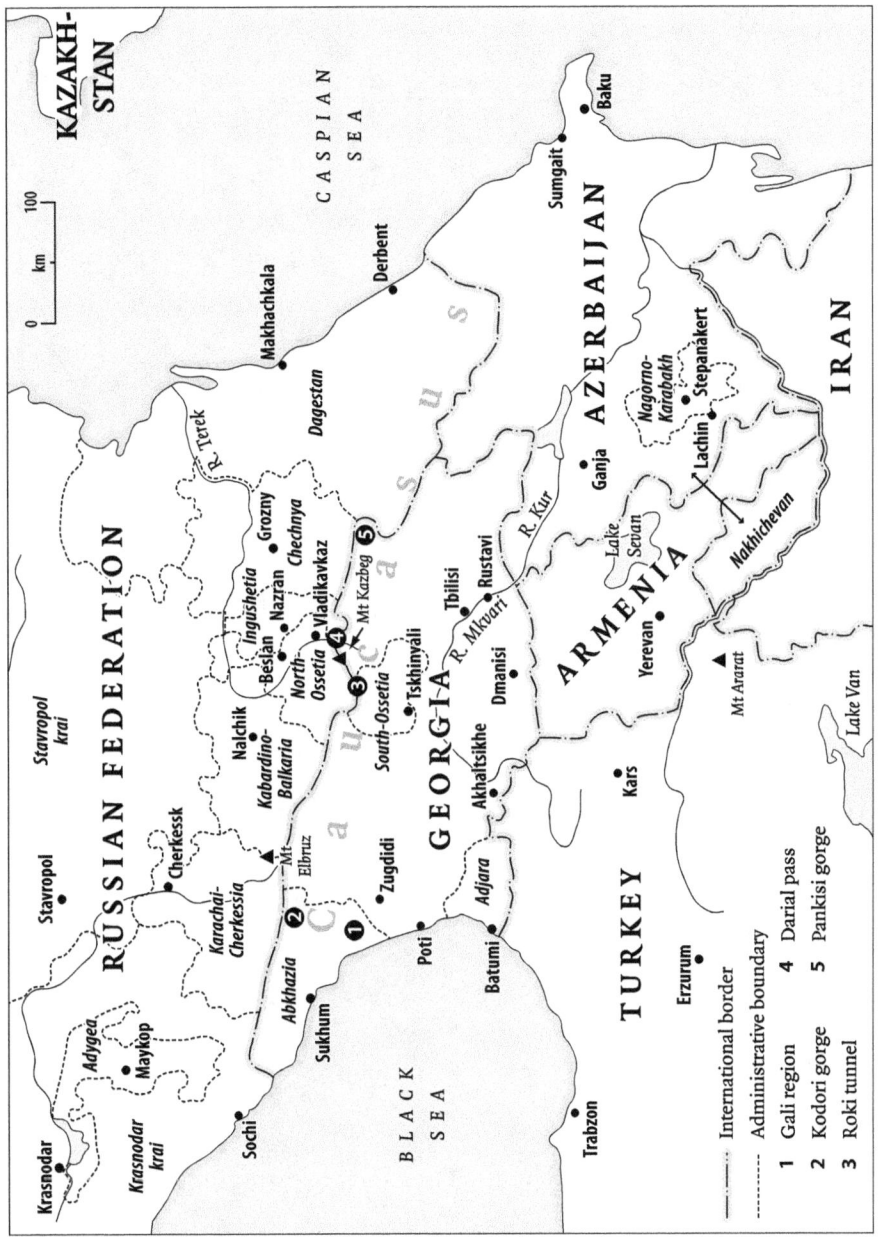

The borders of Abkhazia and South Ossetia are still disputed: Russia recognized these as international but the vast majority of the international community did not.

Introduction

Several events have put the Caucasus on the modern world map after the dissolution of the Soviet Union. Firstly, the break up of the USSR brought independence to the previous Soviet Union Republics. The wars fought about the Autonomous regions (Chechnya, South Ossetia, Abkhazia, Nagorno-Karabakh) within the Union Republics, drew media attention, unlocking an area which had been almost sealed for seventy years. Secondly, the Georgian Revolution of Roses in November 2003 received global media attention. Thirdly, the short, shocking 'peace enforcing' war between Russia and Georgia about the separatist region South Ossetia in August 2008 irrevocably put the Caucasus in the minds of the EU-public at large. Finally, the 2009 memorial of twenty years since the Fall of the Berlin Wall, reinforced the focus on this region, its problems of transition from a closed society based on planned economy and socialism, towards an open society based on a free market economy and democracy.

Since the early nineties, the themes concerning the Caucasus in the public debate have pivoted around transition, energy, Islam, security, and authoritarianism. In the aftermath of the first Iraq war in 1991, the United States of America became interested in Azerbaijan for its strategic geopolitical position and for its energy resources. If not for the force of persuasion by the administration in Washington D.C., the Baku-Tbilisi-Ceyhan pipeline, connecting the Caspian Sea to the Mediterranean, may not have been built. It was opened in May 2005 and since then, a war and a financial crisis later, various other pipelines are in the making.[1]

September 11 unleashed discussions on Islam and on possible threats from Islamic fundamentalists. Specifically related to the Caucasus, the discussion focused on the possible harboring of 'terrorists' or 'freedom fighters' in the Georgian Pankisi gorge, more of a valley really, bordering with Chechnya. These suspicions were an incentive for American training of Georgian border security which was later expanded into a more general training of the Georgian army. With the election of President Saakashvili in January 2004, and his wish to turn westward, the theme of security included negotiations about possibly joining NATO in the future.[2] The necessary preparatory steps thereto also concerned reforms, especially of the judicial system. Western Security Organizations such as the OSCE, which monitor elections, had initially been mild about the standards of fairness of elections and democracy in the South Caucasus. The consistent and increasing authoritarianism reported throughout the Caucasus in UN Human Development Reports this past decade however, caused more discussion on how seriously to assess the wish of some local leaders to integrate into Western institutions.

The heightened media interest and public debates created a need for background information and scientific analyses on how some of these events came about from a historical, cultural and political point of view. This collection of essays exploring the Caucasus in the twenty-first century, aims to provide the reader with such analyses. The task was not easy, because although the term Caucasus in itself has existed for more than two thousand years and may suggest unity and coherence, the region is quite diverse and has multiple linguistic, ethnic, and religious divisions.

Geographically, the Caucasus forms a buffer zone between Russia, Turkey and Iran; between Islam and Orthodox Christianity, divided by a mountain range into a Northern and Southern part. In the north, the Caucasus refers to the republics which are part of the Russian Federation such as Kalmykia, Adygeia, Karachai-Cherkessia, Kabardino-Balkaria, North Ossetia (local name Alania), Krasnodar *krai*,[3] Stavropol *krai*, Ingushetia, Chechnya and Dagestan. The South Caucasus is composed of the Sovereign Republics of Georgia, Armenia and Azerbaijan, including the disputed areas of Abkhazia, South Ossetia and Nagorno Karabakh. Finally, the most Eastern part of Turkey – the strip bordering Georgia (Tao-Klarjeti) to the Turkish port of Trabzon and from Armenia towards the mountain Ararat – can also be included in the Caucasus sphere. Remains of Christian Orthodox churches are still to be found there, and people such as the Laz speak a variation of Kartvelian (Georgian).

It is generally assumed that Aeschylus (525-456 BC) referred to the Caucasus mountains[4] when he described the tragedy of Prometheus who molded man out of clay, taught them arts, brought them fire and civilization, and was chained to a mountain on Zeus' orders as a punishment. A vulture fed each day on his liver, which was restored in the night: a rather powerful image of both birthplace and suffering of mankind. References to the Caucasus are to be found in both the Bible and the Qur'an, with descendants of Noah fanning out towards the East (Caucasus and India) and the West (from Scythes to Germanic tribes). *Genesis* for example cites

Noah's ark as having been stranded on the mountain Ararat (8.4) which is revered by the Armenians as their holy mountain but lies in modern Turkey today. Further down (*Genesis* 10.2,3 and *Ezekiel* 38.4-6), the names of Noah's ancestors are given, of which we cite the line of Japheth, Gomer, Magog and Togarmah. For further information we are dependent on the *Georgian Chronicles*, texts dating from the ninth to the fourteenth century, and the vicissitudes of its translations: the original Georgian text was lost but the Armenian translation survived. In these Chronicles, Kavkas is mentioned as one of Togarmah's (Thargamos') eight giant sons. Thus Togarmah is considered to be a mythical ancestor of the Georgian and Armenian people. In turn, Kavkas' son Dzurdzuk is said to be a mythical ancestor of the Chechens and Ingush.[5]

Linguistically, the term Caucasus can be traced back to the Persian 'kap kah' which means 'big mountain',[6] and was passed on to the Romans and the West through Greek mythology.[7] The Scythian-Türkic *kaukas* can be retraced to *kau/kyu* expressing 'whiteness' (*kyu* meaning swan) and *kas* meaning rock or cliff .[8] Pliny the Elder (Plinius Secundus, first century AD) refers to another word for Caucasus, namely *kroukas*, meaning 'snow-white'. In Türkic *kyrau* is 'frost, icing, snow'. Tolstov in his book *Ancient Khoresm* cites the words of Yakut 'Kas – in the language of the inhabitants of Khoresm is a wall in a desert, surrounded by nothing'.[9] In the Qur'an, in (18:94-98) and (21:96), reference is made to building a protective wall or barrier protecting the civilized nations from the barbarians of the Steppe, such as the biblical tribes of Gog and Magog. Considered to be built by Alexander the Great by some, in Islamic tradition this wall is identified with the sixth-century fortification line at Derbend (today Dagestan). Recent research on its remains claims that the wall must have been built by the Persians who mastered this region until the sixth century.[10]

The Caucasus as a place of origin persists in the hypothesis developed, among others, by the German anthropologist/naturalist Johann Friedrich Blumenbach (1752-1840), namely, that the Caucasus was with great probability the birthplace of (white) mankind, hence the concept of the 'Caucasian race'.[11] He based this idea on 'craniology', the measurement of skulls, finding much resemblance between a skull in Georgia and one in Germany. The association of the Caucasus with place of origin revived when a jaw and partial skulls were found in Dmanisi, Georgia in diggings from 1991 to 1991. These findings were estimated to be about 1.7 to 1.75 million years old (*Homo ergaster*). They were accompanied by stone tools and bones of prehistoric animals such as the saber toothed tiger. The findings posed a challenge to evolutionary and migration theory. In a nutshell, the debate concentrates on whether *Homo Ergaster* (up to 1.8 million years old) found in several places in Eastern and Southern Africa, is a separate species from the younger, Eurasian *Homo Erectus*, or whether they are connected in an evolutionary line. David Lordkipanidze, the leader of the Dmanisi excavation team, has published about these findings in *Nature*.[12] He currently defends the hypothesis (although admittedly the record is still patchy) that *Homo ergaster* is an ancestor of the *Homo erectus*. The findings of Dmanisi are close to the stem from which *Homo erectus* evolved.

Between the myths of ancient Greece, religious texts and present day archaeological findings in the Caucasus, lies a history of conquests, deportations and resistance, dating from Arab, to Mongol, to Persian, to Ottoman, to Russian invasions. The occupation by the nineteenth-century imperialist Russian empire put a halt to further invasions. Of the South Caucasus countries Georgia was the first to be annexed in 1801 by the Russian Czar, in breach of a covenant between Russia and Georgia. It took another decade to take Azerbaijan and Armenia from the Persians and Ottomans, finalizing the treaty by 1829.

Georgia and Armenia are Christian nations with a large aristocratic, affiliated elite. The Armenian-Georgian Bagrationi dynasty for example is said to descend back to King David. This elite was relatively easily incorporated into Russian high society: during the nineteenth century it was common for Georgian aristocracy to serve in the Russian army. It took longer however to pacify the Northern, Muslim Caucasus of 'independent Chechen and Dagestani mountain communities under Imam Shamil in the East (until 1859) and against the Circassians in the West (until 1864)'.[13] But Russification and Sovietization of the whole region did occur, with the exception of a small interval of independence for the South Caucasus republics between 1918-1921.

It is safe to conclude that the Caucasus, rich in cultural, ethnic, and linguistic diversity, and having a history of shifting partnerships – sometimes fighting a common enemy, sometimes each other – does share some commonalities. As illustrated above, the Caucasus has been described as a cradle of mankind, a protective buffer zone and a place of suffering in classical myths, religious texts and early anthropology. From a local, insider perspective, a sense of belonging, 'a feeling of brotherhood'[14] and a love of traditional society transcend equally strong differences in language, religion and ethnicity. In the north-eastern Caucasus, Arabic served as the main medium for inter- ethnic communication for hundreds of years, before it was replaced by Russian in the twentieth century for official purposes. Also the multi ethnic *jihad* movement of the nineteenth and twentieth centuries is a binding force in the Sunni North Caucasus. More generally, other binding elements throughout the whole of the (rural) Caucasus are blood feud, 'bride-nappings', shared sagas and legends (such as *The Knight in the Panther's Skin*, and *Nart*),[15] clans, a strong sense of honor and great hospitality. In short, these are characteristics of traditional society, traces of which can be found in modern life through the essentialist understanding of culture and identity as expressed in national debates on history, ethnicity and religion.

In view of the aforementioned, we chose an ancient map for the cover of this book, with the Darial pass or gorge depending on the precise location, as an insert, for its symbolism: a pass connecting the Caucasus people in spite of the high mountains separating them. Darial originally comes from the Persian, meaning Gate of the Alans. The Scythes passed through there more than two thousand years ago, as did other migrants. Pliny the Elder also noted the 'Caucasian Gate' in reference to the Darial pass;[16] the German army wanted to pass through it during World War II to reach the oil fields of Baku, to no avail. The Darial pass incorporated into the novels of Pushkin, Lermontov and Tolstoy is thus of strategic importance as a symbol of unity and division in the Caucasus.

Since the Caucasus was colonized by the Czarist empire and later incorporated into the Soviet Union, it is not so extraordinary that literature on the (Trans)Caucasus[17] is more abundant from Russian than other sources. Peter the Great (d. 1725), after the reforms following his travels to Europe, encouraged the study of the population of the empire. The first Russian ethnographic surveys were disseminated in the 1730s. From the 1730s to the 1770s the Russian Academy of Sciences sponsored major expeditions dedicated to the study of the empire led by Gerhard Friedrich Müller (1705-1783) and Peter Pallas (1741-1811). These academic expeditions covered a vast area from Siberia to the Caucasus.

The more recent travel accounts are from German ethnographers such as Johann Anton Güldenstädt (1745-1781). His expedition journal was published after his death by Peter Pallas in *Reisen durch Russland und im Caucasischen Gebürge* (Travels in Russia and the Mountains of the Caucasus) (1787-91). A generation later we have to mention two famous and influential people: the universal scholar Alexander Von Humboldt (1769-1859) who led an expedition to Russia in 1829 including the Caucasus; and the linguist and orientalist who only later studied the Caucasus, Julius von Klaproth (1783-1835). The Russian ethnographer, Semyon Bronevskii, in *People of the Caucasus* (1823) popularized the fieldwork of earlier German studies.[18]

The August 2008 war in the context of transition

The two recurrent subjects in this book are the transition process[19] and the Russian-Georgian August 2008 war. After the scare of the Russia-Georgia war the theme of transition gained renewed impetus. For two decades The Newly Independent States in the post-Communist discourse had been presented as countries in transition from a closed, dictatorial society towards an open democratic society with a free market economy. By Western European norms and standards this means having free and fair elections, respect for Human Rights, and to a certain extent the sharing of economic benefits. With the tendency towards authoritarianism in the South Caucasus, and the persisting poverty for a large portion of the population, and the continuing ethnic strife, some authors in recent publications on the Russian Federation and the Caucasus prefer to use the concept *transformation*. The difference between the two concepts is that transformation explicitly means changing from one form into another without alteration of value, whereas the concept of transition refers to a passage from one condition to another, without stressing the necessary change even though heading towards a specific goal. Transformation implies an actual and collective normative change. In this volume the different authors generally refer to transition and sometimes to transformation.

Several themes come to the surface when discussing transition and the background of the August war in South Ossetia. The relations within the Russian Federation with the North Caucasus republics and between Russia and the South Caucasus Republics are historically colored by the former Russian empire and the former Soviet Union. The past political fissures in the Communist Party (Bolsheviks 'majority' and Mensheviks 'minority'[20]), changes in constitutions (Soviet 1936, 1977, and after independence 1995), ethnic-territorial policy and the fights for independence which took place in an anarchic context of the early nineties with many guns available,[21] cash money and kidnappings. All these factors play a role in the transition process and in the various hostilities that have taken place in the past two decades: conflicts which were 'frozen' but not concluded. Let us go over these themes shortly one by one.

Breaking out of the Soviet Union obviously entails a complex process of re-defining one's identity and of one's renewed relation with(in) the Russian Federation. And the same applies to the Russian Federation: how to 'let go'? Where do spheres of influence and responsibilities end? Some Newly Independent States immediately joined the Russian-lead Commonwealth of Independent States voluntarily seeking protection from and cooperation with Russia. Others managed to join yet maintain diplomatic distance; still others chose a clear break yet later had to grudgingly ask for help. Both the large Russian market (importing goods from the Caucasus) and Russian political influence affect the course of the transition and had a negative impact on the negotiations with the break-away regions.

Even former Communist Party politics in the onset to the Russian revolutionary period in 1917 still cast its shadow in today's transition period: the difference of opinion between the Bolsheviks and the Mensheviks. Whilst both Bolshevism and Menshevism were part of the Russian revolutionary movement that emerged in 1903 against the Russian Czar, this distinction became a recurring fault line in Communist Party politics after 1917. As it happened the Abkhazian and South Ossetian leaders had Bolshevik sympathies and used this to try and get more favorable agreements from Moscow to the detriment of Menshevik Georgia; for example with regard to the measure of autonomy allowed on Georgian territory. This political distinction only added to existing constitutional borders influencing the direction of orientation: towards Moscow or Tbilisi.

The Soviet policy of tying ethnicity to territory giving varying degrees of autonomy to Union Republics, Autonomous Republics and Autonomous *oblasts* also lay a foundation for fault lines within the Republics, making it difficult to maintain their territorial integrity. The tying of ethnicity to passports and territory flavors the process of forming a nation next to forming a modern state. Nationhood and statehood in the context of transition need not coincide. Some groups may feel more loyal to their ethnicity or religion than to the state or republic. We see ethnic strife and nationalism in different areas: Alanian in North and South Ossetia, the Abkhaz and the Georgian, the Armenian and Azeri in Nagorno Karabakh, and in Chechnya with two bloody wars for independence.

In Chechnya, as Falkowksi[22] explains, the conflict has shifted somewhat from fighting against the Russian soldiers, to a civil conflict between separatist militants and Chechens who are pro-Russia. The conflict has spilled over into Ingushetia, Dagestan and Kabardino-Balkaria, thereby also becoming a regional fight between Caucasian Islamists and the authorities. Although a renewed outbreak of large scale military force is unlikely in the near future, the demand for an ever-wider autonomy remains: terrorist attacks have resurged recently.[23] Moscow's strategy of buying off corrupt local elites in the region, has according to Trenin, not resulted in deep-rooted stability. Moscow has put a significant amount of money into the reconstruction of Chechnya, which did help pacify the region for a number of years. In everyday practice Chechnya has remained beyond the control of the Russian legal system. Its own laws (traditional, *'adat, sharia*) prevail in the social sphere. But Russia's loosening grip could encourage extremists to rekindle attacks and the demand for formal autonomy. Moreover, by recognizing the independence of Abkhazia and South Ossetia, Russia has created a precedent for Chechnya.

The mentioning of ethnicity/nationality in one's Soviet passport, the tying of ethnicity to territory, besides having a positive side of recognition, also had a downside to it in the way it was effectively put to use. Especially under Stalin,[24] many deportations took place on the basis of ethnicity. He ordered 600,000 Chechens to be deported to Kazakhstan on suspicion of collaboration with the German army in World War II. The Meskhetian Turks, also called Muslim Meskhetians (especially in Georgia) or Ahiska Turks, were deported to the Northern Caucasus and to Central Asia mostly from the Samtskhe-Javakheti region (Akhaltsikhe) in Georgia.[25] This is a region bordering Turkey and Armenia. Interestingly, one of the conditions for entering the Council of Europe was that Georgia should make repatriation and resettlement possible for them. A law on repatriation has been prepared and has recently (2010) been passed in the Georgian Parliament. The first requests for resettlement have been received.[26] Earlier, the USA resettled over 10,000 Meskhetian Turks in the USA from Krasnodar *krai.*

Obviously, this persistent focus on ethnicity and the still unresolved conflicts (for instance Nagorno-Karabakh) does not ease the process of transition to democracy, which is based on the concept of citizenship and statehood. Either culture and identity (the nationhood concepts) should be included or perhaps the term transition should be replaced by transformation?

The elaboration in the chapters[27]

So many interesting accounts exist on exploring the Caucasus in past centuries that we follow suit in the twenty-first century. After all, historical and societal accounts are re-written from a present day perspective and context. Without going into a whole overview of past expeditions through the Caucasus we 'enter' this volume through one expedition leader, the talented Hungarian linguist Count Bálint de Szentkatolna (1844-1913) who studied the Turanian languages.[28] László Marácz (Chapter 1) gives an account of the Hungarian expedition to the Caucasus lead by Count Zichy in 1895. Among the participants was a Hungarian linguist, Gábor Bálint de

Szentkatolna, who took the opportunity to study the Western Caucasian language Kabardian, which he thought was related to Hungarian and other Turanian languages. He compiled a dictionary of Kabardian which today serves as a collective memory for the present-day identity formation of Kabardians. His work serves as a source for them to re-invent themselves in the post-communist transition period today.

René Does (Chapter 2) gives an overview of peoples of the Caucasus in a historical context of deportations and regional conflicts up to the August 2008 war. He explains the soviet territorial arrangements. The relation between passports, ethnicity and nationalism is brought to the fore. This subject also played a role in the onset to the August 2008 war with Russians handing out Russian passports to South Ossetians and Abkhazians. The issue is thorny: sometimes the Soviets and Russians are accused of playing divide and rule politics on the basis of the different ethnicities in the Caucasus. But had they not allowed people to keep their nationality/ethnicity this would have evoked heavy protests as well. The removal of ethnicity from Georgian passports after 1999, for example, provoked a heavy debate in Georgia, as Reisner shows in Chapter 7. In other words, there are arguments for and against whether the Soviet Party rulers used ethnicity as a divide and rule strategy or whether it was a policy respecting ethnicity in an ethno-federal state.

In Chapter 3, Micha Kemper goes back to the colonial past of the great Russian Empire. The process of national awakening and modernization in the Caucasus to a certain extent runs parallel to Czarist and Soviet influence. The Soviets brought industrial and cultural reforms. The use of national languages was encouraged and Russian was used as inter-ethnic idiom. In the Islamic North, education and the learning of Arabic was institutionalized in the religious schools (*madrasas*); therefore the Soviet aim was to eradicate the Arabic as much as possible in favor of local vernacular or Russian. Nevertheless, paradoxically, Soviet scholars after WWII tried to rescue the rich Arabic manuscript heritage of Dagestan.

The Chechen case (Marc Jansen, Chapter 4) is directly related to the August 2008 war by its outcome. Since the Russian Federation has recognized South Ossetia and Abkhazia as independent states, this could be interpreted by Chechens as a precedent to recognize Chechnya as well. Chechnya has fought two bloody wars for its own independence, without formal success so far, but with *de facto* autonomy and chances for *de jure* autonomy growing. Marc Jansen delves into the roots of the Chechen-Russian conflict that has intensified after the collapse of the Soviet Union.

Françoise Companjen (Chapter 5) introduces the concept of transition and then analyses the recent political history of the South Caucasus using this concept as an analytical frame. After twenty years of transition the concept needs to be adjusted for the South Caucasus. The process and context clearly are different than in the West. The South Caucasus history has been one of aristocratic elites in the nineteenth century merging with Russian social structures. The twentieth century Soviet empire had its Communist Party nomenclature elites. For modernization and democratization, a shift from 'empire-soviet-elitist rule' to much more active participation by the people ('the nation', civil society) in reciprocal relations, is needed. Contrary to the West, where civil society emerged more or less against the state, the southern Caucasus countries would need a simultaneous strengthening of the state and of civil society.

Max Bader (Chapter 6) elaborates on authoritarianism in the South Caucasus. According to the literature he draws upon, the South Caucasus states have failed to establish a civil democratic society and can be categorized as authoritarian political systems. He argues just how different parties in the South Caucasus have been from their counterparts in western democracies. They are almost entirely elite-driven. The parties more often serve self-interested financial purposes rather than democratic goals. The institutional arrangements (incentive structures and clans) have constrained the leverage of political parties. Finally he discusses the party types which have been products of authoritarian practices. Of the three dominant types: vote seeking, office seeking and policy seeking (which is the most conducive to democratization) the first two are dominant and the last type is virtually absent in the South Caucasus.

The question whether to mention ethnicity in one's passport (instead of focusing on citizenship) continued well into President Shevardnadze's rule in Georgia (1992-2003). Oliver Reisner (Chapter 7) delves into this debate tied to nationalism and nationhood, as illustrated through an interesting and humorous analysis of Georgian newspapers in the late nineties. Nationalism has a different meaning and importance in the South Caucasus where patriotism is taught as a virtue and where nationalism is a driving force to save the national heritage against Russification or Westernization. Nationhood and statehood need not overlap.

We then move to the war fought in South Ossetia mostly, in August 2008. An EU-Independent International Fact-Finding Mission lead by the Swiss diplomat Heidi Tagliavini presented a three-volume report on September 30th, 2009. The mission's goal was to 'investigate the origins and the course of the conflict in Georgia, including with regard to international law (...), humanitarian law and human rights, and the accusations made in that context (...)'.[29] The war did not end the political conflict. Nor were any of the background issues resolved. The report stresses it cannot claim veracity or completeness, one reason for which publications on the war and the unresolved issues beneath it will continue to appear for some time. A few of the unresolved but related issues are explained in chapters 8 (Companjen) and 9 (Hille) on this interstate and intrastate conflict. This recent example of war in the Caucasus region after many more fights were fought in the past two decades shows the fragility of the transition process in the Caucasus.

Charlotte Hille (Chapter 9) analyses the legal aspects of Georgia's territorial integrity and the legal status of Abkhazia and South Ossetia at the negotiations in Geneva. So far, it is clear that the position of Russia and Georgia is stronger than the position of Abkhazia and South Ossetia. The UN, OSCE and EU have pledged adherence to the principle of Georgian territorial integrity. Hille draws comparisons with Kosovo and Quebec. The possibilities by Georgia to include Abkhazia in a Federal or Confederal State have been severely diminished after the Russian and Nicaraguan recognition of the autonomous regions.

Lia Versteegh (Chapter 10) in the context of transition, continues on the judicial theme and civil society by comparing Freedom of Speech in Azerbaijan and Armenia. She stresses the rights of the victims of violations in proceedings before the Court of Human Rights in Strasbourg. To that purpose she exhibits the working of article 10 of the European Convention under which complaints regarding the lack of commitment to the Convention in Caucasus States are elaborated. Is civil society organized according to the freedoms of the European Convention of Human Rights agreed upon by some Caucasus countries? The Convention takes freedom as a point of departure; only under specific conditions can this freedom be restricted. From the perspective of the Council of Europe the legal situation of civil society should be looked at.

The closest one can ever get to freedom of expression, is probably through the arts. Eva Navarro (Chapter 11) in a personal account gives us an exposé on memory and time as themes in the art of the Caucasus which stands – 'art is unable to lie' – between tradition and modernity: art carries influences of the past. In the case of modern Azeri art, influence from carpet art and miniature paintings can be discerned. In the case of Armenian art, the family is a recurring theme, and the use of color is influenced by the brilliant manuscript illustrations. Applying Barthe's concept of mediation to the visual arts, the paintings mediate ideas, for instance the

Soviet Social Realism versus the European Avant Garde. Navarro demonstrates the 'historical' tension between the artist as an individual defending total freedom of creativity against any system, authoritarian or not.

We hope this introduction will enhance insight on the Caucasus and cogently encourage European Union citizens and civil servants to develop more policy towards the South Caucasus. With the last recent expansion of the EU in 2007 it has become a Black Sea power. After the August 2008 war, the Caucasus in political debates was regularly referred to as 'Russia's backyard' a point which Moscow most likely wanted to stress with its military action. In view of the EU now being a Black Sea power, and with Turkey's preparation for EU standards, perhaps the neighboring South Caucasus should be redefined as 'Europe's front yard'. In any case we should not be hindered by lack of knowledge about the Caucasus to develop policy towards that region. To facilitate the process of transition, the EU has developed several programs, such as the TACIS programme in the early nineties and the EU-sponsored transport corridor TRACE-CA-agreement of 1998 which aims to develop an East-West trade route; the Partnership and Cooperation Agreement (PCA) in 1999, and the European Neighborhood Policy (ENP) since 2004 which has more or less been replaced by the Eastern Partnership (EP) of 2008/2009. But it can be heard regularly that background information on the Caucasus is spread thinly. Hopefully this contribution can help fill this gap.

Notes

1   The BTC pipeline counterbalances the dependency on the Baku-Novorossi-ysk oil line that connects Baku with Southern Russia. Parallel to the oil pipeline of Baku-Tbilisi-Ceyhan runs the so-called Southern Caucasus Pipeline, a gas pipeline that follows the Baku-Tbilisi-Ceyhan oil pipeline until Turkish Erzurum. At both ends of this pipeline two further extensions are planned but are not ready yet. From Erzurum to Central Europe the EU-sponsored Nabucco gas pipeline will be constructed and from Baku to Türkmenbas-sy in Turkmenistan, the so-called Trans-Caspian gas pipeline will be built. These planned gas pipelines should make Europe less dependent on the Blue Stream, a major trans-Black Sea gas pipeline that carries natural gas from Russia into Turkey. The Blue Stream project is dominated by Russia and its state energy company Gazprom.

2   These foresights for Georgia and Ukraine were overshadowed by the war between Russia and Georgia in August 2008.

3   *krai* is a term used to refer to nine of Russia's 83 federal subjects. The term is often translated as territory, province, country or region. It can also mean border, or place of the *cut-off.* There is no difference in legal status between the *krais* and the *oblasts.*

4   Some mention Kazbek in particular: Salkeld, A. & J.L. Bermúdez (1993:2). *On the Edge of Europe. Mountaineering in the Caucasus.* London: Hodder & Stoughton. These authors also mention the mountains of Kaf in the *Arabian Nights* as identified with the Caucasus (1993:3).

5   The following authors all based themselves on the *Georgian Chronicles*: Rapp, S.H. jr. (2003). *Studies in medieval Georgian historiography: Early texts and Eurasian contexts.* Corpus Scriptorum Christianorum Orientalium, 601, subsidia, 113; Qoranashvili, K. (1995). *Questions of Ethnic Identity According to Leonti Mroveli's Historical Chronicles*, Studies, Vol. 1, Tbilisi; Toumanoff, C. (1963). *Studies in Christian Caucasian History.* Georgetown University Press.

6   Gamkrelidze, Th. V. (1998: 40-42) *Postcommunist Democratic Changes and Geopolitics in the South Caucasus.* International Centre for East West Relations. Tbilisi.http://www.parliament.ge/files/327_2288_943216_caucasus.pdf

7   We skip the discussion about the possible (re)invention of classical texts in the Middle Ages.

8   Latyshev, V.V. (1896:185). *News of the Greek and Latin ancient writers about Scythia and Caucasus.* Volume 1, Issue 2 (Russian). In: Mirfatyh Zakiev *Ethnic Roots of the Tatar People.* (The Internet Visited February 19, 2010) http://www.hunmagyar.org/turan/tatar/tatar-origin.html

9   Tolstov, S.P. (1948:11). *Ancient Khoresm.* Moscow. In: *Scytho-Sarmatian ethnic roots of Türks* Origin of Türks and Tatars Part One Scytho-Sarmatian ethnic roots of Türks (Posted: 13-Oct-2009 at 10:02; visited 19 February 2010) http://www.allempires.com/Forum/forum_posts.asp?TID=27833.

10   See Kemper, Chapter 3 in this volume and a recent Hungarian language article by a Dagestan scholar: Murtazali S. Gadzsijev (2009). Hunok és türkök támadásai és a szanszanidák erödítési tevékenysége a kelet-Kaukázusban. (The attacks of the Huns and the Turks and the fortification activities of the Sansanides in the Eastern Caucasus). In: L. Marácz and B. Obrusánszky (2009: 237-264) *A hunok öröksége.* Budapest: Hun-Idea.

11   He was supported in this 'Caucasian hypothesis' by others such as the French doctor and pharmacist Jean Joseph-Virey, Louis Antoine Desmoulines and the French diplomat Arthur de Gobineau.

12   Lordkipanidze, D. c.s. (2007: 305-310). 'Postcranial Evidence from early Homo, from Dmanisi Georgia' in: *Nature* nr 449 xiii 20, September.

13 Kemper, M. (2007: 119). 'Caucasus'. In: Manfred Beller and Joep Leerssen (eds.) *Imagology. The cultural construction and literary representation of national characters*. Amsterdam: Rodopi. King, C., (2008: 77-84). *The Ghost of Freedom: A history of the Caucasus*. Oxford and New York: Oxford University Press.

14 This phrase was used several times during Companjen's interviews with Georgian NGO leaders when talking for example about Chechyans and Zviad Gamsakhurdia's grave in Chechnya in the 1990s.

15 Several translations exist of Shota Rustaveli's *vepkhistqaosani*, for example by Marjori Wardrop (1912) or Vera Urushadze (1979); for *Nart* we refer to Colarusso, J. (2002) *Nart Sagas from the Caucasus: Myths and Legends from the Circassians, Abazas, Abkhaz, and Ubykhs*. Princeton University Press.

16 Kavtaradze, G..L. (2009). *The Geopolitical Role of the Caucasus Mountains from the Historical Perspective. Causes for War – Prospects for Peace* . Patriarchate of the Georgian Orthodox Church. Konrad Adenauer Foundation. http://www.scribd.com/doc/24299269/G-L-Kavtaradze-The-Geopolitical-Role-of-the-Caucasus-Mountains-from-the-Historical-Perspective (Visited January 2010)

17 From the perspective of the Russian Empire and Soviet Union the South Caucasus was seen and named as Transcaucasia [Russ. Zakavkaz'e].

18 King (2008: 106). ibid.

19 See Companjen (2004). *Between Tradition and Modernity*. Ph.d. Amsterdam and Chapter 5 for an elaboration on the concept of transition.

20 Whilst both Bolshevism and Menshevism were part of the Russian revolutionary movement that emerged in 1903 against the Russian Czar, this distinction became a recurring fault line in Communist Party politics after 1917. We skip the nuance Trotsky made between Bolsheviks and bolshevism.

21 For example, the *mkhedrioni*, a militia of about 3000 men with guns, informally 'ruled' over Georgia in 1992.

22 Falkowski, M. (2007). *Chechnya: Between a Caucasian Jihad and 'hidden' separatism*. Warsaw: Centre for Eastern Studies.

23 Trenin, D. (2009:69). Russia Reborn. In: *Foreign Affairs*. Volume 88 nr 6.

24 By birth his name was Soso Djugashvili, born in Gori, Georgia.

25 See Trier, T. & A. Khanzin (eds) (2007). *The Meskhetian Turks at a Crossroads. Integration, Repatriation or Resettlement?* Gesellschaftliche Transformationen/Societal Transformations. Volume 10. Münster: LIT Verlag.

26 Institute for Policy Studies Tbilisi. Personal note to F.J.Companjen

27 The individual chapters may contain points of view which are not necessarily underscored by the editors.

28 'Turanian' covers Central Asian empires such as the Hun, the Turkic, and the

Mongolian. A contested hypothesis in some comparative linguistic analysis is that Hungarian, Turkic, Finnish and a few Caucasian languages are related, hence the interest of some Hungarian scholars for their own linguistic and cultural roots in the Caucasus.

29 Independent International Fact Finding Mission Report (September 30th , 2009) Volume 1, page 5.

1 Gábor Bálint de Szentkatolna (1844-1913) and the Study of Kabardian

László Marácz

Gábor Bálint de Szentkatolna was one of the most talented Hungarian linguists of the late nineteenth century and the beginning of the twentieth century. He devoted his life to the study of the so-called 'Turanian' languages, i.e. the hypothesized language family of Uralic, Altaic and Dravidian languages. In the second half of the nineteenth century, the languages of the Caucasus were also considered to be scattered members of this language family. This Hungarian linguist wrote a number of grammars and dictionaries of these languages.

Bálint de Szentkatolna also wrote a grammar and a dictionary of the Western Caucasian language, Kabardian, which he thought to be closely related to Hungarian. The Kabardian language is presently spoken by 443,000 persons in Russia, who live in the Kabardino-Balkaria and Karachai-Cherkessia native territories. The capital of these territories is Naltshik. The other speakers of Kabardian, more than one million of them, can be found in Turkey and in the Middle East. The fact that half of the Kabardian population has left its Northern Caucasian homeland is due to Russian colonial policy, starting in the beginning of the nineteenth century.

Kabardian is generally considered to be a rather difficult language, and its sound system, especially, is rather complicated. The language counts 56 sounds, having only a few vowels. The set of consonants includes rare fricatives and affricatives, like the ejective ones displaying a clear phonemic distinction. Kabardian is closely related to Adyga that is spoken by 125,000 people in Russia, in the Northern Caucasian Adygeian Republic, of which Maikop is the capital.

Most linguists, including Bálint de Szentkatolna, claimed that Adyga and Kabardian are only dialectical variants of Circassian.[1] In the prefaces of his Kabardian grammar and dictionary, the terms Adyga, Circassian and Kabardian are used as alternates. The term Adyga actually functions as a kind of super-category covering Circassian and Kabardian.[2] According to the Russian scholar, Klimov, (1969, 135) the Adyga-Circassian-Kabardian language is formed with Abkhaz and Ubyx that are no longer spoken in the

Western Caucasian language group. The Western Caucasian languages are related to the Eastern Caucasian languages, including Avar, Chechen and Ingush, yielding the family of Northern Caucasian languages.[3]

In this paper, we will address the question of how a Hungarian linguist became interested in the study of a complicated Caucasian language like Kabardian. It will be argued that this was due to three reasons. Firstly, Bálint de Szentkatolna was of Székely stock. The Székely is an ethnic Hungarian group living in the southern region of Transylvania, the so-called Székelyland at the foot of the Eastern Carpathians. Transylvania belongs presently to Romania but, before the First World War, it was under the sovereignty of the Hungarian Kingdom. Secondly, Bálint de Szentkatolna was a member of the Zichy-expedition to the Caucasus, in 1895, visiting the territories where Kabardian was still spoken. Thirdly, the Székely linguist was convinced of the fact that the so-called Turanian languages, including Kabardian, were related.[4] Finally, we will evaluate Bálint de Szentkatolna's study of the Kabardian language.

The Székely heritage

The Székely, Gábor Bálint de Szentkatolnai, was born on March 13, 1844, to Endre Bálint and Ágnes Illyés, in the village of Szentkatolna, in the County of Háromszék, which was one of the Székely counties of the Hungarian Kingdom. Szentkatolna was a typical Székely village in the so-called Székelyland in the southern part of Transylvania. The Székely were border-guards in the old Hungarian Kingdom, protecting the south-eastern borders, i.e. the mountain range of the Eastern Carpathians. Because of this, most of the Székely were granted nobility by the Hungarians kings or rulers of the semi-independent Transylvanian principality that existed in the seventeenth century, during the Ottoman occupation of Hungary.[5] The ancestors of Gábor Bálint had been granted nobility as well. They received nobility from the Habsburg King of Hungary, Rudolf (1572-1608) and it was reinforced by Prince Gábor Rákóczy I of Transylvania (1630-1648). The Bálint family originally lived in the neighboring village of Lemhény. At the beginning of the seventeenth century, one of their branches moved to Szentkatolna. Hence, instead of referring to Lemhény in their noble title, the branch, to which Gábor Bálint belonged, used the Hungarian style notation *Szentkatolnai* meaning 'from Szentkatolna' or the French style notation with *de*, i.e. 'De Szentkatolna' for international use expressing nobility.[6]

The Székely nobility has always been a group among the Hungarians who have a strong awareness of their Hungarian identity. The Székely military played an important role in the Hungarian Revolution and War of Independence of 1848-1849 against the Austrian absolutism of the Habsburgs. Gábor Bálint de Szenkatolna's father also joined the Hungarian *honvéd* 'army', established by the leader of the Hungarian War of Independence, Lajos Kossuth, in order to fight the Austrian troops and, later in 1849, the Czarist Russian troops that came to the support of the Austrian Emperor, Franz Jozef. The inhabitants of the village of Szentkatolna, just like other Hungarians, were punished severely for their rebellion against the Austrians and the House of Habsburg. The village had to accept the burden of the presence of the Russian soldiers and their horses.[7] Because the Hungarian Revolution and the War of Independence was crushed brutally by the Austrians, the Hungarians took an anti-Austro-German stance in the second half of the nineteenth century, although politically the Austrian and Hungarian conflict was pacified by the *Augleich (Compromise) of* 1867, when the Austrians recognized Hungary as equal to Austria, within the framework of the Austro-Hungarian Dual Monarchy. Hence, little Gábor, who was four years-old at the beginning of the Hungarian Revolution in 1848, grew up in an anti-Austro-German atmosphere in a humiliated Hungary, where the Hungarian defeat at the hands of the Austrians and the Russians was remembered bitterly. Another important feature of the Székely-Hungarian heritage was the legendary remembrance of the Orientalist, Sándor Csoma de Kőrös (1784-1842), who tried to solve the puzzle of the Hungarian *Urheimat* in Central Asia.

Bálint de Szentkatolna was born only shortly after one of the most celebrated fellow Székely heroes of his time, Sándor Csoma de Kőrös, died in 1842, in far away Darjeeling.[8] The remembrance of the Székely Orientalist must have been especially strong in the Székelyland, where Csoma de Kőrös was born. His birth village was actually quite close to Szentkatolna, Gábor's birthplace. Szentkatolna is only twenty kilometres away from Kőrös, both villages lying in the County of Háromszék.[9] Sándor Csoma de Kőrös had studied Orientalism at the University of Göttingen in Germany, and left for Central Asia in 1821 to search for the ancient Hungarian homeland. Csoma de Kőrös, like most of his contemporary Hungarians, was convinced of the fact that the Hungarians were descendants of the Huns and that their ancient homeland must have been somewhere in Central Asia. The belief in the Hunnic origin of the Hungarians is especially strong among the Székely. In their legends and folklore, the Székely are considered to be one of the peoples that succeeded the Huns and who settled, under the leadership of their Prince Csaba, in the southern parts of Transylvania, after the collapse of the Hunnic Empire of Attila.

Csoma de Kőrös arrived on July, 16 1822 in Kashmir, where he met William Moorcroft, an official of the British East India Company. It was William Moorcroft who foresaw a struggle between Britain and Russia for influence in Central Asia, the so-called Great Game.[10] It was the same William Moorcroft, who put the Székely-Hungarian scholar on the track of Tibetan studies, offering him a scholarship from the Royal Asiatic Society to study the Tibetan language and culture. When Csoma de Kőrös died in 1842, in Darjeeling, on his way to the capital of Tibet, Lhasa, it was a complete mystery what he had discovered about the ancient Hungarian homeland in the libraries of the Tibetan monasteries. In any case, a side-effect of his quest for the ancient Hungarian homeland would turn out to be his greatest achievement, namely the publication of a Tibetan grammar and dictionary.

A number of myths, legends and rumors started to spread about Sándor Csoma de Kőrös in his native country, Hungary, after his unfortunate death. These stories had an enormous appeal to the fantasy of young Hungarians. A scholar without any real help, suffering from poverty and tough climate in the Himalayas, had sacrificed his life to solve the puzzle of the origins of Hungarians. The remembrance of Csoma de Kőrös must have had a great appeal also to the young Gábor, a fellow Székely from a neighboring village. In fact, Bálint de Szentkatolna would soon become one of the most important successors of the Central Asian traveler Sándor Csoma de Kőrös.

'The Ugor-Turkish War'

Although the Bálint family was of noble origin, this did not guarantee a wealthy life. Gábor grew up under poor circumstances. After his elementary school years at several schools in his native Székelyland and Transylvania, he took his final examinations at the Catholic Lyceum in Nagyvárad.[11] When he graduated from the Catholic Lyceum, he already knew a dozen European and Oriental languages, including the classical languages. Gábor had a special talent for mastering new languages quickly and, in the years to come, he would acquire some thirty languages, including Esperanto. After his final examinations, Gábor continued his studies at the Faculty of Law at the University of Vienna. The young student also took classes in Oriental Studies and Languages. Because Gábor ran out of money, he decided to finish his law and linguistic studies at the University of Pest. The young Székely graduated from the Hungarian university in 1871. Shortly afterwards, he became acquainted with two other scholars, who were active in Budapest, namely János Fogarasi (1801-1878) and Ármin Vámbéry (1832-1913). These two men had an important influence on his future career.

János Fogarasi was a judge at the High Court of Justice and a member of the Hungarian Academy of Sciences. After his co-editor, Gergely Czuczor died in 1866, he continued to compile the Great Dictionary of the Academy of Sciences alone. This dictionary was the first scientific dictionary of the Hungarian language, organizing the Hungarian vocabulary in terms of the root, i.e. the minimal linguistic entity that has a recognizable phonetic form and semantic identity without suffixes. The co-editor of the Great Dictionary, Gergely Czuczor, was a monk of the Benedictine Order, who wrote romantic poems and, because of his anti-Austrian activities during the 1848-1849 Freedom Fight, he was incarcerated in the prison of Kufstein.[12] A military court, under the leadership of Austrian General Alfred von Windischgrätz, sentenced Czuczor to six years imprisonment in chains because of his poem, *Riadó* 'Alarm', in which he called for the Hungarians to take up arms against Austrian tyranny.[13]

After the defeat of the Hungarian *honvéd* in 1849, the Hungarian Academy of Sciences, established by the liberal Count István Széchenyi, became Germanized in the anti-Hungarian era under the Austrian governor Alexander Bach. In the Bach era that lasted until the *Ausgleich* of 1867, a scholar loyal to the Austrian cause, Paul Hunsdorfer, became one of the leading scholars at the Hungarian Academy of Sciences. Hunsdorfer was a lawyer belonging to the German minority of Upper-Hungary and a representative of the Peace Party in the Hungarian Parliament, which wanted to compromise with the House of Habsburg. He Magyarized his name into Pál Hunfalvy, and was appointed chief librarian of the Hungarian Academy of Sciences in 1851. The Great Dictionary of the Academy of Sciences, also referred to as the Czuczor-Fogarasi dictionary, which was finished in 1874, was heavily attacked by Pál Hunfalvy. Hunfalvy, who claimed that the dictionary was based on false premises, could not, however, prevent its publication.[14]

The other scholar, who played an important role in Bálint de Szentkatolna's further scientific career, was the Orientalist, Ármin Vámbéry. Vámbéry was a traveller to Central Asia and he lectured in Turkish at the University of Pest. Although Hunfalvy had in 1861 already designated the Finnish language as the most influential in the research of Hungarian language relationships, Vámbéry kept advocating the genetic relationship between Hungarian and the Turkish-Mongolian languages, especially from 1870 on, when he published his study on 'Hungarian and Turkish-Tatar Cognates'.[15] In order to prove that the Hungarian language was genetically related to Finnish, Hunfalvy invited the German linguist, Jozef Budenz (1836-1892), educated at the University of Göttingen, to the Hungarian Academy of Sciences. Budenz was however not successful in applying the methods of comparative Indo-Germanic linguistics to Hungarian and Finnish. He at first even thought that Hungarian was related to Turkish.[16]

The debate between the two camps, on the one hand the supporters of the Finnish and, on the other hand, the Turkish relationship to Hungarian, was called the 'Ugor-Turkish War'.[17] In fact, the term 'war' is not as obscure as it seems at first sight because it was actually a continuation of the Hungarian-Austro-German political and military clash of 1848-1849. The 'battlefield' was this time not Hungary but the Hungarian identity, i.e. the quest for the origins of the Hungarians and their language. The German camp, including Hunfalvy and Budenz, pushed the Nordic relationship of the Hungarians; the Hungarian camp, including Fogarasi and Vámbéry, looked to the south for Hungarian relatives. Since the southern option was closer to the cradle of human culture and civilization than the Nordic one, it was favored by the Hungarian camp and disliked by the German camp. Bálint de Szentkatolna joined – how could he do anything else as a Székely – the Hungarian camp. The Székely scholar was of the opinion that it was unacceptable for Germans, like Hunfalvy and Budenz to head the Department of Linguistics of the Hungarian Academy of Sciences and decide on the origin of the Hungarian language.[18] In 1871, Vámbéry urged Bálint de Szentkatolna to study the Central Asian language affinities, i.e. Mongolian, Tatar, Chinese, to the Hungarian language in situ. Fogarasi advised him to take up Mongolian and Russian.[19]

In isolation

Between 1871 and 1874, Bálint de Szentkatolna traveled to Russia, Central Asia and Mongolia to study the so-called Turanian languages. This field trip was sponsored by János Fogarasi, who gave the Székely scholar one hundred golden forints. The amount was doubled by József von Eötvös, the Hungarian Minister of Culture and Education after the *Ausgleich*. In those years, Bálint de Szentkatolna also visited Kazan and the St. Petersburg Academy of Sciences to collect Turkish, Tatar and Mongolian language material. When he arrived back in Hungary in 1874, the Academy of Sciences offered the Székely linguist a monthly salary of 500 forints only, half of the salary of a young university teacher. Because of this, Gábor found it difficult to pay his expenses. His difficult financial situation hindered the elaboration of the enormous files of language material Bálint de Szentkatolna had collected in Russia and Central Asia. It was, however, not by accident that his financial existence was kept uncertain by the Academy of Sciences. By then, Hunfalvy and Budenz had already gained full control over the positions within the Hungarian Academy of Sciences and they were not interested in a scholar arguing for a Hungarian language relationship with Oriental languages, like Turkish or Mongolian. Budenz must have felt personally offended by Bálint de Szentkatolna because the Székely linguist questioned Budenz' study of Cheremiss. Gábor, who had checked Budenz' Cheremiss language study, on his request, with Cheremiss informants in situ, was not able to make anything out of it, because Budenz had mixed up two dialects of Cheremiss.[20] In 1877-1878, Bálint de Szentkatolna again traveled to Eastern Asia, this time as a member of the expedition organized by Count Béla Széchenyi, the son of Count István Széchenyi. During this expedition, Bálint de Szentkatolna focused on his Dravidian and Tamil studies.[21]

In his 1877 study, 'Parallels in the Field of the Hungarian and Mongolian Languages', Bálint de Szentkatolna argued that Hungarian is an independent branch within the family of Turanian languages and cannot be derived from a non-existent Finno-Ugrian *Ursprache*. According to the Székely linguist, there is a genetic relationship between Hungarian and Mongolian, and Mongolian is closer to Hungarian than Finnish.[22] In his 'Parallels (...)', Bálint de Szentkatolna strongly criticizes Pál Hunfalvy for trying to reconstruct the Hungarian *Urgeschichte* on the basis of linguistic affinities only.[23] Hunfalvy and Budenz were embarrassed by the Székely linguist and he became their most important opponent to be marginalized definitively.[24] After the death of his protector, János Fogarasi, in 1878, Hunfalvy and Budenz kept Bálint de Szentkatolna away from Vámbéry, who already had a teaching position at the University of Budapest. Finally Bálint de Szentkatolna tired of the machinations of his enemies and decided to leave his beloved Hungary: 'For me there was no position at the University, at the Academy, at the ministries, or at some foreign embassy, while others, who hardly did anything for Science, were given old and newly established positions with a good income.'[25] The conflict between Bálint de Szentkatolna and Hunfalvy and Budenz inspired the national poet, János Arany (1817-1882), who was, between 1870 and 1879, Secretary of the Academy of Sciences, to write the following epigrams in 1878:

> To Budenz. Bálint is a really iron-headed Székely,
> Who does not go, where Pál Hunfalvy wants him to go.[26]

Arany wrote the following epigram about Bálint de Szentkatolna's pamphlet in which he attacked the Academy of Sciences and the Hungarian Ministry of Culture and Education,

On the pamphlet of Gábor Bálint. Poor Gábor Bálint, unhappy crafty Székely; how much you are suffering, what is the good in it![27]

From 1879 until 1892, the Székely wanderer lived in voluntary exile in the Middle East and Northern Africa. However, with the financial support of his friends and the Székely counties, he was brought home. Finally, in 1893, he was appointed Chair of the Department of Ural-Altaic Languages at the Franz Jozef University in Transylvanian Kolozsvár.[28] Until his retirement in 1912, he would teach the so-called Turanian languages, including Japanese, Turkish, Tatar, Mongolian, Korean and Kabardian and he would study their grammatical and lexical relationships. In 1896, he received an honorary doctorate from the University of Kolozsvár. Bálint de Szentkatolna did not establish a school, however. In 1918, six years after his retirement, the Ural-Altaic Department at the University of Kolozsvár was closed down.[29]

The Caucasian expedition

In 1895, Count Jenő Zichy invited Bálint de Szentkatolna to join his scientific expedition to the Caucasus.[30] The other members of the expedition were his colleague from the Franz Jozef University – the historian Lajos Szádeczky-Kardoss, a specialist on the history and culture of the Székely; Jacob Csellingarian, a Russian interpreter of Armenian origin, who happened to be in Hungary and had traveled in the Caucasus before; and the priest Dr. Mór Wosinszky, a trained archaeologist. The purpose of the expedition was to search for the traces of the ancient Hungarians, who once lived in the territory of the Caucasian region. Count Zichy also had a private agenda. He wanted to meet a Georgian prince named 'Zici' because he was convinced of the fact that the aristocratic family of this Georgian and his noble family were close relatives. This must have been an additional driving force for Count Zichy to initiate this and following expeditions.

Count Jenő Zichy (1837-1906), the leader and the main sponsor of the Caucasus-expedition, was a descendent of the Hungarian magnate Zichy-family, who played an important role in Hungarian history. His father, Count Ödön Zichy (1811-1894), was remarkable for his great activity in promoting art and industry in Austria-Hungary. He founded the Oriental Museum in Vienna and was one of the highest sponsors for the Austro-Hungarian North Pole Expedition to Franz Jozef Land. His son Jenő inherited his father's notable collection and followed in the footsteps of his father. Jenő studied Law in Germany, was a landowner, a member of the Hungarian Parliament and President of the Hungarian National Industrial Council. Because of his activities in the field of economy and industry, he was nicknamed the 'industry count'.

It was not by accident that Count Zichy invited Bálint de Szentkatolna to be a member of his 1895 expedition. The Székely linguist, who only joined Zichy's first expedition to the Caucasus and Central Asia in 1895, and Count Zichy were actually brothers in arms. They shared the same views on the ancient history of the Hungarians. Bálint de Szentkatolna and Count Zichy both strongly opposed a one-sided Finno-Ugric origin of the Hungarians; and they both considered the Hungarians to be descendants of the Huns, hypothesizing that one of the ancient Hungarian homelands must have been somewhere in the area north of the Caucasus, neighboring the South Russian Steppes, continuously inhabited by the Scythians, Sarmatians, Huns, Avars, Magyars and other steppe peoples migrating from the East westwards. Hence, the expedition was meant to contribute evidence to this hypothesis by studying the languages, people and cultures of the Caucasus.

In an interesting public lecture in the National Casino in Budapest on March 31, 1895, a month before the expedition would take off, Count Zichy explained the objectives of the expedition, arguing against an exclusive Finno-Ugric origin of the Hungarians. The 'industry count' claimed that the ancient Hungarians could not have originated from the Finno-Ugrians who wandered from the Gobi Desert, over the Ural Mountains, to their present location but that 'they must have been an ancient race that occupied the space in the Maeotis marshes, i.e. the Caspian Sea, the Sea of Azov and the Black Sea, the Volga and the Don, stretching its influence to the Caucasus region, bordering on the Persian and Babylonian territories'. According to Zichy, the Hungarian tribes settled thousands of years ago in this area. During several westward migrations, some tribes split off and turned to the north at the Volga, meeting the ancestors of the so-called Finno-Ugric peoples, including the Finns, Mordvins and Voguls. 'This is supported by the fact that legends, folksongs and historic memories of these peoples refer to a southern climate.' According to Count Zichy, the ancestors of the Hungarians did not come southwards from the Urals but were living in the so-called Scythian area north of the Caucasus in the first century A.D.

To support his claims, Zichy put forth the following arguments. Firstly, a number of classical Greek, Roman, Armenian and Byzantine sources point to the same people under different names, like Huns, Avars and Magyars. Secondly, in ancient sources, Hungarians are called the Western Huns. Thirdly, Alans, who originated from the eastern part of the Caucasus, joined the armies of Attila the Hun (406?-453). This has also been spelled out in the work of Vámbéry. The remains of the Avar tribe that followed the route of the Huns westward settled in Dagestan and are now referred to as Lezgic. Fourthly, Hunfalvy had neglected the Hungarian chronicles and symbols that shed light on the westward migrations crossing the area neighboring the northern Caucasus. Fifthly, Hunfalvy did not take into consideration the data linking the Huns to the Caucasus region. These data are in correspondence with the ancient sources, however. Sixthly, according to Zichy, there is a relationship between the name of the Huns and the other name of the Magyars, i.e. Hungar. Seventhly, from the fact that the tribes of the Hungars and Onogurs settled to the east of the Sea of Azov in the sixth century A.D., Zichy concluded that the Huns and Hungarians, i.e. the Magyars, were the same people, spoke the same language and must have lived for a long time in the vicinity of the Caucasus area before they started to migrate westwards.

The fact that the expedition was intended to challenge the official view on the Hungarian ancient history that claims that the Hungarians originate from the Nordic Ural area might explain the lack of interest Count Zichy engaged from the Hungarian government and the Hungarian Academy of Sciences. Count Zichy complained: 'I had the duty to ask every minister who was in charge of one of my functions, including my membership of the Industrial Council, the Monuments' Council and so on for a holiday (...) with the only exception of Ernő Dániel, I received no answer (...).'[31] The Academy remained completely silent, although I only asked for a certificate to verify that I am Zichy.'[32] The expedition was, however, welcomed by the Russian Czar, Nicolas II (1868-1918) and his government, although the Hungarians were forbidden to dig in Russian soil.

This Zichy-expedition to the Caucasus has been recorded by Lajos Szádeczky-Kardoss in his stenographic travel diary. The original diary of the 1895 expedition – together with seven original photos – is presently kept in the library of the Hungarian Academy of Sciences. This diary has recently been decoded by the Hungarian stenographer Pálma Schenken, who succeeded in deciphering the 400 handwritten pages denoted in the style of the nineteenth-century Gabelsberger-Markovits version of stenography. The decipherment took Pálma Schenken twenty years of work and the manuscript is extremely hard to read. The travel diary gives a good impression of what Count Zichy and his team were doing in the Caucasus.

The 1895 expedition and the two others to the Caucasus and Central Asia, organized by Count Zichy in the following years, yielded much precious material to the Hungarian researchers of the Caucasus and also to the researchers of the ancient Hungarians. The ethnographical collections and photos of the Zichy-expeditions can be found in the Hungarian Ethnographical Museum in Budapest. The archaeological objects collected are kept in the collection of the Ferenc Hopp East Asian Museum.

In the Caucasus

The expedition to the Caucasus started on April 30, 1895, leaving from Budapest, and ended on August 14 of the same year, when the Russian-Austrian border was crossed. The members of the expedition had to prepare in advance, bringing tents, summer and winter clothes, weapons, ammunition, equipment for horse-riding and mountaineering, a minimum of food, photography equipment, phonographs, maps, books, medical supplies and so on. Within three and half months, they had traveled 20,000 kilometers by train, boat, horse farm-wagons, horse and camel. Count Zichy and his men wandered through deserts, over mountain-tops several thousand meters high, and they visited cities and camps of ethnic Turkish nomads. They had to deal with different weather conditions like storms, rain, hailstones and the expedition members had to stand the heat of 40 degrees Celsius. The travelers visited all the territories of the Caucasus, including Adyge, Circassia, Kabardino, North Ossetia, Ingushia, Chechnya, Dagestan, Abkhazia, South Ossetia, Adzharia, Georgia and Azerbaijan. In all these territories, they stayed overnight in villages and towns.[33] Count Zichy and his research team met with a lot of different Caucasian people and tribes, speaking different languages, like Adyga, Abkhaz, Chechen, Avar, Georgian, Mingrelian, Karatsjaj, Circassian, Lezgic and so on. They took part in interesting meetings, festivities, celebrations, rituals and dinners with princes. Count Zichy and his men kept their supporters and families informed by letters and articles for Hungarian newspapers.

Bálint de Szentkatolna claimed that each of the expedition members was left with his own branch of sciences 'because there was complete freedom of study'. However, this freedom of study was interpreted completely differently by the leader of the expedition. In a letter from Odessa dated May, 10 1895, Count Zichy wrote: 'Szádeczky and Bálint are of no use to me, they are spending the whole day in the libraries. Csellingarian has picked up an ancient Russian with whom he is playing chess all day. Only Wosinszky is doing the research with me.'[34]

From the Szádeczky-Kardoss' diary we receive an image of the somewhat unworldly personality of Bálint de Szentkatolna, the Székely, as a highly talented scholar, always eager to learn, everywhere collecting books and impressing people with his extensive knowledge of languages but also as a hot-headed, opinionated, often quarrelling, eccentric person:

> On May 1-2. The first night on Russia ground: A Greek merchant traveled with us, who spoke French, English, Russian and Greek. He was quickly impressed by Bálint. He came into our department to chat and gave information about Odessa.[35]
>
> On May 2. Odessa. In Odessa, Bálint was looking for stones but the shops were closed.[36] Bálint did not find the book on linguistics and the Caucasus that was published in Tiblisi.[37]
>
> On May 2. Odessa. Bálint dominated conversations with officials. Already in the beginning of the expedition, Count Zichy wanted Bálint to keep his mouth shut because he was dominating the scene during conversations.[38] Count Zichy was not amused by the fact that, at the reception of the Austro-Hungarian Consulate in Odessa, Bálint took the wife of Consul Henrik Müller, a nice Viennese woman, to one side.[39]
>
> On May 3. In Odessa, Bálint met the Director of the City's Museum, W. Jurgewics, who told him much about the Hungarian roots of place names in the Crimea.[40]
>
> On May 7. Jevpatorija. In the morning, it turned out that Bálint has left his purse with 30 rubels and his passport in Odessa.
>
> On May 9. Novorossijs. Bálint had not slept enough and made a lot of noise, this all was terrible.[41]
>
> On May 14. Sometimes Bálint de Szentkatolna was not motivated to join the group for dinner and ate alone, like in Kamennij Most in Circassia.[42]
>
> On May 22. In Voroncovko, the expedition met a Mongolian camel driver; Bálint was extremely happy and started to talk with him about the Hungarian-Mongolian ancestry.[43]

On May 27. The expedition reached Naltshik. In Atazsuk, the Kabardians did a dance performance. Bálint did not want to dance but he walked around with a *burka*, a sleeveless frieze cape that is the typical outfit of the Kabardians, on his head.[44] After the dance, Bálint greeted the Kabardians like brothers.[45]

On May 30. In Gori, Count Zichy asked the way, after having crossed the mountain range of the Caucasus, and Bálint started to quarrel with him.[46]

On May 31. Bálint de Szentkatolna received a letter in Tiblisi that he was appointed as ordinary lecturer at the Franz Jozef University.

On June 3. Tiblisi. Bálint visited Inspector Lopatinsky, who was of Kabard origin and a linguist who had been writing grammars and dictionaries.[47]

On June 9. We arrived in Baku and what did Bálint do? He looked for books.[48]

On July 11. Tiblisi. It was discussed whether the Ossetian language is related to Hungarian. This is true for Alan. Gábor provoked the expedition members, stating that the Huns were just a branch of Hungarian people and spoke Hungarian.[49] The Székely language is simply the ancient Hun language, he said.[50]

On July 13. The Count quarreled with Bálint. Bálint wanted more time to read a book on the 'Huns in Dagestan'.[51]

On July 18. The expedition was received by the Georgian Prince Zicianov. Count Zichy thought they were relatives due to the similarity of their family names. The Georgian noble family complained about Bálint's uncivilized behavior.[52]

On June 25. Petrovsk. Bálint said during lunch that people get lazy and stupid when eating fish.[53]

The last important visit the Zichy-expedition made was to St. Petersburg, where Count Zichy and his team arrived on August 2 and where they would stay until August 11. On August 6, the expedition members met a relative of Count Jenő Zichy, Count Mihály Zichy, the famous Hungarian painter, who was appointed as a court painter in St. Petersburg in 1847. Mihály Zichy was also highly honored in Georgia because he painted illustrations for 'The Knight in the Panther's Skin', the Georgian national epic poem written by the Georgian poet, Shota Rustaveli, in the twelfth century. Only Count Jenő Zichy was allowed to have an audience with Czar Nicolas II, who wanted to know everything about the expedition, asking Zichy whether they had found the Hungarians the researchers had been looking for.[54]

Kabardian dictionary

The classification of languages into three main branches, namely Turanian, i.e. all the agglutinative languages, Aryan, i.e, languages displaying flexion and Semitic, i.e. languages displaying root flexion, was initiated by Max Müller, a German linguist teaching in Oxford. His lectures on linguistics were translated into Hungarian in 1874 and were highly influential.[55] Bálint de Szentkatolna also accepted Müller's classification and distinguished, in his report on his linguistic studies in Russia and Asia, different branches of the Turanian languages, like Manchu, Mongolian, Turkish-Tatar, Finn-Ugric, Hungarian, Dravidian and so on.[56] Bálint de Szentkatolna was highly impressed by the Kabardians during the Zichy-expedition. The Székely scholar was convinced of the fact that their language must be an old Turanian language, as well as being closely related to Hungarian.

The Turanian language family is, however, something highly controversial, referring more to typological relationships than to genetic ones. The genetic relationships, involving massive grammatical and lexical affinities, were not demonstrated convincingly. Bálint de Szentkatolna did not prove the genetic relationship between Kabardian and Hungarian either. However his descriptions of the so-called Turanian languages should deserve credit. The reason that his studies of Kabardian and other so-called Turanian languages stood the test of time is that he correctly considered these languages to be of the agglutinative type. Bálint de Szentkatolna did not waste his time with the reconstruction of phantom roots, unable to prove a genetic language relationship. Instead, he operated with roots and suffixes only.[57] From a methodological point of view, this is the right approach to investigate and analyze agglutinative languages. Bálint de Szentkatolna was a pioneer in comparing agglutinative languages on the root level, as he convincingly demonstrated in his *Parallels in the field of the Hungarian and Mongolian languages*, thereby heavily relying on Hungarian root dictionaries, like the ones of Kresznerics and Czuczor-Fogarasi.[58] As a consequence, the studies of Bálint de Szentkatolna can be used without exception, reflecting the state of the so-called Turanian languages in the second half of the nineteenth century. In conclusion, the relevance of his work on the Turanian languages can be summarized as follows:

Firstly, Bálint de Szentkatolna correctly recognized that the Caucasus, especially the northern parts of it, played an important role in the ancient history of the Hungarians. This area had been used as a transit area by the equestrian people of the Steppes, such as the Scythians, Sarmatians, Huns, Avars and the Hungarians originating from the east and migrating westwards. Hence, due to the fact that the ancient Hungarians had been in contact with the peoples from the Caucasus area, language affinities between Hungarian and Caucasian languages are to be expected. A contemporary of Bálint de Szentkatolna, the Hungarian linguist Bernát Munkácsi, already referred to such affinities, including Hungarian and Ossetian.[59] Kabardian is also a good candidate because, before the Kabardians fell victim to the imperial policy of Czarist Russia in the first half of the nineteenth century, the Kabardians, grouped in twelve tribes, dominated for at least 1,500 years the whole area of the Northern Caucasus, along the Rivers Kuban, Terek and Malka. Only in 1864, long after the equestrian people of the Steppes had crossed the area in front of the Northern Caucasus westward, the number of the Kabardians was reduced heavily and their territory diminished substantially, when half a million Adyga-Kabardians had to leave the Northern Caucasus for Turkey.[60]

Péter Veres, a Hungarian ethnographer and researcher of the Caucasus, has recently observed some interesting linguistic affinities that can be found in the Kabardian dictionary of Bálint de Szentkatolna.[61] So far, Hungarian linguistics has no satisfactory etymology for the word *isten* meaning 'God'. This word is classified as being of unknown origin. In his Kabardian dictionary, Bálint de Szentkatolna links Hungarian *isten* to the Kabardian form *s-te-n* that means 'fire-giver'. The alternate Kabardian form *Ošten* refers to the place where the Gods live at the highest point of the Caucasus, namely at the top of Mount Elbrus that is 5,642 meters high, found in the western mountain range of the Caucasus. Veres correctly hypothesizes that the etymology of Hungarian *isten* might be related to Kabardian *s-te-n* and *Ošten*. This link is of course not a proof of a genetic relationship between Hungarian and Kabardian but it offers a highly intriguing trace of language contact that deserves further investigation.[62]

Secondly, it took Bálint de Szentkatolna nine years to arrange the Kabardian language material he had been collecting in the Caucasus and to publish his Kabardian dictionary. Veres (2007) claims that this dictionary is the first dictionary of the Kabardian language, matching an acceptable scientific standard. It is true that, in the course of the Zichy-expedition, the Székely scholar did everything to extend his knowledge of Kabardian. He collected dictionaries of this language, especially in Odessa and Tiblisi. Furthermore, he contacted Dr. L. Lopatinskij, an education inspector in Tiblisi, who had written a Russian-Kabardian dictionary containing detailed information on the Kabardian language.[63] Finally, he worked with informants. One of his informants was the Circassian officer, Aghir Kanamat, who was for ten days the guide of the Zichy-expedition along the Kuban River in 1895.[64]

Due to the fact that the Kabardian language is so complicated, not everyone is able to transcribe this language properly. In the preface of his grammar, Bálint de Szentkatolna refers to Dr. L. Loewe's *A Dictionary of the Circassian Language: Containing all the most necessary words for the traveller, the soldier, and the sailor: with the exact pronunciation of each word in the English character* (1854, London: Bell) as a bad example of a Kabardian dictionary. The Székely linguist notes that 'the British author writes down the sounds of Adyga with Latin and Arab letters. This English-Adyga-Turkish and Adyga-English-Turkish dictionary is largely an invention, such that no-one is able to understand the Adyga language because the author had no idea of this language.'[65] Bálint de Szentkatolna succeeded however in transcribing the Kabardian items because he had substantial training in writing down complicated languages during his travels in Asia.

Bálint de Szentkatolna's Kabardian dictionary of 611 pages can still be used and it is of enormous value to the researchers of the Kabardian language and to the Kabardians themselves. In fact, Bálint de Szentkatolna's dictionary is a kind of collective memory for present-day Kabardians, reflecting a part of the knowledge of their ancestors. Speakers of Kabardian can find a lot of authentic material in the dictionary, for, under each lemma of a given word, an example sentence with that word is included. Hence, the Kabardian communities were extremely grateful when, in 1994, several photocopies of Bálint de Szentkatolna's dictionary 'returned' to the scientific centers in the cities of Maikop and Naltshik, where the Adyga-Kabardian language is spoken and studied.[66] But not only the Adyga-Kabardian speakers have rediscovered and credited the work of Bálint de Szentkatolna, the underestimated Székely linguist, who published the Kabardian studies at his own expense.[67] In 1994, in his birthplace, Szentkatolna, a scientific symposium took place, supported by the Babes-Bolyai University of Cluj-Napoca, to commemorate the 150th anniversary of the birth of the Székely linguist.[68] In 2006, Budapest was the location of a scientific conference to underline the merits of Gábor Bálint de Szentkatolna for the study of the ancient history of the Hungarians, the Hungarian language and other so-called Turanian languages, like the Caucasian language Kabardian.[69]

Notes

1 See www.ethnologue.com. (last accessed February 20, 2010).

2 Compare Szentkatolnai Bálint, G. (1900). *Kabard Nyelvtan. Grammatica Cabardica, seu lingua progeniei Hunnorum. Chazari et Utiguri dictum.* Kolozsvár; and Szentkatolna Bálint-Illyés, G. de. (1904). *Lexicon Cabardico-Hungarico-Latinum.* Kolozsvariensi.

3 Compare www.ethnologue.com. (last accessed February 20, 2010).

4 Compare Szentkatolnai Bálint, G. (1888: 33-55; 215-236). A Tamul nyelv a turáni nyelvek sanskritja vagy van-e a magyarnak testvére, in *Az Erdélyi Muzeum-Egylet Bölcselet-, Nyelv- és Történelemtudományi Szakosztályának Kiadványai V kötet,* Hegedűs, I. (ed.). Kolozsvár.

5 See Köpeczi, B. (ed.). (1994: 301-355). *The History of Transylvania.* Budapest: Akadémiai Kiadó.

6 See Pálmay, J. (2000: 33). *Háromszék vármegye nemes családjai ABOD-ISTVÁN.* Hasonmás kiadás. Székely Nemesi Családok első kötet. Sepsiszentgyörgy: Charta kiadó.

7 See Bakk, P. (1994: 27-29). Szentkatolnai Bálint Gábor. *Erdélyi Tudományos Füzetek* 220, in Borcsa, J. (ed.). (1994). Kolozsvár: Az Erdélyi Múzeum-Egyesület.

8 Compare Csetri, E. (2002). *Kőrösi Csoma Sándor.* Bukarest: Kriterion.

9 Hence his name in Hungarian transcription: Kőrösi Csoma Sándor 'Sándor Csoma from Kőrös'.

10 See Hopkirk, P. (1992: 88). *The Great Game, The Struggle for Empire in Central Asia.* New York: Kodansha International.

11 Today's Oradea in Romania.

12 Kacziány, G. (2004: 20-21). *Magyar vértanuk könyve.* Reprint of 1905 edition. Keckemét: Nemzeti Kincseinkért Egyesülete.

13 Náday, K. and Gy. Sáfrán. (1984: 38). Történeti kutatások Kufsteinban, Czuczor Gergely rabsága, Historische Forschungen in Kufstein, Die Gefangenschaft von Gergely Czuczor. *Publicationes Bibliothecae Academiae Scientiarum Hungaricae* 14 (89). Budapest: Magyar Tudományos Akadémia.

14 Marácz, L. (2008: 559-570). The *Origin of the Hungarian Language. In Selected Studies in Hungarian History,* Botos, L. (ed.). Budapest: Hun-Idea.

15 See the following studies by Vámbéry: Vámbéry, Á. (1870). Magyar és töröktatár szóegyezések. *Nyelvtudományi Közlemények.* Pesten; Ibid. (1877). A török-tatár nyelvek etymológiai szótára. *Nyelvtudományi Közlemények.* Budapest: A. M. T. Akadémia Könyvkiadó-Hivatala; and Ibid. (1882). *A magyarok eredete.* Ethnológiai tanulmány. Budapest: A M.T. Akadémia Könyvkiadó-hivatala.

16 Marcantonio, A. (2002: 35-42). *The Uralic Language Family*, Facts, Myths and Statistics. In Publications of the Philological Society 35. Oxford: Blackwell

17 Pusztay, J. (1994). Az 'ugor-török háború' után. Fejezetek a magyar nyelvhasonlítás történetéből. Budapest: Magvető.

18 Zágoni, J. (2005: 10). *Szentkatolnai Bálint Gábor*. Válogatott írások. Budapest.

19 Zágoni, op. cit., p. 8.

20 Zágoni, op. cit., p. 124.

21 Szentkatolna Bálint, G. de. (1897: 1-429). *Tamulische (Dravidische) studien*. In Zwei Teilen. I. Grammatikalischer Teil, II. Lexikalischer Teil, Separatabdruck aus dem II. Bande des Werkes: Wissenschafliche Ergebnisse der Reise des Grafen B. Széchenyi in Ostasien (1877-1880). Budapest.

22 Szentkatolnai Bálint, G. (1877). *Párhuzam a magyar és mongol nyelv terén*. Budapest: nyomtatott Hornyánszky Victor-nál.

23 Ibid., Chapter IV.

24 Péntek, J. (1994: 14). Koreszmék és rögeszmék. In *Erdélyi Tudományos Füzetek 220*, Borcsa, J. (ed.). Kolozsvár: Az Erdélyi Múzeum-Egyesület.

25 Zágoni, op. cit., p. 13.

26 Arany, J. (1956: 439). *Arany János összes költeményei I.* Budapest: Szépirodalmi könyvkiadó: 'Budenzhez. Igazi vasfejű Székely a Bálint, nem megy arra, amerre Hunfalvy Pál int.'

27 Ibid. Bálint Gábor röpiratára: 'Szegény Bálint Gábor, Boldogtalan góbé; amennyit te szenvedsz, mi ahhoz a Jóbé!' The Hungarian *góbé* is actually a nickname of the Székely attributing crafty capabilities to them.

28 Today's Babes-Bolyai University in Cluj-Napoca Romania.

29 Péntek, pro. cit., p. 19.

30 See Bodor, A. (1994, 10). Szentkatolnai Bálint Gábor, a nyelvtudós. In *Erdélyi Tudományos Füzetek 220*, Borcsa, J. (ed.). Kolozsvár: Az Erdélyi Múzeum-Egyesület.

31 Baron Ernő Dániel was minister of Trade between 1895-1899 in the Bánffy-government. He was the nephew of the Hungarian *honvéd* general Ernő Kiss, who fought against the Austrians in the Hungarian War of Indepencence, 1848-1849. Kiss was one of the 13 Martyrs of Arad, the thirteen Hungarian freedom fighter generals who were executed on October 6, 1849 in the Transylvanian city of Arad (presently in Romania) to re-establish Habsburg rule over Hungary. The Baron had another reason to support the Caucasian expedition of Zichy. The wealthy Dániel family, who had its estates in Transylvania, was of Armenian origin.

32 Szádeczky-Kardoss, L. (2000: 11). *Zichy-expedíció Kaukázus, Közép-Ázsia, 1895.* Szádeczky-Kardoss Lajos útinaplója. Gyorsírásból megfejtette: Schelken Pálma. Budapest: Magyar Őstörténeti Kutató és Kiadó.

33 See the map in ibid., p. 240.
34 Ibid., p. 241. It is clear from these remarks by a somewhat irritated Count Zichy that the members of the expedition had different research methods. The scholars, Bálint de Szentkatolnai and Szadéczky-Kardoss were trying to find books, documents and written sources to support their claims, whereas Count Zichy was collecting data by the method of oral history, that is by questioning and interviewing older people in remote villages.
35 Ibid., p. 25.
36 Ibid., p. 26.
37 Ibid., p.27.
38 Ibid., p. 27.
39 Ibid., p.29.
40 Ibid., p.28.
41 Ibid., p. 42.
42 Ibid., p. 63.
43 Ibid., p. 91.
44 Ibid., p. 304.
45 Ibid., p. 103.
46 Ibid., p. 114
47 Ibid., p. 128.
48 Ibid., p. 131.
49 Ibid., p. 192-193.
50 In an article written in 1917, Lajos Szádeczky-Kardoss quotes Bálint de Szentkatolna, claiming that the etymology of the name *székély* is derived from the root *zich* 'sik' (compare Szádeczky-Kardoss, L. (1917: 371-372). Magyar-rokon népek a Kaukázusban. *Turán* 1917.). This is the name of the Kabardians in their own language meaning 'chair, dwelling'. The root of *székely*, *szék* in Hungarian has the same consonantal root form and the same meaning as its Kabardian counterpart. According to Bálint de Szentkatolna, the suffix *-ely* of *székely* is related to the suffix *-li/eli* used in the Caucasian languages and Turkish-Tatarian to express origin from a place. If 'szék, sik' is related to the name 'Scythia', then *székely* means 'originating from *szék*', i.e. 'Scythia'. According to Bálint de Szentkatolna, this supports the historic fact that the Hungarians and the Székely come originally from Scythia.
51 Szádeczky-Kardoss, Zichy-expedició, p. 194.
52 Ibid., p. 201.
53 Ibid., p. 158.
54 Ibid., p. 238.
55 Péntek, op. cit, p. 17.
56 Zágoni, op. cit., p. 143.

57   Szentkatolnai Bálint, A Tamul, p. 45.

58   Compare Szentkatolnai Bálint, A Tamul; Kresznerics, F. (1831) *Magyar Szótár gyökérrenddel és deákozattal*. Buda; and Czuczor, G. and J. Fogarasi. (1862-1874). *A magyar nyelv szótára I-VI*. Pest.

59   Munkácsi, B. (1901). *Árja és kaukázusi elemek a finn-magyar nyelvekben*. I. kötet magyar szójegyzék. Budapest: Magyar Tudományos Akadémia.

60   Szentkatolnai Bálint, G. (1901: 10-11). *A honfoglalás reviziója vagyis a hún, székely, magyar, besenye, kún kérdés tisztázása*. Kolozsvár.

61   See Veres, P. (2007: 182-220). Ősmagyarok a Kaukázus előterében, különös tekintettel Bálint Gábor kaukazológiai munkásságának tükrében. In *A magyarság eredetének nyelvészeti kérdései. Szentkatolnai Bálint Gábor emlékkonferencia kiadványa*, Obrusánszky, B. (ed.). Sfântu-Gheorghe: Táltos.

62   The Persian item *Yazdan* meaning 'God' might be a good candidate as the final source of the Hungarian word *isten*. If this etymology turns out to be correct, the Caucasian languages, like Kabardian, where variants of this word appear, might have been mediating between Persian and the languages of the equestrian people of the steppes, including ancient Hungarian. Another option is that the ancient Hungarians originate from an area much closer to Persia, present-day Iran, than the Caucasus.

63   L.G. Lopatinskij's book in Russian-latin transcription is mentioned in the preface of Bálint's Kabardian grammar 'Russko-kabardinski slovar [Russian-Kabardian Dictionary]', in Sbornik materialov dlya opisaniya mestnostei I plemen Kavkaza [Collection of Materials for the Description of the Districts and Tribes of the Caucasus], Tiflis (Tbilisi), vol. 12, 1891. [With index].

64   Szentkatolnai Bálint, Kabard nyelvtan, p. 1.

65   Szentkatolnai Bálint, Kabard nyelvtan, p. 4-5.

66   Veres, op. cit., p. 182-220.

67   His grammar is written with his own hand-writing.

68   See papers in Borcsa, J. (ed.). (1994). Szentkatolnai Bálint Gábor. *Erdélyi Tudományos Füzetek* 220. Kolozsvár: Az Erdélyi Múzeum-Egyesület.

69   See studies in Obrusánszky, B. (ed.). (2007). *A magyarság eredetének nyelvészeti kérdései. Szentkatolnai Bálint Gábor emlékkonferencia kiadványa*. Sfântu-Gheorghe: Táltos.

2 The Ethnic-Political Arrangement of the Peoples of the Caucasus

René Does

The history of the Caucasus is a story of domination and resistance. Mostly the fighting was directed against foreign rulers, but the peoples of the Caucasus also have a rich tradition of feuds against each other. All struggled for self-preservation. This strife is the leading thread running through their common history. Crucial themes from this history are: deportation, emigration, the role of Diasporas, territorial conflicts which were 'frozen', discussions on genocide and ethnic homogenization, and the search for a new ethnic-political federalization. This introductory chapter depicts how these issues shaped the modern ethnic-political composition of the peoples of the Caucasus.

Ethno-political history

Among the Caucasian peoples, only the Georgians and Armenians can boast of an old tradition of statehood. It was King David IV (1089-1125) who collected the Georgian lands into one state and who conquered Tbilisi from the Seljuk Turks in 1122. With his tenure the Georgian Golden Century started, reaching its peak during the reign of Queen Tamar (1184-1213). After this golden age a period of decline started, resulting in the partition of Georgia between a Persian dominated east and an Ottoman dominated west in the fifteenth century.[1] The history of the Armenian state is comparable to the Georgian. Only during the tenth century, under the reign of the Bagrationi royal family, she was mighty and really independent. This was the 'Second Golden Century' of Armenia. The 'First Golden Century' was the period of nearly complete sovereignty within the Roman Empire ten centuries before.[2] Nevertheless, the predominant identity narrative of the indigenous peoples of the Caucasus is about foreign rule. The Caucasus was the playing field of foreign powers penetrating from the west and from the east, such as the Greeks, the Romans, Byzantium, the Khazars, the Mongols, the Persians, the Ottoman Empire, and Russia. Before the Soviet era the identity of the Caucasians was almost solely based on clan, family and village ties. A national identity in terms of statehood is a rather modern phenomenon.

A decisive turning point in the ethnic-political history of the region was the intrusion in the nineteenth century of the Russian empire from the north. The Russians sought to secure their southern borders against 'Tatar' raiders by subjugating the Crimean Tatars and the peoples of the Caucasus. In a series of treaties with Persia and the decaying Ottoman Empire, 'the sick man of Europe', they pushed the Russian borders further and further to the south. After the incorporation of the Crimea into the Russian empire in 1784, the Russians turned their attention in the direction of the Caucasus. At first, in 1801 the Georgian kingdom was annexed. After that milestone, the subjugating of the other Caucasian peoples was a fierce and ruthless fight, which would last almost for the rest of the century. It was general Alexei Ermolov (1777-1861) who deployed the strategy for the conquest of the region.

> Ermolov believed that only the energetic punishment of raiding parties and the full integration of the highland tribes into the political structures of the Russian state could create a completely secure environment. (...) Targeted assassinations, kidnappings, the killing of entire families, and the use of disproportionate force in response to small-scale raids were to become central to Russian operations in the opening decades of the nineteenth century.[3]

Often, also the rebellion of the Caucasian peoples was relentless. Until these days, the fierce resistance of the Dagestan imam Shamil between the 1830s and 1850s is dreaded by the Russians and hailed by the insurgents of the Northeast Caucasus against Russian rule in the region.

In the track of the military followed ethnographers. At first the inhabitants of the mountains were collectively piled together as *gortsy* (highlanders) by the Russians. But soon ethnographers started to categorize the new subjects of the empire. In the 1870s, the classification system of the Caucasian highlanders was refined into the mapping that is more or less known today:

> The universal category of 'highlanders' had disappeared, replaced by an array of terms that closely mapped modern ethnic categories, such as Circassians, Abkhaz, Ossetians, Chechens, Ingush, and Avars.[4]

Along with the ethnographers, Russian writers followed in the track of the military. In the resulting 'border literature' the Russian attitude towards the Caucasian highlanders, that in fact lasts until this moment, is perfectly expressed. Russia perceived for itself a civilization mission towards the new 'barbaric' subjects of the empire by modernizing and Russifying their societies. On the other hand, the Russians were deeply fascinated by the exoticness of this Orient within the boarders of their expanding empire – by its lush and feral landscape, its dark-haired and erotically mysterious men and women and the dichotomy between hospitality towards strangers and resistance against external rulers. The most famous and artistic of these literary works are Alexander Pushkin's *The Captive of the Caucasus* (1822), Mikhail Lermontov's *A Hero of Our Time* (1840), and Lev Tolstoy's *The Cossacks* (1863).[5]

Under communist rule, in the 1920s and 1930s, an important administrative reform took place that would have drastic consequences. A process of ethnically based federalization of the state structure of the Soviet Union was completed, that resulted in the coming into being of thoughts about modern statehood and nationhood among the peoples of the Caucasus. The larger peoples of the Soviet Union got their own demarcated territories. In a hierarchal structure the USSR was administratively divided into union republics, autonomous republics, autonomous provinces and autonomous districts. Georgia, Armenia and Azerbaijan received the status of union republics. In the North Caucasus, part of the Russian Socialist Federal Soviet Republic (RSFSR), three native republics became the homeland of two titular nations: Karachai-Cherkessia, Kabardino-Balkaria and Chechen-Ingushetia, where after the demise of the Soviet Union the two peoples parted their ways into two separate republics, Chechnya and Ingushetia. Some questionable choices were made during the process of federalization. Nagorno-Karabakh, in majority populated by ethnic Armenians, became part of the union republic of Azerbaijan. Ossetia was divided into a southern part situated in Georgia, South Ossetia, and a northern part located in the RSFSR, North Ossetia. Abkhazia could have been fitted into the RSFSR, but became an Autonomous republic within the borders of the union republic of Georgia. While ethnic-political state building got under way, separatist inclinations were severely suppressed.

Until recently, common opinion among 'sovietologists' stated that the drawing of the ethnic borders in the 1920s and 1930s was the result of a deliberate policy of divide-and-rule by Stalin. Allegedly he wanted to avoid the striving to partition among the peoples of the Caucasus (and the peoples of the Soviet Union in general) by incorporating unavoidable ethnic conflicts in the autonomous subjects in case such strife would emerge. Nowadays, this theory is more and more disputed and being replaced by the interpretation that due to the ethnic and environmental diversity of the Caucasus, the drawing of ethnically faultless borders was just impossible. King by example asserts:

> The decision of Soviet leaders to draw boundary lines in one place and not another thus had little to do with any putative grand strategy to make the Caucasus into a ticking time bomb of territorial disputes. Indeed, if Soviet officials had been able to foresee the violence that would erupt over precisely these borders in the 1980s and 1990s, they might have well opted for a different arrangement.[6]

But whether or not foreseen, the policies of *perestroika* and *glasnost* during the Gorbachev era encouraged ethnic nationalism, which was one of the factors next to corruption and bankruptcy that led to the collapse of the Soviet Union.

Deportation

The most extreme and ruthless method both tsarist Russia and the Soviet Union deployed to tame the Caucasus was the deportation of entire peoples. Two episodes stand out: the deportation of the Circassians in 1864 and the expulsion of the Karachai, the Chechens, the Ingush and the Balkars into Central Asia after World War II. (Not only these Caucasian peoples became victims of the deportation drive of the Stalin regime: peoples like the Crimean Tatars, the Kalmyks, and the Meskhetian Turks suffered the same fate.)

During the first half of the nineteenth century, tsarist officials and the Circassians fruitlessly negotiated about the terms on which the latter would become denizens of the Russian state. After the rebellion of imam Shamil in the Northeast Caucasus was finally crushed in 1859 (see the contribution by Kemper in this volume), tsarist Russia wanted to force an end to the constant hassle with the Circassians in the Northwest. It hardened its position and unfolded the idea that the Circassians had to be deported from the mountains if they persisted in their stubbornness. General Dmitry Milyutin of the tsarist army already had formulated the possibility of such a deportation of the Circassians in a memorandum of 1857. In order to establish a strong majority of ethnic Russians in the Stavropol *guberniia* he proposed: 'We have to remove them to the Don region, because there are not enough free lands in the Stavropol *guberniia* (...). In the Don region we have to settle them in special encampments like colonies. We must keep this idea meticulously secret to the government of the highlanders as long as the time for its implementation has not come.' In 1860, Milyutin proposed an alternative place for the resettlement of the Circassians: Turkey. The time came in 1864. The implementation of the deportation was handed to the merciless general Nikolai Evdokimov, who hated the highlanders and viewed them as enemies. Tens of thousands of Circassians were driven away from the mountains to the Black Sea coast. 'The entire northwest coast of the Black Sea was scattered with dead bodies and dying people. Between them a few oases of nearly living, waiting for their turn to be deported to Turkey, did hold on,' an eye-witness wrote.[7]

Nowadays, a discussion has unfolded about the question of whether this deportation has to be labeled as 'genocide'. The Russian historian Yakov Gordin answers this question in the affirmative: 'Yes, the fact of genocide against the Circassian people is beyond doubt.'[8] His vision is shared by Walter Richmond, a specialist on the Northwest Caucasus: 'I believe that the Circassian deportation was the first modern genocide and ethnic cleansing.'[9] In the republic of Adygeia, the Circassian non-governmental organisation Circassian Congress has as their primary objective that the Russian government recognizes the fate of the Circassians in the nineteenth century by the Russian government as 'genocide'.[10] Every year, the Circassians in the Diaspora, who are mainly living in Turkey, remember 28 May 1864 as Deportation Day.[11] During the Second World War, a new round of deportations took place. Immediately after the Germans were ousted from the Caucasus, all the Karachai, Ingush, Chechens, and Balkars were removed in cattle-wagons to the most inhospitable places of Central Asia, mostly in Kazakhstan.[12] Officially, these peoples were accused of large-scale collaboration with the Nazis. Aside from some individuals, these accusations were false. King writes:

> Some 70,000 Karachai were removed to Kazakhstan in November 1943. More than 300,000 Chechens and 80,000 Ingush were sent to various parts of Central Asia in February 1944. Over 37,000 Balkars were deported in March. The populations of entire villages and districts were wiped away, their places taken by new (usually Russian) migrants.

> Among those sent into exile were significant numbers of people who had actually served in Soviet forces during the war. (...) Focusing on the question of collaboration thus misses the essential point, namely, that the deportations of the Second World War were part and parcel of the persistent Soviet – and earlier Russian – insistence on demographic engineering as state policy.[13]

As a result of the anti-Stalinism campaign of partyleader Nikita Khrushchev, the Karachai, Ingush, Chechens, and Balkars were allowed to return to their homes in the second half of the 1950s. But how about the deported Circassians? Murat Berzegov, an activist member of the Circassian Congress organization, who claims that about four million ethnic Circassians (or 'Adygi') are living in Diaspora, hopes a lot of them will return to the Caucasian homeland of their forefathers: 'The most numerous Diaspora lives in Turkey – nearly three million people in 900 places. Seventy percent of them lives on inferior farmlands and would joyfully return in case Russia provides them a shelter and the Russian citizenship.'[14]

The deportations remain black pages in the collective memory of the Caucasians. Furthermore, this memory is the breeding ground of everlasting distrust towards the Russians and of the latent fear that their existence in their homelands is never secure.

Emigration and Diasporas

Besides the forced deportations, many Caucasian peoples have a tradition of more or less voluntary emigration. Individuals from the region escaped political oppression or economic hardship, or both. In the nineteenth century many Caucasians fled for the Russian rule. During the Civil War that followed upon the First World War, nationalist Georgians, Armenians and Azeri fled for the coming communist regime.

Among the peoples in the region, the Armenians stand out. About four million ethnic Armenians live in Diaspora, that is one million people more than the number of Armenians living in Armenia apart. But in Diaspora the Armenians steadfastly hold on to their national culture. 'The Armenians barely integrated and formed firm and closed communities. Private education was especially stressed with the purpose to preserve their own culture also abroad.'[15] For Armenians, economic hardship has always been the principle motive to leave their country. The last large group of Armenian emigrants left after the collapse of the Soviet Union, almost 700,000 people in the period 1991-1996.[16] For the same economic reason, about one million Azeri men are now living as migrant workers in Russia.

As a result of the Second Chechen War in the autumn of 1999 and the successive Russian suppression of the Chechen nationalist and Islamic forces, Chechen Diasporas are the newest communities of expatriates. This is remarkable, because the Chechens are known as people that are emotionally strongly tied to their native places. So, since 2000 there exists a Chechen parliament and government in exile, mostly in the Arab countries and the United Kingdom. In 2007, under the rule of commander Doku Umarov, a North Caucasus emirate was proclaimed, of which Umarov declared to be the leader.[17] A second Chechen Diaspora exists in Russia. According to Russia's 2002 census, out of the 1,360,253 Chechens in the Russian Federation, 260,000 were living in Russian regions outside Chechnya, including 14,500 in Moscow. The Diaspora within Russia is strongly divided between the supporters and the opponents of Chechen separatism. The supporters are mostly represented among the young, who are more radical in their nationalist and religious views than the elderly.[18] By the way, logically all the other peoples of the Russian Federation that have their own ethnic republic, also have larger or smaller Diasporas in Russia.

As a rule, emigrants in the Diaspora tend to be stronger nationalists than those who remained. In this respect the Armenian example once more stands out. The Armenian Diaspora has politically, morally and financially always been of great importance in the promotion and protection of the Armenian case, like the lasting fight for the official acknowledgment by Turkey of the mass murder on the Armenians in 1915 as a 'genocide'. So, Diasporas can be strong political players in the region itself.

'Frozen' conflicts

After the collapse of the Soviet Union in 1991, only the fifteen union republics were recognized as new independent states. But nationalism was getting a grip on all its peoples. Besides the union republics, five autonomous formations declared unilaterally their own independence: Chechnya, the Armenian enclave of Nagorno-Karabakh in Azerbaijan, the Georgian autonomous territories of Abkhazia and South Ossetia, and the Moldovan republic of Transnistria. Their declarations of independence were not recognized, neither by their metropolitan states, nor by the international community. Nevertheless, the armed struggles between these self-proclaimed republics and their metropolitan states, which already had started at the end of the 1980s, continued with full fervor. In 1992 and 1993 the armed conflicts were 'frozen', that is militarily brought to an end by the signing of ceasefires. The Chechen rebellion was militarily crushed by the Russian army in the fall of 1999. Concerning the other four separatist states, lasting political settlements are still some way off. Three of the four current 'frozen conflicts' are thus Caucasian ethnic conflicts.

Although not recognized as independent states, the separatist regions have acted as relatively strong states, except South Ossetia, that was numerically divided between Ossetians and Georgians and weakened by their continuing ethnic conflicts before the August 2008 war.[19] Democratic elections are part of their internal political life. Their governments function rather effectively and have the support of a large majority of the population. Therefore these non-recognized states are indeed stronger and more organized than a multitude of independent but weak or even failing states all round the world. Since the beginning of the 1990s, it became more and more difficult to reintegrate them into the metropolitan states from which they did split off. They rightfully suppose that time is on their side. Lynch calls them *de facto* states, which are defined as follows:

> A de facto state exists where there is an organized political leadership, which has risento power through some degree of indigenous capacity; receives popular support; and has achieved sufficient capacity to provide governmental services to a given population in a specific territorial area, over which effective control is maintained for a significant period of time the de facto state views itself as capable of entering into relations with other states and it seeks full constitutional independence and widespread international recognition as a sovereign state.[20]

So, at the time the Soviet Union collapsed, the striving for greater sovereignty and even total independence was virulent in the autonomous formations lower in the federal hierarchy of the Soviet state as well. This political phenomenon has been called '*matryoshka* nationalism' and revealed itself strongest in the Caucasus, due to its kaleidoscopic ethnic diversity.

The question is why some separatist regions could develop into 'de facto states' and others were not able to reach this 'halfway stadium' of state building. Two factors turned out to be decisive: strong and effective internal leadership combined with comprehensive external support. With respect to the second element, South Ossetia, Abkhazia and Transnistria were supported by Russia, and Nagorno-Karabakh was supported by Armenia and Russia – in all cases the support included military assistance.[21]

Ethnic homogenization

The ethnic strife that has engulfed the Caucasus has been accompanied with ethnic homogenization within the state and republican borders in the region. This process occurred as the result of sneaking emigration, war, and ethnic cleansings. In the Caucasus the formerly complex ethnic composition is unraveling into increasingly ethnically homogenous states and regions.

All the recent wars in the region were accompanied by ethnic cleansing. In 1988, the first year of the war between Armenia and Azerbaijan over Nagorno-Karabakh, nearly 200,000 Armenians were driven out of Azerbaijan. About the same number of Azeri escaped Armenia and Nagorno-Karabakh. After the Abkhaz victory in the war against Georgia, realized thanks to the support of volunteer fighters from the North Caucasian peoples and of weapons from Russia, the whole ethnic Georgian population of more than 200,000 persons departed to Georgia proper. This has resulted in the current desolation of large parts of Abkhazia. And recently, following upon the Russian-Georgian war of August 2008, South Ossetia was cleansed of its ethnic Georgians.

Aside from these massive ethnic cleansings in the South Caucasus as the result of (civil) wars, strained ethno-social relations and some other factors produced a process of sneaking homogenization in the North Caucasus:

> By 1989, with the exception of Circassians/Adyga in Adygeia, titular nationalities formed an absolute majority in their homelands. Most dramatically, the Chechen and Ingush populations increased from around 41 percent of their region's total in 1959 to 80 percent in 1989. The proportion of ethnic Russians, by contrast, had fallen precipitously during the preceding decades. Emigration by Russian and other minorities, higher birth rates among some Muslim groups, and the return of formerly deported peoples from Central Asia all contributed to the relative homogenization of the north Caucasus. According to official

rhetoric, the Soviet Union was meant to encourage the fusion of nation-alities into a single Soviet people. In reality, the Soviet experience made the political units of the Caucasus considerably less ethnically diverse and more clearly national than they had been in the past.[22]

In Chechnya an almost total ethnic homogenization has occurred since the Russian minority has left in the wake of the two Chechen wars. Ac-cording to Mavlit Bazhaev, the president of the Association of Chechen Social and Cultural Organizations: 'At present, in the republics of the North Caucasus all the conditions for the founding of mono-cultural and mono-ethnic societies are formed.'[23]

A new federalism?

The former Soviet Union was a multi-ethnic empire. An important cause of its collapse was that there was a tolerance towards non-Russian popu-lations expressing their nationalist feelings and conducting nationalist policies. The fact that separatism is still a source of political turmoil and military violence, especially in the Caucasus, can be explained by the cir-cumstance that two of the Soviet successor states were, although smaller, empires on their own: the 'big empire' of the Russian Federation and the 'small empire' of Georgia.

Independent Georgia became too weak a state to resist the separat-ism in Abkhazia and South Ossetia. After having been *de facto* 'states' in a situation which was 'frozen' by the international players in the field (UN, OSCE, etc.), the two separatist entities since the war of August 2008 constitutionally still find themselves in dire straits. Only a few countries besides Russia have recognized their independence. Nevertheless, their reintegration into the Georgian state at this point appears to be difficult, though it is decreed by the western powers. These separatist conflicts are a source of tension between Russia and the West.

The independence of South Ossetia is rather unlikely to be sustain-able. There are two possibilities for the near future: South Ossetia will be merged with North Ossetia and incorporated into the Russian Federa-tion as the southern part of 'Ossetia', or the present state of limbo will be frozen. The independence of Abkhazia, on the other hand, is not unjus-tifiable. This region can develop into a viable state. Among the Abkhaz a discussion is going on about two scenarios for the future of their indepen-dent state: to remain an unobtrusive vassal state of the Russian Federation or to escape from underneath the current Russian domination as well. The founder and the editor of the newspaper *Chegemskaya Pravda* has been a staunch and loud supporter of real Abkhaz independence: 'Now, after recognizing Abkhazia, Russia is swallowing us. This is happening economically, politically, militarily, and socially. Every day we are becoming more and more dependent.'[24] Unlike South Ossetia, Abkhazia could turn out to be a new geopolitical nuisance for the Russians.

On the other side of the mountain ridge, the Russian North Caucasus remains marred by political violence, clannish politics, Islamic insurgencies and poverty. The Russian authorities seem unable to develop a viable regional policy, besides outsourcing government to local elites. But this system is not working either, according to Alexei Malashenko, a specialist on the region. 'This spring (2009 – RD) the situation has got worse in Dagestan, in Chechnya and in Ingushetia.'[25] In Dagestan blood feuds and gang wars are rampant. On June 5, 2009, Adilgeri Magomedtagirov, the interior minister of Dagestan, was murdered in a spray of bullets.[26] Two weeks later, on June 21, the president of Ingushetia, Yunus-Bek Yevkurov, was severely wounded in an attempted murder. Yevkurov had recently replaced the unpopular Murat Zyazikov and tried to restore order. He started an anti-corruption campaign. The shooting is said to have been the initiative of a local coalition of corrupt state officials and Islamist insurgents ('Pokushenie...'). After the assassination of Magomedtagirov, Russian president Dmitry Medvedev told the security council of Dagestan 'that since the beginning of the year, a total of 235 people – 48 civilians, 112 bandits and 75 law enforcement officials – have been killed in the North Caucasus'.[27] In Chechnya, the merciless president Ramzan Kadyrov restored order and rebuilt the capital Grozny, but he is also suspected of stealthily building a quasi-independent *sharia* state.[28] Specialists on the region agree that the North Caucasus is slipping out of the Kremlin's control.

The logical solution for ethnic separatist problems in a multi-ethnic state is ethnic federalization. But in the former Soviet Union ethnic federalization of the state has also been the root cause of separatist aims. Paradoxically, ethnic federalization is both the most reasonable solution and the root cause of ethnic separatism.

Russian authorities are unsure about how to increase the governability of the North Caucasus. A few scenarios are conceivable. Firstly, a comprehensive recentralization, but this strategy seems very unlikely due to a severe lack of political will and financial-military resources. Secondly, Russian specialists on the region are discussing the outlines of 'a new federalism'. The renowned ethnographer Emil Pain argues that Russia still has to make the transformation from being an empire into being a real ethnic federation: 'The federation is a form of historical compromise that provides an opportunity for the relatively independent development of a given territorial community while preserving the integrity of the polyethnic state.'[29] Maybe Pain is right. In that case he also gives an explanation for the question why the ethnically based federal structures of the Russian Federation are not functioning: the country is still conceived as an empire by its non-titular nationalities, above all the 'stubborn' North Caucasian peoples.

Appendix. The peoples of the Caucasus

The Russian part of the Caucasus, the North Caucasus, is home to approximately five million people. The region is divided into three zones: Northwest, Central, and Northeast. In the Northwest zone three ethnic republics are situated, from west to east Adygeia (pop. 447,100), Karachai-Cherkessia (pop. 439,500), and Kabardino-Balkaria (pop. 901,500). This part of the Caucasus can be called 'Circassian'. The Northwest and the Northeast are separated by the Central republic of North Ossetia (pop. 710,300). While the peoples of the Northwest and the Northeast are Muslim, the North Ossetians are Orthodox Christians. The Northeast consists of the republics of Ingushetia (pop. 467,300), Chechnya (pop. 1,1 million) and Dagestan (pop. 2,6 million). The republic of Dagestan is in itself also a colorful mosaic of 32 distinct indigenous ethnic groups, of which the most numerous are the Avars (758,400 people, or 29.4% of the Dagestan population), the Dargins (425,500; 16.5%), the Kumyks (365,800; 14.2%) and the Lezgins (336,700; 13.1%). These seven North Caucasian republics are 'subjects' of the Russian Federation.[30] (The number of inhabitants is gathered from Wikipedia and based on the census of 2002.)

The ethnic diversity of the Caucasus is matched by its linguistic variety. Fifty languages are indigenous to this region. They are part of five language families. These languages can be extremely complex. Nearly all of the Caucasians are bilingual: besides their mother-tongue, they speak Russian. Religiously, the Caucasians are Muslims or Orthodox Christians. The Orthodox churches of Armenia and Georgia are auto-cephalic. Religious traditions form a basic part of the national identity of the Caucasians.

Table 1   Ethnic composition of the states and regions in the Caucasus (%)

People	Adygeia	Karachay-Cherkessia	Kabardino-Balkaria	North Ossetia	Ingushetia	Chechnya	Dagestan	Georgia	Armenia	Azerbaijan
Russian	64.5	33.7	25.1	23.2	1.2	3.7	4.7	6.3	–	1.8
Adyga	24.2									
Armenian	3.4			2.4				8.1	97.9	1.5
Ukrainian	2.0									
Karachay		38.5								
Cherkes		11.3								
Abaza		7.4								
Nogais		3.4					1.5			
Kabardin			55.3							
Balkar			11.6							
Ossetian			1.1	62.7				3.3		
Ingushetian				3.1	77.3					
Georgian				1.5				70.1		
Chechen					20.4	93.5	3.4			
Avar							29.4			
Dargin							16.5			
Kumyk							14.2			
Lezgin							13.1			
Lak							5.4			2.2
Azerbaijan							4.3	5.7		90.6
Greek								1.9		
Abkhaz								1.8		
Kurdic									1.3	
Total number (1000)	444.4	434.5	896.9	704.4	481.6	1,141.3	2,621.8	4,474.0	3,016.0	8,388.0

NB Only peoples with a share of at least one percent are mentioned; the number of Chechens is probably an overestimation.
Source: *Fischer Weltalmanach 2008/Volkszählung Russische Föderation 2002* (www.perepis2002.ru)

Notes

1   Van der Schriek, D. (2004: 7). *Georgië*.Amsterdam: Koninklijk Instituut voor de Tropen/Novib.
2   Termeer, S. and Zeynalian, E. (2000: 7-8). *Armenië*. Amsterdam: Koninklijk Instituut voor de Tropen/Novib, Amsterdam.
3   King, C. (2008: 48). *The Ghost of Freedom. A History of the Caucasus*. Oxford: Oxford University Press.
4   Ibid., p.144.
5   Hokanson, K. (2008). *Writing at Russia's Border*. Toronto: University Press.
6   King, C. (2008: 198). *The Ghost of Freedom. A History of the Caucasus*. Oxford: Oxford University Press.
7   Gordin, Y. (2007). 'Cherkessia – "Kavkazskaya Atlantida"', *Zvezda*, No. 12. (http://magazines.russ.ru/zvezda/2007/12/g06-pr.html)
8   Ibid.
9   Richmond, W. (2009, June 10). '*Interview with Walter Richmond*', www.circassianworld.com, (taken from the news site David Johnson's Russia List).
10 Gordin, op cit.
11 Colarusso, J. (1997). 'Peoples of the Caucasus', in: *Encyclopedia of Culture and Daily Life*. Pepper Pike, Ohio: Eastword Publications, hhttp://www.circassianworld.com/colarusso_2.html).
12 See Jansen, Chapter 4 for a detailed discussion of the case of the Chechens.
13 King, op cit, pp. 196-197.
14 Gordin, op cit.
15 Termeer, S. and Zeynalian, E. (2000: 27). *Armenië*. Amsterdam: Koninklijk Instituut voor de Tropen/Novib, Amsterdam.
16 Ibid.
17 Fuller, L. (2007, November 11). 'Chechen Leadership In Exile Seeks To Salvage Legitimacy', *RFE/RL*.
18 Vatchagaev, M. (2008, March 27) 'The Chechen Diaspora in Russia', *Jamestown Foundation Chechnya Weekly*, (taken from the news site David Jonhson's Russia List).
19 See the contributions of Companjen, Chapter 8 and Hille, Chapter 9 in this volume for further discussion of the Russian-Georgian War in August 2008 and the cases of separatism in Georgia.
20 Lynch, D. (2004: 15). *Engaging Eurasia's Separatist States. Unresolved Conflicts and De Facto States*. Washington D.C.: United States Institute of Peace Press.
21 Cornell, S. E. (2002: 232-235). *Ethnoterritoriality and Separatism in the South Caucasus – Cases in Georgia*. Department of Peace and Conflict Research, Uppsala University, Uppsala.

22 King, op cit, pp. 205-206.

23 Maksimov, V. (2008, July 28). 'Prezident Assotsiatsii chechenskich obsh-chestvennykh I kuluturnykh obyedinenii Mavlit Bazhaev: "V odinochku re-spubliky Severnogo Kavkaza s problemami ne spravyatsya"', *Noviye Izvestiia*.

24 Whitmore, B. (2009, June 19). 'Abkhazia and the Perils of Independence', *RFE/RL*, 2009 (taken from the news site David Johnson's Russia List).

25 Humphries, C. (2009, June 12) 'Kremlin faces fresh challenges in Muslim south', *Reuters*, (taken from the news site David Johnson's Russia List).

26 Kamenev, M. (2009, June 12) *Has Russia Lost Control of the North Cauca-sus?*, Time.com, (taken from the news site David Johnson's Russia List)

27 Ibid.

28 Clover, Ch. (2009, January 13). 'Chechnya's ruler puts his faith in Islam – and a leadership cult', *Financial Times*, (taken from the news site David Johnson's Russia List).

29 Pain, E. (2008, December 17), 'From Empire to Federation and Back: Ethno-political Trends and Their Trial by Crisis', *Nezavisimaya Gazeta*, (taken from the news site David Johnson's Russia List).

30 Colarusso, op cit.

3   An Island of Classical Arabic in the Caucasus: Dagestan

Michael Kemper

Introduction

With its strong and resilient tradition of Arabic, multi-ethnic and multi-lingual Dagestan (today a republic in the Russian Federation) assumes a special place not only in the Caucasus but also among all other Muslim areas of the former Soviet Union. For more than a thousand years Arabic served as the main medium for interethnic communication. Introduced in the South of Dagestan during the first Islamization wave by the Arabs in the late seventh century, Arabic literature in Dagestan flourished during the medieval period when all Khanates and mountain village communities became Muslim. Arabic language and literature, in manuscript form, went through a new period of blossoming during the anti-colonial *jihad* movement (*c.* 1828-1859), and even after the defeat of the *jihad* it continued to be in official use in the Russian colonial times.

In the early twentieth century, Dagestani modernizers started debates on how to reform the teaching of Arabic, and whether Arabic should be replaced by Turkic or Russian as the medium of interethnic communication in the North Caucasus. At the same time, these Jadid reformers started the mass publication of books in the Turkic and Caucasian vernacular languages of the region, especially Kumyk, Avar, Dargi, and Lak. In the 1920s the Soviets continued and even enforced this support of the Dagestani national languages for literature, and strongly promoted the spread of Russian for official and interethnic communication instead of Arabic. The 1930s saw the full-blown attack on Islam in the Caucasus, and everything connected to the language of the Qur'an was to be eradicated. Still, Arabic continued to be studied in private, and some Dagestani authors made huge efforts to save the Dagestani Muslim literature in Arabic from extinction. Paradoxically, after World War II these attempts at rescuing the rich Arabic and Islamic manuscript heritage of Dagestan were continued by Soviet academic institutions in the country. With the Islamic boom of the late 1980s and 1990s, Arabic regained its high prestige, and resurfaced as the language for religious instruction; but the Soviet traditions were so strong that Russian has become the main language of Islam in Dagestan.

Arabic as Dagestan's Midwife

The Arab conquests of the late seventh and eighth centuries touched Dagestan only in its extreme South, in Derbend and its environs of Tabasaran. The ancient Persian city of Derbend was turned into an Arab garrison city and Arab armies made incursions into areas further north. However, the invaders could not obtain a permanent foothold in Central and Northern Dagestan. What followed was a centuries-long process of gradual Islamization that was not propelled by the Arab conquerors but by Dagestanis themselves. Conversion probably proceeded by force, by peaceful missionary work, and above all by political opportunism and alliance-making. Christian sacred items excavated in Central Dagestan reveal that a Christian past of parts of Dagestan, with a Georgian outlook, was literally being buried under growing layers of Islam.

Dagestan's Islamization was completed only by the fifteenth century; and with Islam, Arabic became the most common written language in the whole of the country. This process can best be followed with inscriptions on tombstones, from the coastal city of Derbend in the South to the alpine mountains of Dagestan. Dagestan is still home to a wealth of Arabic inscriptions from the tenth century, and a Kufi-style Arabic inscription dating back to as early as 770 CE (153 of the Islamic calendar) was still visible in Derbend's city wall when the Russian scholar Nikolai Khanykov visited the place in 1862.[1] Also, until the turn of the twentieth century, Arabic was still spoken as the native language in a small Tabasarani village whose inhabitants regarded themselves as descendents of the Arab conquerors.[2]

Also, the oldest known works of Dagestani authors are written in Arabic; this is the case, for example, with the outstanding Sufi biographical dictionary *Rayhan al-daqa'iq* ('Basilicum of the Niceties') of Abu Bakr Muhammad al-Darbandi (d. 1145), the only existing manuscript which has recently been thoroughly analyzed by the Moscow-based Arabist Alikber Alikberov.[3] A huge part of the Arabic heritage of Dagestani literature is made up of Islamization legends, like the 'Book of Derbend' (*Darband-nama*) and the 'History of Dagestan' (*Ta'rikh Daghistan*), which have survived in manuscript copies of the sixteenth to nineteenth centuries. The latter two works describe the Islamization mainly in political terms:

typically, they depict a dynasty as having ruled in a certain area already in pre-Islamic times and then to have taken on Islam in the course of the Arab invasions, or by Arab missionaries. Through marriage alliances the ruling dynasties then obtained an Arabic genealogy reaching back to the tribe of Muhammad, the Quraysh. With this construction of spiritual and genealogical Arabic pedigree, the rulers who ordered these works not only defended their hold on their individual provinces (which were often meticulously described by lists of place names) but also laid claim to leadership over the whole of Dagestan, against other Dagestani Muslim leaders. Thus already in these early works, Islam appears as a political factor for potential unification.[4]

It is in these Arabic books that the name Dagestan makes its first appearance – the 'Land of the Mountains'. It signified something that would be understood as a coherent region, defined mainly by Sunni Islam and by the Arab ancestry of their leaders, fictitious as they may be in our eyes. Not being derived from the name of an ethnic group, 'Dagestan' was a geographical concept with borders defined through its neighbors – the mainly Shii communities of Azerbaijan in the South, the Christian Georgians in the South and East, and the Chechens in the East; in the North, Dagestan's neighbors were various Turkic ethnic groups and Buddhist Kalmyks, as well as Cossacks communities and finally the Christian Russians. Sunni Islam became the strongest common denominator of Dagestani identity.

Another factor that seems to have given Dagestan a coherent form is its peculiar economy, which is characterized by the exchange relations between the highlanders (who speak Caucasian languages like Avar, Lak, Dargin, Lezgi, Tabasarani and others) and the Turkic-speaking Kumyks of the Caspian littoral of Eastern Dagestan. Dagestani mountaineer communities needed the plains as winter pastures for their cattle, and this gave the Kumyk principalities in the plain a strong leverage on the 'free' mountain communities. Mountaineers also rented or took pastures in Chechnya and Georgia, and they regularly raided Georgian villages south of the Great Caucasus range for slaves and booty. With raiding often being a permanent part of the Dagestanis' economy, warrior virtues had a prominent place in their code of honor, and accordingly the Dagestanis enjoyed a bad image among their neighbors.

Paradoxically, also multiethnicity worked as a uniting factor in Dagestan: the number of ethnic groups (or 'Dagestani nations') in the country amounts to twenty or more, depending where one would draw the line between language and dialects. None of them has a clearly dominant position; today the largest language group is that of the Avars, comprising roughly a third of the population but kept in check by the other peoples of Dagestan. This multiethnic balance of the country stands in stark contrast to the more homogenous populations of Dagestan's neighbors, especially the Chechens. The latter also joined Sunni Islam, but Dagestanis usually regarded the Chechens as primitive and uneducated in Islamic matters. By contrast to the characteristic tribal/clan structure of Chechen society before the twentieth century, the Dagestanis identified mostly with their place of birth and dwelling – in fact, with their local village or valley. For the Dagestanis, this geographic identity with their settlements and neighborhoods weighed more than family or clan relations (which, however, still played a role in the internal affairs of the village community).

Under these circumstances the Arabic language obtained a special importance as a medium for interethnic communication in Dagestan; and skills in Arabic became equivalent to education. In spite of Soviet suppression of Islam and Arabic literature, thousands of Arabic manuscripts are still preserved in the country's public and private libraries, most of them from the eighteenth to early twentieth centuries. While folk literature (tales, songs and poetry) was mostly transmitted in the local Caucasian and Turkic languages and rarely written down, Arabic was reverted to for almost everything that needed to be fixed in writing. Arabic was the language par excellence for religious literature, education, and historiography, but it was also the main idiom for correspondence between Dagestani local rulers (Beks and Khans) and village communities, for documenting contracts, testaments and pious donations as well as for genealogies, memorial inscriptions and epitaphs, and, as we will see below, for customary law. Arabic thus connected the politically and ethnically diverse Dagestani communities and principalities with each other, and it also served as a cultural bridge to the Arab world. In the Caucasus, however, Dagestan became an Arabic-writing island, cut off by its neighbors geographically and politically from the Arab World.

While Arabic was certainly most important as a medium for writing, one should not underestimate the Dagestanis' abilities also to *speak* Arabic. Dagestan was home to a plethora of village schools (*madrasas*) where Arabic was the language of instruction; and while most of these schools were ventures of only one renowned teacher, certain villages (like Kumukh/Ghazi-Ghumuq, Khunzakh, Kakhib, Kudutl and many others) became famous as centers of learning where education was offered through many centuries. Next to Arabic books on Islamic law, classical works on Arabic grammar, syntax, rhetoric and lexicography made up the bulk of each library at these *madrasas* as well as in mosques and private homes. Dagestani students went from village to village for learning, and many also traveled to Arabia for studies and for the *hajj* pilgrimage. In Mecca and Medina, the local Arab scholars were sometimes surprised and amazed by the Dagestanis' excellent command of the Arabic literary language, the *fusha*, which they found was not 'polluted' by interferences from Arabic dialects.[5] In their geographical isolation from the Arab lands and with their 'bookish' Arabic, the Dagestanis obviously maintained an Arabic that was regarded as 'ancient' or 'pure', and therefore as highly cultured.

As to written Arabic, Dagestanis introduced one curious change to improve the Arabic script: since the middle of the seventeenth century (and maybe earlier) Dagestanis used additional diacritical markers in their Arabic texts, little 'saddles' inserted over individual words. These additional signs have long been a riddle to Russian Orientalists, and it was only in the 1940s that their nature was revealed by the young Arabist Barabanov (who soon after perished in the World War): not to be confused with the usual dots and strokes that determine the consonants and vocalization of Arabic letters, these little signs are in fact syntactical aids, making a connection between the verb of a sentence and its subject.[6] With this easy system, Dagestani copyists eliminated the uncertainties of unvocalized Arabic texts where subjects (nominatives) could often be confused with objects (accusatives), which lent themselves to opposite interpretation. We now find these helpful signs back in many Dagestani manuscripts of the eighteenth and nineteenth centuries, and even in every-day notes.

The Great *Jihad* as Reflected in Arabic Documents and Literature

In the Dagestani communities, Arabic was of course used for Islamic law; especially legal issues like personal status, marriage and divorce as well as testaments were treated according to the Shafi'i school of Islamic law, and administered by the local mullahs or *qadis* (Islamic judges). But in other legal relations Dagestanis did not necessarily implement Shari'a but followed customary law (*'adat*), that is, what people believed were the customs of their forefathers. Customary law for example provided the regulations for treating cases of theft, murder, manslaughter, and other crimes, in much detail and always according to local circumstances. In general, customary law proscribed that a murderer would be expelled from the community, with his property being confiscated; usually the perpetrator's party had to give a negotiated sum of blood-money to the victim's side to avoid retaliation. The individual rulings often contradicted Islamic law, and they were not pronounced as verdicts by the Islamic *qadis* but were mediated by the village council of elders, in which the most important households were represented. Similarly, violations of property and injuries were punished by fines and restitution payments to the victims. What is more, customary law also regulated the community's use of its resources: the exploitation of pastures, fields, and water, and it also organized the administration and military defense of the village.

The concept that customary law is the 'unchanged ancient practice of the forefathers' is naturally a construct: in reality, customary law has constantly been changed, enlarged, or cut, and adapted to new circumstances. The idea of 'ancient practice' then legitimizes what the community has recently decided. In many societies, customary law lends itself to transformation and manipulation at the hands of the community leaders because this law is usually not written down. This was certainly also the case in many North Caucasian communities. However, at some point in history some Dagestani villages started to fix their customary law decisions in writing: once the council of elders made a decision on a new case, this decision was added to the communal law paper. Over the decades and centuries, these *'adat* papers grew into veritable books of local customary law. These manuscripts also included other important community decisions, for example on an enlargement of mountain pastures and the establishment of new settlements, or on alliances with other parties and on the amount of taxes or services communities had to pay to a certain prince. These historical cases, often provided with dates and signatures, were then copied several times, and have thus survived into our time as testimonies of communal decision-making over the decades and centuries. Typically, community documents of these kinds were called *ittifaqs*, the Arabic word for 'agreements' – they were regarded as consensus decisions of the village community in question.[7] Customary law was thus thoroughly local (produced by the local community for its members), comprehensive (covering items from law, custom and morality to economy and politics), and historical (reflecting historic events of the given communities). In short, customary law personified the identity of the given village community. And again, in the overwhelming majority of cases the customary law books that have survived from the eighteenth and nineteenth centuries were written in Arabic.

Starting in the late seventeenth century, however, opposition rose against this 'consensual' customary law. Some eminent Dagestani scholars demanded that all legal relations be governed by God's Shari'a only, not by the manifold versions of man-made customary law. In the eighteenth and early nineteenth centuries, this opinion found more followers, and some 'agreements' testify to the gradual inclusion of more Islamic elements. At the same time, other Muslim scholars resisted the change of the status quo; they pursued Islamic studies in their schools and scholarly writings but refrained from the revolutionary demand to apply all regulations of Islamic law in their communities. These debates and disputes between Dagestani Muslim scholars are preserved in Arabic fatwas and legal treatises of that time.

By the early nineteenth century, the scholarly opposition against customary law grew into a broader movement for the introduction of Shari'a law. This movement prepared the ground for the Great *Jihad* of the Dagestanis and Chechens against Russia (known in Russian literature as the 'Great Caucasian War'). This *jihad* was, as is the case with most modern *jihad*s, as much a civil war among Muslims as it was a defensive struggle against Western encroachment. The conflict started when local students of Islamic law, led by young charismatic preachers, rebelled against the Muslim elders and local petty princes of their communities (and in some instances against their own teachers), whom they declared apostates for not following Islamic law. When these young men seized power in some Avar mountain villages around 1828, the Russians supported the traditional leaders against this rebellious movement, and the war started. The *jihad* unfolded under the leadership of three subsequent Imams (i.e., *jihad* leaders) from the Avar regions of Central Dagestan, Ghazi-Muhammad (1828-1832), Hamzat Bek (1832-1834) and Shamil (1834-1859). They attempted a political unification of the Sunni Dagestani ethnic groups – scattered as they were over dozens of small principalities and federations of village communities; and at times their *jihad* state also comprised parts of Chechnya. The establishment of a Dagestani state based on Islam (and not on dynasties) and unified by permanent *jihad* was completely new for the Caucasus. The princes had never been able to enforce their rule on so many parts of that rigged country, or to mobilize so many Dagestani communities for a war effort. And the *jihad* was successful: putting the Russian forces under permanent strain, the Imamate lasted for thirty years – longer than the contemporary *jihad* of 'Abd al-Qadir against the French in Algeria.[8]

The establishment of administrative structures in the multi-ethnic regions would not have been possible without the Arabic language, and Arabic-language literature flourished in Dagestan during the *jihad* period. A huge wealth of Arabic documents was produced by the *jihad* leaders and their scribes, and by their correspondents in the villages.[9] Propaganda was also conducted in the Arabic-language. Shamil's scholars began to write fatwas and whole treatises, using the huge spectrum of Islamic law to find arguments why Shamil's rule was legitimate, and why Muslims in the Russian-ruled areas of the Caucasus had to obey Shamil's order to leave their homes and emigrate into Shamil's territory. Other scholars wrote polemics against Shamil, arguing that Shamil was just a self-appointed oppressor with no Islamic credits who only brought misery to the Muslim communities.[10] Shamil himself issued several Arabic law texts, including his famous *Nizam* ('System'), which contained regulations about the Dagestanis' military duties, taxes, prisoners, and the integration of migrant communities into his realm.[11] Also, both before and during the *jihad* Shamil compiled a considerable collection of Arabic books, and several manuscripts from this library, some of them copied by Shamil's own hand, are today preserved in the library of Princeton University.[12]

The *jihad* was also a stimulus for developing literary genres that had previously not found much attention. This is especially visible in the case of historiography; three magnificent Arabic works on Shamil stand out from among the numerous historical writings produced during this period. The most well-known is 'The Shining Dagestani Swords', written by Shamil's court chronicler, the scholar Muhammad-Tahir al-Qarakhi (d. 1881) from the Avar mountain village of Karakh. In this volume, al-Qarakhi describes the rise of the *jihad* movement and the reign of the three Imams, with a focus on Shamil, whose campaigns the author partly accompanied.[13] The work celebrates Shamil's Islamic virtues and praises his capacity as a leader, but it also gives quite a balanced account of his defeats and failures; al-Qarakhi's work also makes it clear that Shamil spent at least as much time subduing Dagestani Muslim communities and keeping them under control as he did fighting Russians. Interestingly, after Shamil's defeat al-Qarakhi was employed by the Russian administration as a *qadi* in one of the Dagestani regions; in fact, the Russian administration needed local personnel with qualifications not only in military and judicial matters but also in Arabic writing, since also the Russians kept their administrative correspondence with the village communities in Arabic.

The other two major volumes on Shamil were produced by 'Abd al-Rahman al-Ghazighumuqi, a son-in-law of Shamil. 'Abd al-Rahman accompanied Shamil into Russian exile in 1859, and it is in Kaluga (south of Moscow) that he wrote his two books. The first of these volumes, whose title can roughly be translated as 'The Epitome of Shamil's Time', differs from al-Qarakhi's account of Shamil's reign; instead of following the *jihad* movement chronologically, 'Abd al-Rahman treats his subject topicwise, with several chapters on Shamil's administration, on the scholars and the state of the Islamic sciences under Shamil, and on individual events.[14] The book thus provides an institutional overview of the *jihad* state, with a wealth of information also on the periods before the *jihad* movement. It is quite possible that it was partly written on Russian demand, or at least with Russian support, for the colonial administration was very interested in how Shamil managed to establish his state (and in fact, Shamil himself was repeatedly interviewed about his time in power, the results of which were published in Russian). 'Abd al-Rahman's second work, 'The Book of Memories', is wholly dedicated to Shamil's personality and his family, and especially to Shamil's time of luxurious house arrest in Kaluga.[15] The captive Shamil was treated by the Russian Tsar with much honor, and in the Russian press Shamil was portrayed as an object of the Russian civilizing mission, as a symbol of Russia's military greatness and an exotic trophy. When it was clear that Shamil ceased to pose any danger he was allowed to leave for Mecca and to Medina, where he died peacefully a year later, in 1871.

Arabic and Vernacular Languages after the *Jihad*

The flourishing of Arabic writing continued after the Shamil period – and again often by Muslim scholars who found themselves in Russian service but still took pride in the achievements of Shamil and his companions. Thus the second half of the nineteenth century saw a new wealth of historical works, and of course of religious genres.

Sufism (Islamic mysticism) assumes a special place in Dagestani literature, and we already mentioned the twelfth-century Sufi encyclopedia of al-Darbandi as the oldest existing Dagestani Arabic work. In the later periods up to the eighteenth century, Sufism was certainly present, but we have no clear picture yet in which forms and brotherhoods it unfolded. The *jihad* period in the first half of the nineteenth century coincided with the spread of the Naqshbandiyya Khalidiyya Sufi brotherhood, which came to Dagestan from the Ottoman Empire via Azerbaijan in the 1820s. Gradually spreading from the South to the North of the country, this brotherhood found adepts in most parts of mountainous Dagestan during the *jihad* period, and it built up a stronghold in Avaria, the core region of the *jihad* movement. Some Dagestani Sufi shaykhs began to compose Arabic Sufi educational literature.

In fact, the whole *jihad* has often been explained as 'Muridism', that is, as an Islamic movement in which the disciples (Arab. *murid*) of the Naqshbandiyya Sufi brotherhood served as the inspiration for the resistance, and as the organizational backbone of the *jihad* state and army.[16] New studies on Dagestani manuscripts from the Shamil period, however, led us to the conclusion that this was not the case.[17] To be sure, some influential Sufi shaykhs played a role in *jihad* propaganda, and one of them, Shaykh Jamal al-Din al-Ghazighumuqi (the father of the above mentioned 'Abd al-Rahman), accompanied Shamil for much of his time in power. But the three Imams themselves did not function as Sufi shaykhs, and they did not educate Sufi disciples. Documents and correspondences from the *jihad* period do not indicate that Sufis played a role in the Imams' troops or in the administration of the *jihad* state. The *jihad* had little to do with Sufism; it emerged not out of Sufi concepts but out of the struggle for Islamic law, as seen above. Tellingly, the major Sufi works produced during the *jihad* time, one of them by Jamal al-Din himself, are works on Sufi ethics and education, and they do not even mention the obligation of *jihad*.[18] The term 'Muridism', used in Russian and many Western sources as equivalent to *jihad*, therefore appears to be a misnomer. It seems to go back to a comparison: Shamil's warriors were found to be as obedient towards their leader as Sufi *murids* are towards their shaykhs. A Sufi brotherhood is in the first place a loose network of teachers and students, united by a shared tradition of moral and spiritual teaching but oftentimes in competition with each other; it is not a military organization.

The ethical and educational aspects of Sufism are also central in Sufi writings produced after the *jihad*. In the latter half of the nineteenth and in the early twentieth centuries the most widespread Sufi brotherhood in mountainous Dagestan was the Mahmudiyya, an offshoot of the Naqshbandiyya khalidiyya brotherhood. The Mahmudiyya shaykhs ostensibly stayed aloof from *jihad*, and they criticized the older Dagestani Naqshbandiyya khalidiyya for their propagandistic support of Shamil's fight against the Russians, which was regarded as senseless by the Mahmudiyya, and as a perversion of Sufi ideals. This Mahmudiyya branch left us with an exceptional set of works on Sufi practice and education as well as an outstanding biographical book on Dagestani Sufis of the nineteenth and early twentieth centuries and volumes of the shaykhs' correspondences. All of these Sufi works were produced in the Arabic language, and they were recently printed in Damascus.[19]

Another genre that was deeply rooted in Dagestani literature but that underwent a significant boom during and after the *jihad* is Arabic poetry.

For the scholar Hasan al-Alqadari (1834-1910) from the Lezgi village of Alqadar in Southern Dagestan, Arabic poetry was not just an aesthetic art: it was a means of communication with fellow Muslims. Hasan, himself a loyal administrator in Russian service, wrote poetry on all occasions, commemorating in his Arabic verses all kinds of anniversaries, reunions of friends, professional promotions of his acquaintances and the births of their children. He maintained a huge network of correspondents; Dagestanis exiled to Russia and Siberia would send him poems about their dreadful situation, knowing that Hasan would reply artfully in the same metrum. Another Arabic medium for long-distance correspondence were fatwas. Fatwas are Islamic legal opinions, and as such an excellent means to express one's opinion on current affairs in the terminology of Islamic law and tradition. The above-mentioned Hasan al-Alqadari, for example, wrote fatwas legitimizing the use of the gramophone and modern geography schoolbooks.[20]

Up to the early twentieth century, Dagestani literature was exclusively a culture of manuscript production, and it was a culture of the Arabic language in the first place. To be sure, there had always been some literary production in the Persian language, mainly in the Southern regions close to Azerbaijan, and Turkic was used next to Arabic for writing in the lowlands, among the Kumyks. The Caucasian vernacular languages were widely used for oral genres like poetry and tales, but not much for writing before the late nineteenth century. To be sure, we know of some impressive monuments of literature in the Caucasian languages of Dagestan. For example, there is an interesting manuscript of customary law, the 'Codex of Rustam Khan' from the Dargi region of Kaytak, that has survived as a manuscript in the Dargi language copied in 1244 AH (1828-29 CE) but certainly going back to earlier times. Similarly, in 1734 the scholar Damadan al-Muhi, from the Lak village of Megeb, compiled a book on medicine in the Lak language. As to Avar, notes in that language are known since at least the late sixteenth century, and in the second half of the eighteenth century the Avar scholar Dibir-Qadi al-Khunzakhi (1742-1817) even developed a system for writing his Caucasian mother tongue in Arabic script with the help of some additional signs.[21] Future research will certainly bring to light more manuscripts in the Caucasian vernacular languages, but it is not probable that this will change the general impression that before the twentieth century, writing in the North Caucasian vernaculars was mostly confined to short notes, often in the margins of Arabic books to clarify an Arabic expression to the reader (Dargi marginal notes are known from a Dagestani copy of al-Ghazali's [d. 1111] Arabic *Minhaj al-*

'abidin from as early as 1497 CE). Thus in most cases, the vernacular language was a supplement and auxiliary to the Arabic, with the small local languages remaining in the shadow of that international giant. Still, some *jihad* proclamations were also produced in Avar, and while the multi-ethnic *jihad* movement in the nineteenth century meant a push for the development of Arabic literature in the first place, it also seems to have produced the general increase in literacy that prepared the ground for a later upsurge in the literatures also of the vernaculars.

This development seems to have gained momentum with the advent of the printing press to Dagestan in the early 1900s. The most successful non-Russian printing house in Dagestan was the 'Islamic Printing House' of Mirza Mavraev from the Avar village of Chokh (1878-1964), founded in 1905 in Temir Khan Shura (today Buinaksk).[22] A huge part of the early printed output was, as could be expected, in Arabic: in addition to Qur'ans and popular Islamic calendars, Mavraev edited classics of moralistic and legal literature and some Sufi works. But Mavraev also printed works in Dagestani vernacular languages (in Arabic letters with some additional signs), especially in Kumyk and Avar followed in numbers by Dargi and Lak, plus some in Chechen – all in all 308 vernacular titles are reported. Many of these works were translations, but they also included innovative historical writings of Dagestani authors (for example by 'Ali Kaiaev in the Lak language)[23] as well as books on geography and small dictionaries of the Dagestani languages; a curious case in point that reflects the multilinguality of the area is Abu Sufyan Akaev's 'Five Tongues' (*Khamsat alsun*, 1910), a pocket guide with word lists in Arabic, Kumyk, Avar, Russian and Chechen!

Printing thus reflected the Arabic character of Islamic literature in Dagestan but also strongly promoted the vernacular languages. As in many other places of the Muslim world, printing targeted a readership broader than the learned circles of Islamic scholars and their students: the new readers obviously had a basic literacy – which means: literacy in Arabic, for the vernacular languages were still written in Arabic letters – but definitely preferred books in their own, spoken languages over Arabic works. The new trend seems to be connected to the Jadid movement in the Turkic-speaking world of the Russian Empire. This 'new method' (*usul-i jadid*) movement was initiated in the late nineteenth century by Tatar educators from the Crimea and the Volga-Urals region (today's Tatarstan and Bashkortostan), and strove for the modernization of the Muslim educational system by using new pedagogical methods (a new method for teaching students to learn to read, modern schoolbooks, and a division of the pupils into grades of peers instead of common classes for all), and they also introduced modern subjects like geography, history and natural sciences as well as Russian language into the Muslim classroom. Due to their attempts to use a form of Turkic (in fact, a Tatar with Ottoman-Turkish interferences) that would be understandable to readers from the various Turkic-speaking peoples of the Russian Empire, Jadidism has often been depicted by Russian and Western observers as conveying a 'pan-Turkic' or 'pan-Islamist' political agenda, aimed at unification of Central Asia, Tataria and the Caucasus with the Ottoman Turks. This interpretation of the Jadidiyya is misleading and even wrong; while there certainly was a feeling of linguistic, cultural and religious connectedness between the modernist elites of various Turkic peoples, we hardly find any evidence of such political dreams in their writings. In addition, the 'pan-Turkic' interpretation is absurd because in Central Asia of the early twentieth century, most Jadids wrote in Persian, not in Turkic.

As to Dagestan, the modernizing movement of the first decades of the twentieth century is only now becoming a topic of research. What is already discernible from the few pioneering works is that Turkic (in its regional variant of Kumyk) was obtaining more importance in Dagestan since the late nineteenth century, to the detriment of Arabic; at the same time, however, the Dagestani modernist movement also included scholars and intellectuals from the Caucasian ethnic groups who developed the use of their particular vernaculars for literature.

At the same time the Muslim intellectuals of the early twentieth century still used Arabic when a country-wide readership was addressed. The most outstanding example for this feature of North Caucasian Muslim modernism is the 'Newspaper of Dagestan' (*Jaridat Daghistan*), the first Muslim newspaper in Dagestan which appeared between January 1913 and 1918.[24] Originally designed as an Arabic mouthpiece of the Russian administration (which might have eased its way through Tsarist censorship), *Jaridat Daghistan* had sections on politics, society and sciences authored by Muslim intellectuals and scholars; its most active contributor was the already mentioned Ali Kaiaev from the Lak town of Kumukh ('Ali al-Ghumuqi, 1878-1943), and it was produced at Mavraev's printing house. The journal soon became a forum for Dagestani and also Chechen and even Cherkess authors, and it included a column for letters to the editors where readers brought up all kinds of political, social and cultural issues. The three central topics of the discourse of that time were language, education and Islam. Kaiaev and many others deplored the ignorance of the Dagestanis, which they explained by poverty, neglect, and especially by the supposedly dreadful state of education in Dagestan. In their eyes, the classical Dagestani *madrasa*s were largely a waste of time because of their inept teaching methods: as Kaiaev explained, students were already at the beginning of their studies confronted with the most difficult texts of Arabic grammar and syntax, which they were expected to simply learn by heart; the idea was that comprehension would come by itself at a later stage, after a decade or two of studying. In reality, most students understood hardly anything, lost interest in their studies and dropped out. Like the Jadids elsewhere, Kaiaev demanded that new pedagogical methods had to be elaborated; students should first read easy texts, with the teachers giving elucidations in their native languages, followed by more difficult texts as the study proceeds. Equally important for Kaiaev was the introduction of modern 'rationalist sciences' in the schools, so that in fact he called for a comprehensive *madrasa* reform. Kaiaev was not sparing with criticisms of the Muslim scholars of Dagestan, which paradoxically must have made up a huge part of his readership.

Another important matter of debate in *Jaridat Daghistan* was which language should be promoted as *lingua franca* for interethnic communication. Defenders of the Arabic argued that parting from the emphasis on Arabic would lead to a decay of Islam and morality in Dagestan. Kaiaev himself was more nuanced: like the Jadids elsewhere, he saw a language reform as a means for a renewal of Islam, and especially for a return to the original texts of Islam, the Qur'an and the Sunna of the Prophet. In his articles he discussed the merits of Turkic, which was anyway widely spoken in some areas of Dagestan, and which would unite Dagestan with the Turkic peoples to the North and South. On the other hand, he showed himself deeply impressed by the success of Russian schools, which seem to have served him as a model for his pedagogical reforms. The most ardent proponents of Russian teaching among the Muslims of Dagestan on the pages of *Jaridat Daghistan* were, however, Socialists like Said Gabiev.

With their push for reforms in the field of language, education and religion, the debates in *Jaridat Daghistan* demonstrate how tightly the Dagestani modernists were embedded in the broader discourse of Jadidism, and indeed they often implored the names of leading Tatar thinkers, like the religious reformer and historian Shihab al-Din al-Marjani from Kazan (d. 1889) and the Crimean Tatar pioneer of Jadidism, Ismail Gasprinskii (d. 1914). This Muslim modernism of the early twentieth century, in Dagestan as elsewhere, prepared the ground for the promotion of the national languages by the Bolsheviks in the 1920s.

Saving the Heritage: Arabic Literature in the Soviet Period

After the October Revolution of 1917 and during the Russian Civil War (1918-1921), the country was in political turmoil; the White and Red Armies crisscrossed Dagestan, devastating villages and killing and expelling populations. At the same time there were several contradicting attempts at state-building in Dagestan. While the Socialists set up a wider North Caucasian republic, some religious leaders in the mountains tried to establish an Islamic state: the old scholar Uzun Hajji from Salta (d. 1920) proclaimed himself head of a North Caucasian Emirate, and also the Avar nobleman Najmaddin Gotsinskii (d. 1925) set up military resistance to the Bolsheviks. Other scholars, like Ali Akushinskii, tried to cooperate with the Bolsheviks, but were liquidated in the process.[25] In 1921, the Dagestan region of Tsarist times was transformed into the Dagestan Autonomous Soviet Socialist Republic within the Russian FSR. Attached to the new Dagestani ASSR were some Nogai lowlands in the North that did not belong to historical Dagestan.

Soviet rule in the Muslim regions of the Soviet Union is often depicted as equivalent to heavy persecution, and to the uprooting of anything that had to do with Islam. While this view is largely correct, some important nuances have to be made. In general, Muslims welcomed the overthrow of the Tsarist regime in February 1917 as an end of Tsarist repression; and Lenin's and Stalin's promise of national self-determination for the peoples of the former Empire instilled hopes. Some Muslim intellectuals from Dagestan – mostly of a conservative or liberal persuasion – had been represented in the Russian State Duma since 1906. Dagestanis were thus drawn into the new forms of Russian politics, which led to more contacts with Muslim politicians and intellectuals from other parts of the Empire, especially with Tatars.

When the Bolsheviks established their rule in Dagestan in the 1920s, they did not have a power base in the mountains, and were desperately in need of local cadres to staff the regional administration and Party offices. We know from Central Asia and Tatarstan that the Bolsheviks were forced to cooperate with the Jadids, the reformist-minded Muslim intellectuals, throughout the early 1920s. For the Jadids, the Bolsheviks' push for national (indigenous) forms of modern education in the republics seemed to converge to a certain degree with their own interests, and for a while an uneasy alliance between Bolsheviks and Muslim reformists came into being. There is no post-Soviet study on these developments in Dagestan as of yet, but we can assume that things went in a similar direction.

Some scholars and Sufi shaykhs, like Sayfallah al-Nitsubkri (Bashlarov, d. 1920), cooperated with the Bolsheviks, and our printer Mirza Mavraev took on a leading position in the new Dagestan Publishing House; many others at least did not openly oppose the Soviet programs. In the first half of the 1920s, Islamic education in mosques and *madrasa*s was still widespread and largely unmolested in Dagestan. This changed, however, around 1927/1928, with the start of the huge Stalinist collectivization and witch-hunt campaigns that were accompanied by the closure or destruction of most Islamic institutions, including mosques, schools, libraries, and Islamic pious foundations; in the late twenties and throughout the thirties, thousands of Islamic scholars and Muslim intellectuals were arrested, exiled, sent to the GULag camps, or shot. After the years of the Red Terror, 1936-1938, most of the Muslim intellectuals were dead or deported. The broken fates can be illustrated by our main protagonists from above: the Lak publisher and educator Ali Kaiaev was arrested for the first time in 1930 on charges of 'counterrevolutionary activities' and exiled to the Urals; after four years he was released by mediation of Korkmasov, the then chairman of the DASSR government. In 1938 Kaiaev was again arrested, this time because of his connections to the former chairman who had by then fallen into disgrace, in addition to charges of espionage for the Turks. Kaiaev was exiled to Semipalatinsk, Kazakhstan, where he died of typhus in 1943. The first Dagestani printer, Mirza Mavraev, had more luck; he saw a smear campaign building up against himself in 1928 and escaped arrest by fleeing from Dagestan. After a failed attempt to leave the USSR via Baku, he also ended up in Kazakhstan, where he found a modest job as mechanic under a false name. He died in Akmolinsk in 1964.[26]

The Party's all-out attack on Muslim scholars and intellectuals as well as on Islam and Arabic had its 'positive' side in the Soviets' promotion of vernacular languages. Here the Bolsheviks de facto continued – albeit in a much more radical and centralized fashion – what the Muslim modernists had started. While the latter had argued for the use of improved and adapted Arabic letters for the regional languages, the Soviets opted for the wholesale liquidation of the Arabic alphabet. As a result, two contradicting radical script reforms hit Dagestan – just like all other Muslim regions of the Soviet Union – in the 1920s and 1930s.

In 1926 the decision was made to abolish the Arabic script used for the languages of the Muslim minority nations of the Soviet Union. As the introduction of the Russian (Cyrillic) alphabet for the small nations would have smelled of Russian nationalism and chauvinism, the Soviets introduced the Latin alphabet, that is what we would call European letters (again with some modifications for the phonetic peculiarities of each language). In 1927, almost overnight everything had to be written in the new alphabet. For the Turkic-speaking nations of the Soviet Union, the script reform was devastating because it deprived the young generation of access to works written before the change. At the same time, many elderly people – and also most Muslim scholars, hitherto the main bearers of Arabic literacy – were suddenly 'illiterate' in everything that was newly produced. This was fully intended.

This abrupt change was part of a broader policy that has recently been called the Soviet 'Affirmative Action Policy' for the minority nations of the USSR.[27] The Soviets spent a lot of effort and resources on upgrading many small languages that hitherto had no or only a limited written literary tradition, to full-fledged literary languages. In Dagestan, the 1920s saw a significant production of literatures and school books in languages such as Avar, Dargi, Kumyk, Lezgi and Lak, in addition to Chechen and Azeri. In order to demonstrate the blessings they brought to the Dagestani nations, the Soviets even declared that before 1917 the Caucasian languages never had any written tradition – a blatant lie, as can be seen from the many historical examples of Kumyk, Avar, Lak and Dargi writings mentioned above.

The active promotion of small nations' literatures and national cultures was a measure to educate and mobilize Muslim society for the Bolsheviks' political purposes; it also allowed the Bolsheviks to pose as defenders of national cultures, thus taking the wind out of the nationalists' sails. It was also a clear and successful strategy to eliminate the influence of Arabic: Arabic was denounced as the language of the Qur'an, as a language that by its very nature transports religiosity; it was a tool in the hands of the class enemies, and especially the parasitic Muslim 'clergy' (scholars and Sufis) who exploited the Muslim working population by their 'superstitions'. In addition, the Soviets feared Arabic because it allowed international contacts with Muslims in the Middle East.

In Dagestan, the strong encouragement of national written languages, together with the open persecution of Arabic, paved the way for the Russian language to replace Arabic as a Dagestani means of interethnic, republican-wide communication. In the 1930s, Russian became mandatory at schools, and Dagestan inevitably became a Russian-speaking republic. This is the other side of the Bolsheviks' affirmative action policy towards the Dagestani languages: as the use of the small languages and literatures was restricted to small pockets of Dagestan, their actual sphere was minimal. Due to the Soviets' national policy of 'compartmentalization', not the Dagestani languages but Russian became central in the public sphere –

and also in the countrywide Dagestani literature and the media. The national languages smacked of provincialism, while Russian was the gateway for a career. As if that was not enough, the Soviets dealt another blow to the national literatures in 1937-1940, when the recently introduced Latin alphabets were replaced by Cyrillic – with the same devastating results as ten years earlier. The change to Cyrillic must be seen against the background of Stalinism. Stalin, although himself of Georgian nationality, pushed the interpretation that the Russians were historically the leading nation in the Russian Empire and the Soviet Union, so that the introduction of Cyrillic for the small nations were to be regarded as a step towards their 'drawing closer' (Russ., *sblizhenie*) to the advanced culture of the Russians.

The remaining Muslim scholars in Dagestan must have perceived this language policy with utmost horror. Not only that they saw their leading social position eroded by the new generations of intellectuals; now Islam was to be wiped out, and with it Dagestani literature in Arabic – in fact, everything that was Dagestani Muslim history and identity!

One of our witnesses from that time is Nadhir al-Durgili (1891-1934), a Muslim scholar from the village of Durgeli in Northern Central Dagestan. Nadhir left us with a wealth of Arabic papers, mostly short writings and excerpts from other authors' books – nothing spectacular in itself but extremely interesting as a whole. In an effort to save from destruction what could still be saved, Nadhir gathered all information on Dagestani scholars of the previous centuries until his own times, the late 1920s and early 1930s, and compiled them in one book. The outcome is a fascinating biographical and bibliographical dictionary, preserved only in a small number of Arabic manuscripts before it was finally edited in 2004.[28] This compilation was a desperate attempt to save the Islamic memory of the Dagestanis against the ongoing Soviet attack on Islam and Arabic culture. Nadhir's book can also be read as a literary anthology, with many long excerpts from Arabic prose and especially poetry written by Dagestani scholars of the eighteenth to early twentieth centuries. This poetry is at times closely related to the political events, and provides valuable insight into how Dagestani Muslims perceived the *jihad* and its leaders. Interestingly, the work does not include any texts in languages other than Arabic. A similar but shorter attempt at a biographical dictionary of Dagestani scholars, in the Kumyk/Turkic language in Arabic script, was made by the above-mentioned Ali Kaiaev, and has not yet been published.[29] In the 1920s and 1930s other authors produced local histories in the vernaculars (like the Kumyk historian al-Qarabudakhkenti)[30] that equally remained unpublished.

The history of Dagestani Islam in the Soviet period is only beginning to be studied seriously.[31] We now know that Sufi education never ceased to be transmitted in the remote Dagestani villages, and with it also a rudimentary teaching of Arabic in private houses, in small circles isolated from each other and under the threat of denunciation to the authorities. We can also assume that Muslim education in private enjoyed a certain comeback in the mid-1950s when many Dagestani mullahs returned from exile and from the GULag camps. Interestingly, a good deal of this modest revival took place within the Dagestani branch of the Soviet Academy of Sciences.

With the Soviet abolition of the Arabic script for Dagestani languages, not only Arabic literature was on the verge of annihilation but also the pre-revolutionary heritage in North Caucasian languages in the Arabic script. In the newly established Soviet research institutions, there was a chronic shortage in personnel trained in Muslim languages. While Soviet historians usually saw their foremost task in the revolutionary rewriting of history in a Marxist framework, against 'bourgeois' historiography and with tight ideological dogmas, they still could not completely do without some knowledge of Arabic and of the Arabic script. It is therefore in the newly established museums and research institutes that we find some people busy with cataloging and describing Arabic and 'ajam manuscripts of Dagestan's Islamic past. As Arabic was hardly taught any more in Soviet Dagestan, the institutions had to rely on persons who still had a thorough classical education from pre-revolutionary times. As these persons were regarded as ideologically unreliable, and as they had no formal academic degrees from the Soviet educational system, they worked in modest positions, mostly as clerks and assistants in the institutes' libraries. Today, their casual writings are much more interesting and helpful than the thick books of their institute's directors.

One of these scribes and assistants was Muhammad Inkvachilav, an Avar scholar who, probably since the 1920s and 1930s, had copied Arabic and Avar documents and transcribed them into the new Latin alphabet for Avar. He thus preserved the texts of many Dagestani historical documents for us, the originals of which have in the meantime been lost. Another person to whom we owe the survival of many Dagestani texts is the Kumyk school teacher Mansur Gaidarbekov, who seemingly worked part-time at the newly established Institute for History, Language and Literatures (IIIaL) in Makhachkala. In 1965 Gaidarbekov compiled, like Nadhir al-Durgili thirty years before him, an anthology of Dagestani Arabic poetry.[32] He copied the Arabic originals by hand (there was no means for typing or printing Arabic letters at the Institute), and supplied them with typewritten provisional Russian translations; these translations show that Gaidarbekov was probably more at home in Arabic than in Russian. His work, a treasury of Dagestani poetry in Arabic, has remained unpublished to this day, and it has rarely been used by scholars.

Another example of Muslim scholars who became integrated into the Soviet academic system without ever aspiring for a doctorate was the Arabist Magomed-Said Saidov (Muhammad-Sa'id al-Awari, d. 1985), who was in charge of the manuscript collection of the Institute in Makhachkala. Saidov wrote a brief but ground-breaking survey of the history of Dagestani Arabic literature, which was published in 1963 in the Russian-language proceedings of a Congress of Orientalists (it seems he held his paper in the Arabic language, and it was also published separately in that language).[33] Another major work of his, a translation of the above-mentioned 'Abd al-Rahman al-Ghazighumuqi's historical account of Shamil's *jihad*, obviously did not pass censorship, and it could only be published in book form in 1997, long after Saidov's death.[34] Less problematic was Saidov's work as a linguist; his Avar-Russian dictionary, a great source that also includes historical material, did indeed go to the press. Saidov also produced the first small catalog of Arabic manuscripts of the Institute, published in 1977.[35]

This combination of traditional and Soviet education still lives on in the work of the now elderly generation of post-war scholars in the Dagestani research institutions, personified in the eminent Arabist and scholar of Islam, Prof. Amri Shikhsaidov (b. in 1928) from the Lezgi town of Kasumkent in Southern Dagestan. A disciple of the famous Leningrad Arabist Ignatii Krachkovskii (d. 1951), Shikhsaidov against all ideological odds defended his doctoral and habilitational dissertations on Islamic history and the Arabic manuscript culture of Dagestan; his work repeatedly earned him 'strong reprimands' from Party offices.[36] Still working at the Institute for History, Archeology and Ethnography in Makhachkala, Shikhsaidov has been conducting archeographical expeditions into the Dagestani mountains since the 1960s, documenting, studying and publishing Arabic inscriptions and manuscripts in private possession. Next to the Avar Timur Aitberov (a specialist in Arabic sources on Dagestani customary law at Makhachkala University) and a few other specialists still trained in Oriental languages, Shikhsaidov has been encouraging a new generation of Arabists who now study aspects of recent and contemporary Islamic culture that had been completely taboo in the Soviet period. Supported by the academic interest in Dagestani history and Islam, a significant movement of local history has emerged since the 1990s, with valuable amateur publications on local sources (especially connected to Shamil's *jihad* in the regions) and accounts of oral history.

The 'Islamic Boom' since the 1990s: Russian as the New Language of Islam

The new rise of Islam in Dagestan in the 1990s brought renewed attention to the importance of Arabic religious literature. This Islamic boom was usually understood in the dichotomous terms of 'traditionalism' versus 'Islamic fundamentalism' or 'Wahhabism'. This binary opposition, however, is a gross simplification.

Already in the 1940s the USSR had established Muslim spiritual boards (Muftiates), with the Muftiate in the Dagestani town of Buinaksk (later transferred to the capital Makhachkala) as a kind of small-scale administration for Islam in the whole of the Sunni North Caucasus. These Muftiates, under tight ideological control, gave the semblance of a self-representation of Islam in the Soviet Union, and were mainly in charge of maintaining and staffing the few surviving mosques in their respective areas. Since Brezhnev's reign, the Soviet struggle against Islam had been significantly scaled down, and was most of the time limited to propaganda, atheist education and surveillance. While Dagestan had officially not more than some twenty to thirty mosques, many prayer rooms had been reopened without official licenses in the villages and kolkhozes,[37] with the authorities closing their eyes as long as no political problems ensued. The relationship between the Soviet Muftiate and these community mosques outside of their purview has often been described in terms of an opposition between 'official' and 'parallel' Islam; recent research, however, has made us understand that one can better speak of a continuity, and a division of functions and labor, between the official and 'unofficial' institutions of Islam and Islamic education. Glasnost' further eroded the state control over Islam, and the end of the Soviet Union brought a new dynamic to the Islamic sector. Mirroring the dissolution of the USSR itself, the four official Soviet Muftiates fell apart into numerous republican Spiritual Boards, with the one in Makhachkala now reduced to a solely Dagestani Muftiate.

The Soviet propaganda efforts to reduce the influence of Islam among the population were, above all, aimed at the eradication of Sufism, which was portrayed as 'superstition' and as the deception of the working population. Paradoxically, in their struggle against Sufism the Soviets at times found allies in fundamentalist-minded Salafists, who also condemned Sufism as anti-scientific, and as a deviation from the scriptures of Islam.[38] The Soviet Muftiates stood somewhere in between these two trends: they were often manned by scholars who had Sufi backgrounds, but they also issued fatwas against 'popular', uncontrolled religious practices.

After the dissolution of the USSR, the formerly Autonomous Socialist Soviet Republic of Dagestan remained in the Russian Federation, now known simply as the Republic of Dagestan. The republican parliament and government continued to be composed on the basis of 'consociationalism', that is, with institutionalized quotas that secured the top functions in politics and economy to the major ethnic groups of the country, but that also secured the smaller ethnic groups representation in parliament and councils. In this system, the Avars secured the Muftiate and most of the Islamic establishments for themselves.[39] Competing religious boards of the Kumyks, Laks, Nogays and other small nations were set up in the 1990s in a wave of nationalist movements of these groups that threatened to lead to a dissolution of Dagestan as a single republic; however, these 'ethnic' Muftiates were quickly dissolved by governmental decree. Today, the Spiritual Board, the Dagestani Council of Islamic Scholars and most of the private Islamic institutes that survived after the Islamic boom of the 1990s in Dagestan are controlled by the Mahmudiyya branch of the Naqshbandiyya brotherhood, with the shaykh Said Apandi Chirkeevskii pulling the strings. Muslim traditionalism, and more precisely a combination of the major Dagestani Sufi tradition of the Naqshbandiyya and the legal tradition of the Shafi'i school of Islamic law, are now presented as the rightful, because autochthonous, form of Islam that needs to be defended against intrusions of foreign, 'alien' Islams. The emergence of this monopolizing form of 'traditional Islam' as a backbone of the secular Dagestani republic in the Russian Federation occurred against the background of the conflict in neighboring Chechnya, where nationalist separatism had been hijacked by Islamic radical groups since the early 1990s. The two Russian wars in Chechnya (1994-1996, and 1999 to the present time) have significantly destabilized Dagestan, and radicalized parts of its Islamic youth.

With the Naqshbandiyya in control of the official Islamic institutions in Dagestan and backed by the state, all other trends of Islam have come under suspicion, and are often associated with 'Wahhabism'. Wahhabism has become a key term in the post-Soviet discourse of Islam in the former Soviet Union, and also in Dagestan. The term is derived from the teaching of the eighteenth-century preacher Ibn 'Abd al-Wahhab in what is today Saudi Arabia. As the Saudis and Saudi-Arabian based Islamic institutions and NGOs have, since the 1970s, increasingly used the revenues from oil and the Mecca pilgrimage to propagate the Saudi model of Islam in the rest of the Sunni world, 'Wahhabism' has today become a synonym for world-wide 'fundamentalism'.[40] Both 'fundamentalism' and 'Wahhabism' are today applied almost interchangeably to various forms of Islamic movements, from a-political pious community lifestyle over Salafism to terrorism. Following an attack of Chechen Islamists/separatists on Dagestani villages in the summer of 1999, the Russian Federation and the Republic of Dagestan issued an official state ban on 'Wahhabism', without clarifying what this term comprises and what not. Today, any sort of Islamic expression can be suppressed under this vague title. This indiscriminate state measure outrages the pious mountain communities that try to defy the control of the state and the Avar-dominated Muftiate.

The end of Soviet control also led to a boom of the Islamic book market in Russia, and in Dagestan in particular. Interestingly, literature of Islamic thinkers from Egypt or Pakistan were sold in Dagestan mostly in Russian translations, reflecting the fact that only Russian was accessible to readers from all Dagestani ethnic groups. Also the Dagestani religious leaders, like the above-mentioned Said Apandi, published mainly in Russian,[41] and the same holds true for most Islamic newspapers. While Russian is also the language of the public discourse against 'Wahhabism', also the Islamic opposition in Chechnya and Dagestan uses Russian for its internet publications; Shamil Basaev wrote his 'Jihad Manual' in Russian, and also the declaration of the 'Caucasian Caliphate' by the Chechen underground leader Dokku Umarov in fall 2007 was published in that language.[42] Thus Russian became the language of Dagestani Islam that once was Arabic; a curious result of Soviet politics.

At the same time, Arabic is still enjoying high prestige as the language of Islamic learning. Many Dagestani students acquired Arabic language skills when studying in Turkey and the Middle East, and teaching Arabic is also central to the sixteen or more Islamic institutes or *madrasas* that now function in the Republic of Dagestan, and is also offered at the University of Makhachkala and many public and private institutes. While the current book market offers many Islamic primers in the Arabic language, most of these are reprints from the period before 1917, plus some modern Arabic textbooks of Russian provenance. To my knowledge, Dagestani religious authorities have not yet rediscovered Arabic for writing original works, and thus for re-establishing a learned discourse of Islam that would be targeting only the *madrasa*-educated elite; this place is held by Russian.

Contemporary Islam in Dagestan is thus a curious mixture of indigenous traditions from the medieval past and the nineteenth-century *jihad* period, of Soviet administrative and educational traditions, of post-1991 Russian attempts to create a loyal state Islam, and of various international influences. This combination is unique in the world; each of its elements unites Dagestanis with Muslims elsewhere, but as a whole Dagestani Islam is still very specific, and struggling to maintain its interior balance against all domestic and foreign challenges. Dagestan will probably continue to be a small but very peculiar island between the Oceans of Russia and the Middle East, and situated between other specific blends of Islam emerging in the neighboring republics.

Notes

1   Lavrov, L.I. (1966: 57). *Epigraficheskie pamiatniki Severnogo Kavkaza na arabskom, persidskom i turetskom iazykakh*, part 1. Moscow.
2   Genko, A.N. (1941: 85-86). 'Arabskii iazyk i kavkazovedenie', *Trudy vtoroi sessii arabistov 19-23 okt. 1937*. Moscow, Leningrad.
3   Alikberov, A.K. (2003). *Epokha klassicheskogo islama na Kavkaze*. Moscow.
4   Orazaev, G.M.-R. and A.R. Shikhsaidov (1992). *Mukhammed Avabi Aktashi, 'Derbend-name'* Makhachkala; Shikhsaidov, A.R., T.M. Aitberov and G.M.-R. Orazaev (1993). *Dagestanskie istoricheskie sochineniia*. Moscow; Kemper, M. (2005: 75-111). *Herrschaft, Recht und Islam in Daghestan*. Wiesbaden.
5   Reichmuth, S. (1998: 26-29). 'The Interplay of Local Developments and Transnational Relations in the Islamic World', *Muslim Culture in Russia and Central Asia*, vol. 2, Kügelgen, A. v., M. Kemper and A.J. Frank (eds.). Berlin. Compare Krachkovskii, I. Iu. (1937: 288-296). 'Daghestan et Yémen', *Mélanges Gautier*. Algiers.
6   Barabanov, A.M. (1945: 183-214). 'Poiasnitel'nye znachki v arabskikh rukopisiakh i dokumentakh Severnogo Kavkaza', *Sovetskoe vostokovedenie* III.
7   Bobrovnikov, V.O. (2002: 21-27). 'Ittifāq Agreements in Daghestan in the Eighteenth-Nineteenth Centuries', in: *Manuscripta Orientalia* 8:4; Kemper, M. (2004: 115-151). 'Communal Agreements (*Ittifāqāt*) and *'ādāt*-Books from Daghestani Villages and Confederacies (18th-19th Centuries)', *Der Islam* 81. For customary law in general see also Bobrovnikov, V.O. (2002). *Musul'mane severnogo Kavkaza. Obychai, pravo, nasilie*. Moscow.
8   For comparisons with Algeria see Kemper, M. (2007: 28-58). 'The Changing Images of Jihad Leaders: Shamil and Abd al-Qadir in Daghestani and Algerian Historical Writing', *Nova Religio* 11:2.

9   For Shamil's correspondences see Omarov, Kh. A. (1997). *100 pisem Shamilia*. Makhachkala; and Sharafutdinova, R. Sh. (2001). *Araboiazychnye dokumenty epokhi Shamilia*. Moscow.

10 Kemper, M. (2002: 265-278). 'The Daghestani Legal Discourse on the Imamate', *Central Asian Survey* 21: 3.

11 Kemper, *Herrschaft*, p.366-381.

12 Kemper, M., A.R. Shikhsaidov and N.A. Tagirova (2002: 121-140), 'The 'Shamil Collection' of the Princeton University Library', *The Princeton University Library Chronicle*, vol. LXVI, no. 1.

13 Muhammad-Tahir al-Qarakhi, *Bariqat al-suyuf al-daghistaniyya fi ba'd al-ghazawat al-shamiliyya*, Arabic ed. Barabanov, A.M. and I.Iu. Krachkovskii (1946). Moscow; Leningrad; *Khronika Mukhammeda Takhira al-Karakhi o dagestanskikh voinakh v period Shamilia*, Russ. transl. Barabanov, Krachkovskii (ed.). (1941). Moscow; Leningrad.

14 'Abd al-Rahman al-Ghazi-Ghumuqi, *Kniga vospominanii saiiida Abdurakhmana [Tadhkirat 'Abd al-Rahman]*, Russian transl. Saidov, M.-S., Shikhsaidov, A.R. and Kh.A. Omarov (eds.). (1997). Makhachkala. (with Arabic facsimile).

15 Al-Gazikumukhi, A. (2002). *Kratkoe izlozhenie podrobnogo opisaniia del Imama Shamilia*, Arabic facsimile and Russian transl. by Natal'ia Tagirova. Moscow.

16 Zelkina, A. (2000). *In Quest of God and Freedom. Sufi Responses to the Russian Advance in the North Caucasus*. London. More nuanced is Gammer, M. (1994). *Resistance to the Tsar: Shamil and the Conquest of Chechnia and Daghestan*. London.

17 Kemper, M. (2006: 111-126). 'The North Caucasian Khalidiyya and ,Muridism': Historiographical Problems', in: *Journal for the History of Sufism* vol. 5. See also *Severnyi kavkaz v sostave Rossiiskoi imperii*, Bobrovnikov, V.O. and I.L. Babich. (eds.). (2007: 97-99). Moscow.

18 Kemper, *Herrschaft*, pp. 224-234.

19 The most important of these publications are: Shu'ayb b. Idris al-Bagini. (1417/1996). *Tabaqat al-khwajagan al-naqshbandiyya*, ed. 'Abd al-Jalil al-'Ata'. Damascus; Mir Khalid Sayfallah b. Husayn Bashlar al-Nitsubkri al-Ghazi-Ghumuqi al-Daghistani (Damascus, 1998). *Maktubat Khalid Sayfallah*; Hasan Hilmi b. Muhammad al-Qahi, *Maktubat al-Qahi* (Damascus, 1998). Compare Kemper, M. (2002: 41-71). 'Khālidiyya Networks in Daghestan and the Question of *Jihād*', *Die Welt des Islams* 42:1.

20 For Hasan al-Alqadari's poetry see his *Diwan al-Mamnun* (Temir-Khan-Shura, 1913); for fatwas see his *Jirab al-Mamnun* (Temir-Khan Shura, 1912). For an analysis, see Kemper, M. (2006: 95-107). 'Daghestani Shaykhs and Schol-

ars in Russian Exile: Networks of Sufism, Fatwas and Poetry', *Daghestan and the World of Islam*, Gammer, M. and D. J. Wasserstein. (eds.). Helsinki.

21 Isaev, A.A. (1991: 85-89). 'K voprosu o datirovke darginskikh zapisei na poliakh arabskikh rukopisei XV v.', *Istochnikovedenie istorii i kul'tury narodov Dagestana i Severnogo Kavkaza*. Makhachkala; Magomedov, R. (1965). *Pamiatnik istorii i pis'mennosti dargintsev XVII veka*. Makhachkala; Saidov, M.S. (1948: 136-140). 'Vozniknovenie pis'mennosti u avartsev', *Iazyki Dagestana* 1. Makhachkala.

22 Isaev, A.A. (2003). *Magomedmirza Mavraev: Pervopechatnik i prosvetitel' Dagestana*. Makhachkala, for Mavraev's work and biography.

23 Isaev, A.A. (1986: 104-112). 'Al-Khikaia al-madiia – pamiatnik dagestanskoi istoriografii', *Istochnikovedenie srednevekovogo Dagestana*. Makhachkala,.

24 For the following discussion see the pioneering work of Navruzov, A.R. (2007: 14-73). *Gazeta 'Dzharidat Dagistan' (1913-1918) kak istoriko-kul'turnyi istochnik*. Makhachkala.

25 For a first post-Soviet study on these events see Sulaev, I. Kh. (2004). *Musul'manskoe dukhovenstvo Dagestana i svetskaia vlast': bor'ba i sotrudnichestvo (1917-1921)*. Makhachkala.

26 Compare Bobrovnikov, V.O. (2006: 192-194). 'Kaiaev, Ali', *Islam na territorii byvshei Rossiiskoi Imperii: Entsiklopedicheskii slovar '*, in Prozorov, S.M. (ed.). vol. I. Moscow, and Isaev, *Magomedmirza Mavraev.*

27 Martin, T. (2001). *The Affirmative Action Empire: Nations and Nationalism in the Soviet Union, 1923-1939*. Ithaca.

28 *Die Islamgelehrten Daghestans und ihre arabischen Werke. Naḏir ad-Durgilīs (st. 1935) Nuzhat al-aḏhān fī tarāǧim 'ulamā' Dāġistān*, Arabic ed., German transl. and comm. by Kemper, M. and A.R. Šixsaidov (2004). *Muslim Culture in Russia and Central Asia*, vol. 4. Berlin.

29 Ali Kaiaev, *Tarajim 'ulama' Daghistan*, IIAE, fond 25, opis' I, no. 1678.

30 Compare Orazaev, G.M.-R. (2001). *Istoriia Karabudakhkenta Dzhamalutdina-Khadzi Karabudakhkentskogo*. Makhachkala.

31 For a first overview see Bobrovnikov, V.O., A. Navruzov and Sh. Shikhaliev (2009: 107-167), 'Islamic Education in Soviet and Post-Soviet Daghestan', *Islamic Education in the Soviet Union and Its Successor States*, Kemper, M. R. Motika and S. Reichmuth (eds.). London: Routledge.

32 Gaidarbekov, M. *Antologiia dagestanskoi poezii*, typoscript IIAE Makhachkala, fond 3, opis' 1, no. 129.

33 Saidov, M.-S. (1963: 118-123). 'Dagestanskaia literatura XVIII-XIX vv na arabskom iazyke', in: *Trudy dvadtsat'-piatogo Mezhdunarodnogo kongressa vostokovedov*, tom II. Moscow; also published in Arabic: Muhammad Sa'id al-Awari, *Ta'rikh al-adab al-'arabiyya fi Daghistan* (Baghdad, s.a. [1963?]), 14 pp.

34 *Kniga vospominanii saiiida Abdurakhmana*, transl. Saidov, M.-S. and Shikhsaidov, A.R. and Kh.A. Omarov (eds.). (1997). Makhachkala.

35 *Katalog arabskikh rukopisei IIIaL Dagestanskogo filial AN SSSR* (Moscow, 1977).

36 Shikhsaidov, A.R. (2008). *Ocherki istorii, istochnikovedeniia, arkheografii srednevekovogo Dagestana*. Makhachkala.

37 Bobrovnikov, V.O. (2004: 563-593). 'Arkheologiia stroitel'stva islamskikh traditsii v dagestanskom kolkhoze', *Ab Imperio* 3; Bobrovnikov, "'Traditionalist" versus "Islamist": Identitites in a Dagestani Collective Farm', *Central Asian Survey* 25 (2006: 287-302).

38 Muminov, A. (2007: 249-262). 'Fundamentalist Challenges to Local Islamic Traditions in Soviet and Post-Soviet Central Asia', *Empire, Islam and Politics in Central Eurasia*, Tomohiko, U. (ed.). Sapporo: Slavic Eurasian Studies No. 14; Babajanov, B. (2001). 'O fetvakh SADUMa protiv "neislamskikh obychaev"', *Islam na postsovetskom prostranstve: vzgliad iznutri*, Malashenko A. and M. B. Olcott (eds.). Moscow.

39 Bobrovnikov, Navruzov, Shikhaliev , 'Islamic Education in Soviet and Post-Soviet Daghestan', p. 141-169. Compare Matsuzato, K. and M.-R. Ibragimov (2005: 753-779). 'Islamic Politics at the Sub-regional Level in Dagestan: Tariqa Brotherhoods, Ethnicities and the Spiritual Board', *Europe-Asia Studies* 57:5 (with interesting case studies).

40 Knysh, A. (2004: 3-26). 'A Clear and Present Danger: Wahhabism as a Rhetoric Foil', *Die Welt des Islams* 44:1.

41 Said-afandi al'-Chirkavi, (2003). *Sokrovishchnitsa blagodatnykh znanii*. Moscow.

42 Roshchin, M. (2009, March 13). 'Caucasus Emirate: Virtual Myth or Reality?' *Jamestown Foundation North Caucasus Weekly*, vol. 10:10. http://www.jamestown.org/single/?no_cache=1&tx_ttnews%5Btt_news%5D=34708 (last accessed June 21, 2009).

4 Chechnya and Russia, between Revolt and Loyalty

Marc Jansen

In the late twentieth century, seemingly out of the blue, they were suddenly brought to international notice: one million Chechens with their small country in the northeastern Caucasus mountains, less than half the size of the Netherlands. Does Chechnya have a right to independence, and is there any chance of recognition of this status? Or is it rather a part of Russia? Two wars have been fought over this issue since then, killing tens of thousands of people. A little study of history could have taught the Russians that these were formidable opponents indeed.

Thousands of years ago, the Chechens' ancestors settled in this mountainous and woody territory, managing to hold their own against other mountain peoples as well as against foreign invaders. Relatively late, they converted to Islam (Sufism), preserving some animist left-overs. Belief was at the centre of their resistance to foreign rule. Strongly egalitarian, Chechen society is based on clans ('teips'); loyalty to the clan comes first, blood feud being practiced. Far into the twentieth century, national consciousness was lacking, until it was encouraged by a deportation in 1944 and the struggle for independence after 1991.

During the second half of the eighteenth century, under empress Catherine the Great, the Russian army started establishing permanent stations in the North Caucasus, then an Ottoman protectorate, as a first step in the subjection of the mountain peoples. Then and there, Chechen opposition to Russian rule began. It was 'unparalleled among other colonial nations', according to Marie Bennigsen, who deems the resistance led by the Chechens and the Dagestanis 'the longest of any Muslim nations against a western colonizer'.[1] Moshe Gammer, however, makes some distinctions with respect to the idea of resistance as a distinguishing feature of Chechen culture, pointing out that it always originated with a minority, whereas the majority was prepared to compromise.[2]

From 1785 to 1791, Sheik Mansur led the first major revolt. Meanwhile, helped by Christian nations like the Georgians and the Armenians, the Russians moved down south along the coast of the Black Sea, cutting off the

North Caucasians from the Ottoman Empire. In subjecting the mountain peoples, the Russian commander in the Caucasus, General Alexei Yermolov, used cruel methods. 'Condescension' he thought a 'sign of weakness' in the eyes of 'Asiatics'. 'Born rebels', the 'bold and dangerous' Chechens were to be 'constrained within their mountains'. Yermolov's chief-of-staff, General Alexei Veliaminov, wanted to starve them into submission: 'Let the standing corn be destroyed each autumn as it ripens.' Forests were cut down, crops devastated, villages sacked, men massacred and women raped or sold as slaves.[3] These are familiar colonial methods. In 1818 the fortress Groznaia (Russian for 'menacing') was founded as headquarters in the subjection campaign (later, Grozny became Chechnya's capital).

The campaign took a heavy toll. During four decades of war, some 77,000 Russian soldiers were killed,[4] along with a much higher number of indigenous victims. In 1829 a large-scale revolt broke out, led by Imam Shamil, an Avar from Dagestan. His assistant Hadji Murat, known by Lev Tolstoy's novel of the same name, deserted to the Russians. Even Shamil's surrender in 1859 did not finally break Chechen resistance, and regular smaller revolts were to follow. The Russians had their hands full not only with the Chechens. Hundreds of thousands of Circassians and other mountain dwellers, mainly from the western part of the North Caucasus, were put to flight or deported to Ottoman territory. According to Peter Holquist, between 1859-1879 two million inhabitants left the Caucasus, approximately a quarter of them perishing.[5] Some historians qualify it as 'genocide'.[6]

Chechen combativeness has always aroused contradictory reactions. In his *Cossack Lullaby*, the poet Mikhail Lermontov, a participant in the campaign of conquest of the Caucasus in the early nineteenth century, enters 'the evil Chechen', 'sharpening his dagger', as bogeyman.[7] They might be 'robbers', according to a character from his novel *A Hero of Our Time*, but they were also 'daredevils'.[8] Whereas some observers see them as wild cutters of throats, others think them noble freedom fighters. The Russian Pan-Slavist Nikolai Danilevskii was irritated by the indignation and complaint provoked in Europe by the subjection of the Caucasians, a task Russia had undertaken in civilization's name. In *Russia and Europe* (1869) he wrote:

> The fact that these Caucasian mountain dwellers, by their fanatic religion and their way of life, by their habits, and by the very character of the land they inhabit, are kidnappers and robbers who can and will never leave their neighbors in peace, is not taken into account. Warriors without fear and rebuke, they are 'lords' of freedom, and that is all! (...)

Under threat of being labeled as a persecutor and oppressor of freedom, Russia has but to endure the million or so warriors that have nested in the unchartable crevices of the Caucasian mountains, who impede all peaceful settlements for hundreds of kilometers around. And while waiting for the inevitable Caucasian alliance with the first chance enemy who is ready to attack it, Russia infinitely has to keep its army of two hundred thousand men standing by to guard all entrances and exits of these robbers' dens.[9]

Lev Tolstoy, however, mopped the floor with arguments like self-defense or civilization mission. These were mere pretexts, he wrote in a draft of *Hadji Murat* (1896-1904), to 'commit all sorts of villainy against small peoples'.[10]

According to Ehren Park and David Brandenberger, the subject's historiography is also 'highly partisan', 'oscillat[ing] wildly between celebration of the Chechen people's epic struggle and condemnation of its stubborn refusal to accept the geopolitical realities of the North Caucasus'.[11]

Following the Revolution of 1917, the Chechens first joined the Bolsheviks against the Whites, aiming to restore the Russian empire, after all. When the victorious Bolsheviks did not want to part with their territory either, they took up arms against them as well. In the early 1920s the Chechens were part of the autonomous North Caucasian Mountain Republic. Later on, together with their relatives the Ingush, they were given their own autonomous republic. Soviet government fought Islam, replacing the Arabic by the Cyrillic alphabet. Around 1930 the Chechens resisted forced collectivization of agriculture, and in 1937 Stalin's Great Terror. This is all the more striking compared to the passivity towards the terror of most Soviet citizens.

When in June 1941 the Germans invaded the Soviet Union, another revolt was going on in the Chechen mountains. The rebels welcomed the Germans to the Caucasus as guests, on the condition that they recognized their independence.[12] This was unacceptable to the Germans, who only reached the farthest northwest of Chechnya, however, mainly inhabited by Russians, whereas thousands of Chechens fought against the Germans in the Red Army.[13] Nevertheless, after liberation several complete peoples were deported from the North Caucasus on a charge of collaboration. In this strategically and economically important region, made vulnerable by internal disunity, Stalin lacked trust in their loyalty. Late in February 1944, in an action personally overseen by state security chief Lavrenti Beria from Grozny, over 600,000 people were deported from the North

Caucasus, two thirds of them Chechens, the rest Ingush, Karachai and Balkars. After thousands of people considered 'untransportable' had been liquidated on the spot, in three to four weeks they were brought in sealed freight trains, with dozens of people packed into each carriage, to the steppes of Kazakhstan and Kirghizia. The 'special settlements' there were absolutely not designed to hold them all; hunger and illness raged, health care being utterly insufficient. According to state security, between 1944-1948, and apart from transport's toll, almost a quarter of the deportees perished.[14] A few thousand Chechens and Ingush managed to escape deportation, and as late as 1953 Soviet police continued hunting remnants of guerrilla opposition.[15]

In all, during the 1930s and 1940s, over three million Soviet citizens were subjected to ethnic-based resettlement. The French historian Nicolas Werth quotes the words of Beria's deputy Bogdan Kobulov that the regime had tried to 'solve the Chechen problem once and forever'.[16] Most Chechen historians call it genocide. As deportation did not explicitly aim at extermination, however, other, mainly Western, historians prefer to speak of ethnic cleansing. In any event, in 2004 the European Parliament qualified the deportation as an act of genocide.[17]

Exile also was incapable of breaking the Chechens. Mixing admiration with awe, Alexander Solzhenitsyn writes in *The Gulag Archipelago*: 'There was one nation which would not give in, would not acquire the mental habits of submission (...). These were the Chechens.' The Soviet regime did not manage to have them respect its laws: 'The Chechens walk the Kazakh land with insolence in their eyes, shouldering people aside, and the "masters of the land" and non-masters alike respectfully make way for them.'[18] The Chechens and Ingush were thus unmanageable, to the extent that finally, in 1952, the Kazakh authorities proposed that Moscow deport a substantial number of them further away to even more remote areas of Kazakhstan. In a reaction, the State Security Department confirmed that the Chechens and Ingush were 'totally incorrigible'. They refused to work, organized mass disturbances, committed banditry and engaged in anti-Soviet activities. 'Police infiltration is hopeless, because the Chechens and the Ingush have a specific genotype and are fanaticized by pan-Islamism.' Nevertheless the MGB considered 'a second deportation [to be] inappropriate and useless. (...) Deporting these people to ever more remote areas will not solve the problem'.[19]

In this way, the Chechens preserved their identity even in exile. Their drive to survive was so great that, in spite of the toll deportation took upon them, after the rehabilitation of 1956 following Stalin's death more

Chechens returned to the North Caucasus than had been deported in 1944. The Russians, having replaced them, attempted to block their return. In early 1957, however, the Chechen-Ingush autonomous republic was restored, minus some fifteen percent of the former territory going to neighboring regions.

While semi-tribal, egalitarian traditions were Chechen society's strength, the clan system no less suited Mafia practices, and under Brezhnev Chechen criminal gangs became quite active in Moscow. Indomitability resulted not only in resistance to subjection, but in an almost anarchistic attitude towards all authority, fitting in badly with the development of a modern democratic nation.

The First Chechen War

The Chechens were back home, but as second-class citizens. Key posts in their republic were given to Russians and other non-Chechens. This lack of a loyal Chechen elite, capable of playing a stabilizing role, is considered by Christof Zürcher to be one of the causes of the post-1991 radicalization.[20] When in the late 1980s the Soviet Union disintegrated, the Chechens did not lag behind. In 1990, a Chechen National Congress elected air force General Dzhokhar Dudaev, stationed in Tartu, Estonia, as president and commander of the national guard. When in the following year the Union republics of the collapsed Soviet state proclaimed independence in accordance with their constitutional right, Dudaev and his allies claimed this right as well, although the constitution did not assign it to autonomous republics like Chechnya. They proclaimed the independent republic of Ichkeria, from which the Ingush broke away, staying within the Russian Federation. Following the disintegration of the Soviet Union, Russian authorities now feared the same would happen to Russia.

Park and Brandenberger reject the idea that Chechen independence fits smoothly into the age-old rebellious tradition. The Chechen nationalism of 1991 was non-existent in Mansur's and Shamil's times, after all.[21] In any event, in these chaotic days Russia's President Boris Yeltsin for a long time did almost nothing to contain the Chechens. His policy was inconsistent. The use of force was rejected at this stage. The Russian army even withdrew from Chechnya, leaving behind enormous supplies of weapons, sold by corrupt officers and soldiers, to a large extent; afterwards, they functioned as the backbone of Chechen defense. In the literature one comes across the thesis that Yeltsin let the opportunity slip to negotiate an acceptable alternative for independence with Dudaev, like a 'Tatarstan-plus' type of agreement after the example of the Russian Federation's Tatar Republic, having managed to get hold of a large extent of autonomy. J.B. Dunlop considers this a 'cardinal error'.[22] Yeltsin was too busy with the internal struggle for power, first with Gorbachev, then with Parliament, to pay serious attention to the problem.

Meanwhile, Chechnya's situation deteriorated. Towards domestic opposition, Dudaev behaved in an increasingly dictatorial manner. A sort of criminal free state developed, a paradise of counterfeiting and smuggling in weapons, narcotics and oil, with the Russian Mafia also taking advantage. Regularly, people were being kidnapped as well. Under the circumstances, during the early 1990s tens of thousands of Russians and other non-Chechens left the region.

After his policy of democratization had reached an impasse, during the autumn of 1994 Yeltsin increasingly came to be influenced by a 'Party of War' that had developed within his entourage. It thought a small victorious war in Chechnya suitable to strengthen the state and show the regime's effectiveness. Defense Minister Pavel Grachev boasted that one airborne regiment was able to accomplish the job within two hours.[23] After attempts to overthrow Dudaev by other means had failed, Yeltsin brought the army into action. On 11 December 1994, 23,700 men, supported by 80 tanks and 208 armored vehicles, invaded Chechnya.[24] The stubborn resistance to be expected from the Chechens against Russia's 'rickety, corrupt, and collapsing military machine' had insufficiently been taken into account, however.[25] The invading army mainly consisted of unprepared recruits with low morale.[26] Only after heavy losses did they manage to seize the flattened capital Grozny (with 400,000 inhabitants before the war), at the expense of the lives of thousands of inhabitants, many of them Russians. Estimates of the number of civilians killed soon ran up to 25,000 if not twice as much; according to Anatol Lieven, however, until late January 1995, 5,000 civilians at most had been killed.[27]

There were mutual outrages. Many Chechens became victims of 'filtrations' or purge operations by the Russian army, aimed officially at separating peaceful citizens and militants. For their part, the rebels took hostages. So, in June 1995 a group of rebels commanded by Shamil Basaev set off for Moscow with the aim of carrying out a spectacular action there, taking along nine thousand dollars to bribe Russian soldiers on the way. By Budennovsk, two hundred kilometers north of Chechnya, all the money had been spent, and in a hospital there they took over a thousand people hostage. During a failed assault over a hundred Russian soldiers were killed. In the end, Prime Minister Viktor Chernomyrdin managed to talk the hostages out, in exchange for the hijackers' unopposed withdrawal. In January of the following year, Basaev's colleague Salman Raduev took several hundred people hostage in Kizliar, just over the Chechen border in Dagestan, resulting in 78 people killed.

In April 1996, tracing him through his satellite telephone, the Russians eliminated Dudaev with a rocket. In August of the same year, however, the rebels managed to retake Grozny. Russian media reported relatively unhampered on the horrors of the Chechen war, thus contributing to its unpopularity among the Russian public. The situation was so hopeless that after 21 months of war the Russian authorities finally opted for a settlement. On 31 August 1996, the Secretary of the Russian Security Council, General Alexander Lebed, in Khasaviurt in Dagestan concluded an agreement with the commander of the Chechen rebels, Aslan Maskhadov, ending the war and *de facto* confirming the seceded province's independence, although the exact regulation of the relation with Russia was suspended for five years.

Estimates of the number of civilians killed during the war of 1994-1996 vary from 20,000 to as much as 100,000. Zürcher thinks the number of civilians killed amounted to some 40,000, apart from the 4,000 Chechen militants killed. According to him, the number of Russian soldiers killed, officially around 4,000, could well be 7,500. Approximately 250,000 people escaped the violence, mainly to the neighboring provinces.[28]

The Resumption of War

The Russian army withdrew, and in early 1997 Maskhadov was elected Chechnya's President. In May of the same year he was received by Yeltsin in the Kremlin to confirm the peace agreement. However, Maskhadov did not manage to rein in Basaev, Raduev and the other warlords having gathered more and more power during the fighting. They were supported by a few hundred foreign Muslim militants or *mujahedin* commanded by the Saudi Afghan war veteran Emir Khattab, through whom they also received money from international Islamic funds. It may have contributed to their increasing appeals to a radical interpretation of Islam. Although originally Dudaev had not aimed at making Chechnya, traditionally a tolerant country with respect to religion, an Islamic republic, during the war he gradually changed his mind. In early 1999, subjected to great pressure, Maskhadov introduced Sharia legislation.[29]

The situation in Chechnya got off the rails. In an explosion of banditry, over a thousand Russian citizens as well as some Westerners were kidnapped. Reacting against the radicals, Maskhadov made overtures to Moscow, declaring himself ready to negotiate. However, just as Moscow had not been prepared at an earlier point to meet Dudaev's wishes, it now ignored an increasingly impotent Maskhadov; meanwhile Basaev's authority was growing. According to the Polish journalist Wojciech Jagielski, as each other's opposites Maskhadov and Basaev were condemned to each other. A former Soviet Colonel, a perfect soldier for whom duty and order came first, Maskhadov was averse to impetuous adventures. The charismatic Basaev, on the other hand, was a daredevil wanting to attract attention with spectacular actions; having started as a jovial fellow selling used computers, he finally grew into a devout Muslim. Under his influence, after the war's resumption in 1999, the Chechen revolt degenerated into a fight for the forming of a caliphate from the Black Sea to the Caspian Sea, if not the Volga; a holy war against Russia, justifying a carnage. Jagielski emphasizes, however, that the Russians left the Chechens little choice.[30]

Meanwhile, in the neighboring republic of Dagestan, part of the Russian Federation, a small Salafist minority had become active also. In discord with traditional Sufi practices of official Islam here, striving for a 'pure' Islam, Salafists reject regional variants. There was a social element as well. With a corrupt and impotent local government, large-scale poverty and unemployment increased the Islamist movement's attraction. Under the circumstances, during the second half of the 1990s in a number of villages in Mid-Dagestan a *de facto* independent 'Wahhabite reservation' developed.[31] For some time, the Islamic enclave was tolerated by Dagestani and Russian authorities. When in late 1997 an anti-Wahhabite law on religion became effective in Dagestan, however, Dagestani Islamists got support from Khattab, who was married to a woman from the enclave. With some one hundred armed adherents from Chechnya, he organized a raid against a Russian military base nearby. The Russians concluded that the Chechens were seeking to expand their Islamic state.[32] In August 1999 Khattab and Basaev, together with a few hundred men, invaded Dagestan once again; unwelcome with the local inhabitants, however, they were soon driven away. Speculations that the invasion was orchestrated by Moscow have not been substantiated. Now, the Wahhabite enclave was forcefully disbanded, resulting (according to Russian officials) in the death of over two thousand militants as well as 281 Russians; over 20,000 Dagestani's took flight.[33]

During the same summer a series of explosions took place in apartment buildings in Moscow and a number of other Russian cities, killing
over 300 people. The facts of the case have never been fully clarified.
According to the Russian authorities it was the work of Chechen rebels. Together with the invasion of Dagestan it induced them to resume
the war in Chechnya. Vladimir Putin, recently appointed Prime Minister
by Yeltsin, held the Chechens responsible for the acts of terror and announced his intention to chase after the bandits 'up to the loo' and finish
them. Again, it went round that Russia's state security service FSB had
itself organized the attempts in order to discredit the Chechens and create a motive for resuming the war. One of the arguments was that around
the same time explosives were found in the basement of an apartment
building in Riazan, with the FSB maintaining an implausible story about
an exercise.[34]

The fact is that Russia had never accepted Chechen independence.
Promises of help to be provided had not been fulfilled. Generals were
intent on revenge for the humiliation of 1996. So, after the series of explosions and the invasion of Dagestan, the Russian government revoked the
Khasaviurt agreement concluded three years ago and in October sent the
army back to Chechnya, arguing that the region had gotten in the grasp
of lawlessness and had since become the scene of a jihad. This time, the
war was more effective than in 1994-96. The invasion was more massive
and the troops were more professional, consisting mainly of contract soldiers. Now, the war was supported by the Russian population, who saw it
as proof of the decisiveness of the new leader Putin, who on the last day
of 1999 succeeded Yeltsin as President. Admittance of the media to the
scene of battle was much more controlled than in the first war. After the
resumption of the fight Maskhadov and the radical warlords joined forces,
whereas the highest Chechen Muslim leader, Mufti Akhmad Kadyrov, dis-
satisfied with the growing Wahhabite influence, went over from the rebels' side to the Russians. No longer recognizing Maskhadov, Moscow saw
Kadyrov as Chechnya's new leader.

For Putin, the Chechen rebels were no separatists but terrorists, aiming not at independence but at forming a 'caliphate' and at Russia's disintegration. The only regime recognizing Chechen independence were
Afghanistan's Taliban, opening a Chechen embassy in Kabul under Ze-
limkhan Yandarbiev. Not a single other Islamic country officially supported the rebels or condemned Russia's intervention. In return for Russian support of Tehrans's nuclear program, Russia especially could look
for assistance to Iran, as chair of the Organization of the Islamic Con-

ference discouraging any public criticism of the Chechen campaign by Muslim partners.[35]

Although the West did not condemn the fight against separatism, to Russia's great dissatisfaction it did criticize the excessive use of force. After the terrorist attacks of 11 September 2001 in the United States, however, Putin's thesis that Russia was at the forefront in the struggle against international terrorism, found a willing ear in the West. The country joined an international anti-terrorist coalition, and Western criticism of the Chechen war diminished. According to the Russians, the rebels were supported with money, equipment and men by Islamic fundamentalists from abroad. Indeed, already during the First Chechen War foreign militants had formed an Islamic battalion commanded by Khattab. It does not seem to have counted more than a few hundred men, however, although the Russians were inclined to exaggerate its size. Khattab was also said to have had connections with Arabic financial backers, according to the Russians, including al-Qaida and Bin Laden.

Others objected that, as Sufists, most Chechens were averse to Islamic fundamentalism, and that the rebels' weapons mainly originated from the corrupt Russian army. Julie Wilhelmsen argues that the conflict had really begun because of separatism, and that initially Islam had played only a marginal role. Only later, political, radical Islam became part of the ideology and methods of many Chechen rebels. They radicalized, while foreign Islamists got involved in the conflict with money from international Muslim organizations (Wilhelmsen has doubts about much of the influence from al-Qaida's side). According to her, this development was greatly promoted by the tough, uncompromising Russian policy, giving no chance to moderates like Maskhadov.[36]

As a matter of fact, Gordon Hahn thinks Sufist tradition to potentially be no less extremist than Islamist jihadism.[37] Robert Bruce Ware objects to arguments like Wilhelmsen's, saying that in 1994 Russia had not started the war in order to annul Chechen independence, but because Chechnya had become a *safe haven* for organized crime. The second war had been initiated because Chechnya had become 'a base for internationally supported irredentist attacks aimed at the violent separation of the North Caucasian republics from the Russian Federation and the imposition of Wahhabite Islamist fundamentalism upon their unwilling inhabitants'. According to Ware, Islamist extremism was not (as Wilhelmsen thinks) a result but a cause of the Chechen wars.[38] Yagil Henkin is of the opinion that, while the Chechens basically fought a nationalistic war, Chechen Islamists 'embraced extremist ideals, adopted extremist rhetoric and employed extremist means learned from fighters from abroad'. Moreover, 'radical Islamists around the world view[ed] the events in Chechnya as part of a global struggle'.[39]

The Second Chechen War

Heavy fighting occurred during the first several months of the Second Chechen War, resulting in the killing of some 2,500 Russian soldiers along with thousands of civilians. In all, during both wars nearly 10,000 Russian soldiers and police perished, while many more were crippled. Roughly 80,000 civilians lost their lives, or eight percent of the prewar population, whereas at least 200,000 people were displaced.[40] Again, the Russian army subjected civilians to large-scale atrocities. On suspicion of contacts with rebels, during so-called purge operations, many people were arrested, often robbed, tortured, raped, killed, or they disappeared. Only very exceptionally were proceedings instituted against the guilty. The most well-known exception was Colonel Yuri Budanov, who in 2000 had raped and killed a Chechen girl. At first, the court imposed only psychiatric treatment, as he was supposed not to have been responsible for his actions. The Supreme Court revoked the sentence, however, whereupon he was condemned to ten years imprisonment. In early 2009 he was released before his time, to the utter dismay even of many Chechens loyal to Moscow.[41] Before having been able to challenge the decision, the lawyer of the family of Budanov's victim, Stanislav Markelov, was shot in Moscow's centre in broad daylight. Later the same year the police arrested a suspect, a Russian nationalist unconnected to Budanov's case.

The other side also committed excesses. Radicalized by violence, Chechen rebels perpetrated a number of spectacular terrorist attempts, including in the very heart of Russia. In October 2002 militants took hundreds of visitors to a Moscow theatre hostage, until a mysterious gas was pumped into the building, taking the life of 129 of the hostages, apart from the terrorists. Uninformed about the composition of the opium-like substance, rescuers were unable to treat the victims appropriately. Basaev claimed responsibility for the action, but the Russians also suspected Maskhadov of involvement. Although the latter has never been proved, Maskhadov turned out to be unable to restrain Basaev and his allies. Independent researchers have also come to the conclusion that, for want of alternatives, he moved ever closer to the radicals.[42]

Hereupon Basaev organized suicide attempts after the Palestinian model. In the summer of 2004 the terror reached a new height. In August 'black widows' blew up two Russian airplanes containing ninety passengers, while a bomb attack in Moscow's subway took ten lives. In early September a major hostage action took place in a school in Beslan in North Ossetia, with a bloody result; also as a consequence of the rather unsubtle methods of Russian special commands, 331 people were killed, more than half of them children. As usual, Russian authorities blamed international terrorism, without, however, producing evidence. For the time being, it was the last attempt on this scale.

Neighboring countries also got involved in the conflict. During the Second Chechen War the Pankisi valley, an inhospitable, rather inaccessible region just across Chechnya's border in Northeast Georgia inhabited by the Chechens' relatives, the Kists, became a shelter for thousands of fugitives. According to the Russians, there were hundreds of rebels among them. They depicted the region as an international centre of crime, drug trafficking, arms smuggling and kidnapping, as well as a base for terrorist preparations. Minister of Defense Sergei Ivanov spoke of a 'mini-Afghanistan on Russia's doorstep'.[43] The Americans took the matter seriously, sending elite troops in order to train Georgian army units in counter-terrorism, with Russia only agreeing gnashing its teeth. The Russians bombed the region, threatening to intervene if the Georgians stayed inactive. In September 2002 a Georgian purge action resulted in the arrest of some fifteen Arabic militants, including at least one mid-level al-Qaida leader; they were handed over to the United States.[44]

Chechenization

After heavy fighting during the first several months, from mid-2000 onwards the Second Chechen War increasingly evolved into what Mark Kramer has called 'a classic insurgency'.[45] The Russian army drove the insurgents into the mountains, and although guerrilla attacks continued from there, Putin declared the war ended, announcing a 'normalization'. As part of a 'Chechenization', local administration was handed over to loyal Chechens. According to official results, in March 2003, 96 percent of Chechnya's voters (turnout being 89 percent) by referendum approved a new regional constitution. There were doubts with respect to the procedure's fairness, however; not only were Russian soldiers allowed to take part in the vote, according to rumors many thousands of 'dead souls' were also counted, people who had in fact been killed or taken flight. Most Chechens were so tired of war, however, that they probably preferred this solution to fighting on. The constitution contained concessions that Putin had denied other regions; although independence was out of the question, Chechnya was given considerable autonomy. For the time being, an agreement on the division of power between Moscow and Chechnya has not yet been concluded; the special status Tatarstan managed to maintain recently might be an example.

In October 2003, without serious rivals, Akhmad Kadyrov was elected President with over 80 percent of the vote. Already in May of the following year he had been blown up, apparently by his former colleagues, but the process of Chechenization continued. In late 2005 a regional parliament was elected, with a majority for Kadyrov's loyalists under the flag of Russia's party of power, United Russia. Early 2007, following an interlude under Alu Alkhanov, Kadyrov's son Ramzan, straight after reaching the required minimum age of 30, was appointed the new President by Putin (after already having been Prime Minister).

Pro-Russian Chechen military units received an increasingly important role. The number of federal soldiers diminished from 80,000 to less than half in early 2006. Together with a force of 30,000 Chechens loyal to Moscow (often former rebels granted amnesty), they opposed 1,000-1,500 rebels plus 100-150 foreigners. Following the beginning of wars in Afghanistan (2001) and Iraq (2003), the interest in Chechnya of foreign Muslim militants and financiers declined considerably. One after the other, leading rebels were liquidated. Late in 2001, after his arrest, Raduev was condemned to life imprisonment, dying in prison under unclear circumstances a year later. In March 2002, Khattab died after reading a poisoned letter, an action for which Russian state security claimed responsibility. In February 2004, Yandarbiev was blown up in Qatar; two Russian military intelligence officers were condemned to life imprisonment but were exchanged with Russia later. In March 2005 Maskhadov was killed, just like his successor Abdul-Khalim Sadulaev in June of the following year, and finally Basaev in July; the FSB claimed responsibility for the latter action as well, others calling it an accident.

Since late 2005 the armed conflict has lost much of its intensity. We are being told that only a few hundred rebels are still active in Chechnya, operating in isolated groups and directed by Doku Umarov. Large-scale military operations are no longer needed, Russian losses having diminished considerably. Officially, war is over. After almost ten years, in April 2009 the end of the 'counterterrorist operation' (CTO) regime in Chechnya was announced, which was to result in the pullout of some 20,000 federal troops; the 46th Brigade of the Ministry of Internal Affairs and the 42nd Motorized Infantry Division of the Defense Ministry, together over 10,000 men, were to stay. In fact, the CTO regime might remain in force in certain regions of Chechnya, as well as Ingushetia and Dagestan.

Many observers, however, doubt whether normalization is an appropriate term and whether things can indeed be left to Ramzan Kadyrov, a potentate notorious for his cruelty. Human rights organizations connect him, together with his guard, thousands of so-called *kadyrovtsy*, with numerous murders, disappearances and cases of torture of alleged terrorists and their sympathizers.[46] In October 2006, journalist Anna Politkovskaya, investigating torture practices in prisons under Kadyrov, was killed in Moscow. Even outside Russia, Kadyrov's opponents have to fear for their life. In January 2009 his former bodyguard Umar Israilov was killed in Vienna, where he had taken refuge.[47] Later the same year, a number of human rights activists were killed in Chechnya. Although some opponents have accused Kadyrov at least of creating an atmosphere of lawlessness and impunity in which such murders could be committed, in none of these cases it has been possible to demonstrate his involvement so far.

What Kadyrov is offering Moscow is loyalty. So, in the Russian parliamentary elections of December 2007, with a devastating war still fresh in mind, turnout in Chechnya, according to official results, was over 99 percent, with over 99 percent of the vote going to United Russia, the party of Putin, the man who had waged the war. The latter thought the result completely credible.[48] Several months later, during regional elections, Kadyrov boasted that if necessary he could also manage a turnout of *over* 100 percent.[49] Emphasizing his loyalty, he named Grozny's main street after Vladimir Putin.

Most of the money for Grozny's reconstruction and other projects to win support among the population, Kadyrov gets from Moscow. Formerly, Moscow has attempted to restrain Kadyrov through the forming of rival armed units (also mainly of former rebels) formally subordinate not to Kadyrov but to federal departments. They were to function as counterbalance in order to guarantee Kadyrov's loyalty and curtail his ambitions. The no less ambitious warlords commanding these heavy armed battalions who were supported by Moscow belonged to competing clans and contributed to new mutual violence between their followers and the *kadyrovtsy*. So, in April 2008, a confrontation between *kadyrovtsy* and the *Vostok* battalion commanded by Sulim Yamadaev and formally subordinate to the GRU (military intelligence), took the lives of eighteen people.

Yamadaev tasted defeat and lost his function, his battalion being disbanded. In September of the same year his brother Ruslan, a former State Duma deputy, was killed in Moscow, and in March 2009 Sulim himself was shot in Dubai. The local police concluded that Kadyrov's confidant and intended successor Adam Delimkhanov, a Duma member and former Deputy Prime Minister, had commissioned the murder. In any case, Moscow's strategy to restrain Kadyrov through his rivals had failed, resulting in the solidification of Kadyrov's personal control over Chechnya.

The *Ramzanizatsia* of Chechnya[50] leaves no room for civil society. With a mix of Stalinism, Sufi-Islam and Chechen nationalism,[51] Kadyrov advocates legalizing polygamy, the wearing of headscarfs by female public officers, schoolgirls and students, and school education in Islam. He defends honor killings and is even said to intend the introduction of Sharia legislation.[52] Late in 2008, an immense mosque arose in Grozny, allegedly the largest one in Europe. As part of this retraditionalization of Chechnya, Islamic dissidents, on the other hand, are dealt with harshly.

It is doubtful whether Putin's solution of the Chechen problem can guarantee long-lasting stability. Some Kremlin leaders question Kadyrov's loyalty, suspecting it to be coupled with attempts to transform Chechnya into something bordering on an independent state. And if ever Moscow might want to dump Kadyrov, he could easily rejoin the other side. Apart from that, since the summer of 2009 there has been a steep increase in the number of terrorist acts committed in Chechnya, ruining the image of 'normalcy'.

In the rest of the North Caucasus the situation has also deteriorated. On a massive scale, Russians have left the ethnically and religiously complicated region, hit hard by socio-economic decline after 1991. The local political system is extremely closed, suffering from nepotism and corruption. Especially unemployed youth, not only in Chechnya, but also in the neighboring republics of Ingushetia, Dagestan, Kabardino-Balkaria and Karachaevo-Cherkessia, easily take refuge with radical movements. Quite often they are believers who are labeled Wahhabite only because they don't go along with Islamic establishment. The authorities crack down on radicalization, real or supposed, people are arrested or disappear, and unofficial mosques are closed down. In this way frustrated believers are incited to join the radicals, and social protest can grow into Islamic fundamentalism. In the summer of 2005, in a report that had leaked out, Putin's plenipotentiary in Southern Russia, Dmitri Kozak, warned that the corruption and nepotism of the closed North Caucasian political caste could foster extremism among the population, possibly bringing about

'Islamic Sharia enclaves'. According to Kozak, continuing to ignore the social, political and economic problems, or trying to violently smother them, could result in 'an uncontrolled chain of events'.[53]

Ingushetia, the Russian Federation's poorest region, wrestles with tens of thousands of refugees, fierce clan competition and, until recently, the incompetent, corrupt and repressive leadership of regional President Murat Ziazikov, a former FSB officer, appointed by Putin as successor of the popular Ruslan Aushev in 2002. Moreover, there is a conflict with the Ossetians, against whom the Ingush in 1992 fought a brief but severe war about Prigorodny district (in 1957 having been assigned to North Ossetia, although before 1944 it had been Ingush). Russian authorities intervened in favor of the Ossetians, thousands of Ingush from the contested territory taking refuge in Ingushetia. Quite a few Ingush also feel attracted to the rebel movement of their close relatives, the Chechens. Thus, in June 2004, Ingushetia was the target of an attack by a group of local militants allied with Basaev, killing nearly 90 officials and plundering arms depots. A wave of disappearances has created an explosive situation, in October 2008 resulting in the resignation of Ziazikov. Quite differently, his successor Yunus-Bek Yevkurov started a policy of dialogue with Ingush society, declaring war on corruption; in June of the following year, however, he was heavily injured in a terrorist attempt. It was only a link in a chain of unrestrained violence continuing during the succeeding months, killing dozens of functionaries, human rights activists and civilians. It is to be feared that after Yekvurov's attempts at consensus the Russians may again resort to pure force.

In Dagestan also an undeclared, violent war is raging between the police and groups offering resistance for various reasons. The other North Caucasian republics are only relatively quieter. So, in October 2005, in a battle between security forces and alleged rebels in Nalchik, capital of Kabardino-Balkaria, almost 150 people were killed. During the summer of 2009, violence in the North Caucasus hit levels unseen for years, resulting in the killing of more than 400 people. Again, violence could not be contained within the North Caucasus. In November of the same year, a bomb attempt on the Moscow-St. Petersburg express took the life of 28 passengers, some of them Russian senior officials. Chechen rebels claimed the attempt had been carried out on the orders of their commander, Doku Umarov, a claim that was taken serious by the Russian investigators.

Having in mind that some observers designate the North Caucasus as Russia's 'inner abroad', only formally still part of it, Russia's policy towards neighboring Georgia has not contributed to decreasing the tension. After a war of five days, in August 2008, Moscow recognized the independence of two Georgian seceded provinces, South Ossetia and Abkhazia. This step has restored hopes of representatives of national minorities in Russia, after the frightening example of Chechnya following the proclaiming of independence in 1991. The Abkhazian President Sergei Bagapsh has stated in an interview, probably not according to Moscow's wish: '[C]ertainly, Chechnya will be independent one day, as will the other republics of the Caucasus. The time of empires is over.'[54] Quite understandably, Chechens are surprised that Moscow has recognized the independence of Abkhazia and South Ossetia, after having denied with so much violence the same right to Chechnya.

Notes

1 Bennigsen, M. (1999: 536-537). 'Chechnia: Political Developments and Strategic Implications for the North Caucasus', *Central Asian Survey* 1999 (18), No. 4.

2 Gammer, M. (2006). *The Lone Wolf and the Bear: Three Centuries of Chechen Defiance of Russian Rule*. London.

3 Dunlop, J.B. (1998: 14-15). *Russia Confronts Chechnya: Roots of a Separatist Conflict*. Cambridge.

4 Trenin, D. (2002: 70). *The End of Eurasia: Russia on the Border between Geopolitics and Globalization*.Washington, DC.

5 Holquist, P. (2001: 119). 'To Count, to Extract, and to Exterminate: Population Statistics and Population Politics in Late Imperial and Soviet Russia',Suny, R.G. and Martin, T. (eds.), *A State of Nations: Empire and Nation-Making in the Age of Lenin and Stalin*. Oxford.

6 Shenfield, S.D. (1999: 149-162). 'The Circassians: a Forgotten Genocide?', Levene, M. and Roberts, P., (eds.), *The Massacre in History*. Oxford; Leitzinger, A. (2000). 'The Circassian Genocide', *The Eurasian Politician*, No. 2; *Johnson's Russia List, Research and Analytical Supplement*, (2008, May) No. 42, Special Issue 'The Circassians'. According to Dana Sherry ('Social Alchemy on the Black Sea Coast, 1860-65', *Kritika*, (2009: 7-30) (10), No. 1), between 1860-1865 at least 370,000 Caucasians moved from the Black Sea coast to Ottoman territory, although there was no determined Russian deportation policy behind it.

7 'Kazach'ia Kolybel'naia Pesnia',Lermontov, M. (1969:130-131). *Stikhotvoreniia, Poemy, Drama, Proza*. Moscow.

8 Ibid., p. 453.

9   Gordin, I. (2000: 39). *Kavkaz: Zemlia i Krov': Rossiia v Kavkazskoi Voine XIX Veka* .St. Petersburg.

10 Dunlop, op. cit., p. 19.

11 Park, E. and Brandenberger, D. (2004: 543). 'Imagined Community? Rethinking the Nationalist Origins of the Contemporary Chechen Crisis', *Kritika*, 2004 (5), No. 3.

12 Dunlop, op. cit., p. 58.

13 Burds, J. (2007: 299-300; 303). 'The Soviet War against "Fifth Columnists": The Case of Chechnya, 1942-4', *Journal of Contemporary History*, 2007 (42), No. 2.

14 Werth, N. (2006: 357-358). 'The "Chechen Problem": Handling an Awkward Legacy, 1918-1958', *Contemporary European History*, 2006 (15), No. 3 (the Karachai were deported in November 1943, the Balkars in March 1944).

15 Burds, op. cit., pp. 304-305; 307.

16 Werth, op. cit., p. 348.

17 Campana, A. (p.8). 'The Massive Deportation of the Chechen People: How and Why Chechens were Deported?', www.massviolence.org.

18 Solzhenitsyn, A. (1992: 401-405). *The Gulag Archipelago*, Vol. 3, New York.

19 Werth, op. cit., pp. 347-348.

20 Zürcher, C. (2007: 74). *The Post-Soviet Wars: Rebellion, Ethnic Conflict, and Nationhood in the Caucasus*. New York.

21 Park and Brandenberger, op. cit., passim.

22 Dunlop, op. cit., p. 215.

23 Cheterian, V. (2008: 257). *War and Peace in the Caucasus: Russia's Troubled Frontier*. London.

24 Dunlop, op. cit., p. 209.

25 Ibid., p. 222.

26 Babchenko, A. (2008). *A Soldier's War in Chechnya*. London.

27 Lieven, A. (1998: 107-108). *Chechnya: Tombstone of Russian Power*. New Haven.

28 Zürcher, op. cit., pp. 99-100.

29 Ibid., p. 87; Jaimoukha, A. (2005: 69). *The Chechens: A Handbook*. London.

30 Jagielski, W. (2009). *Towers of Stone: The Battle of Wills in Chechnya*. New York.

31 Malašenko, A. (2002: 553). 'Islam im postsowjetischen Raum', *Osteuropa*, 2002 (52), No. 5.

32 Lanskoy, M. (2002: 170; 175-178). 'Daghestan and Chechnya: The Wahhabi Challenge to the State', *SAIS Review*, 2002 (22), No. 2.

33 Hunter, S.T. (2004: 228-229). *Islam in Russia: The Politics of Identity and Security*. Armonk, N.Y.

34 Felshtinsky, Y. and Litvinenko, A. (2002). *Blowing up Russia: Terror from Within*. New York.

35 *RFE/RL*, 11 February 2003.

36 Wilhelmsen, J. (2005: 35-59).'Between a Rock and a Hard Place: The Islamisation of the Chechen Separatist Movement', *Europe-Asia Studies*, 2005 (57), No. 1.

37 Hahn, G.M. (2008: 21). 'The *Jihadi* Insurgency and the Russian Counterinsurgency in the North Caucasus', *Post-Soviet Affairs*, 2008 (24), No. 1.

38 Ware, R.B. (2005: 80; 83-84). 'A Multitude of Evils: Mythology and Political Failure in Chechnya', Sakwa, R. (ed.), *Chechnya: From Past to Future*. London.

39 Henkin, Y. (2006: 199). 'From Tactical Terrorism to Holy War: the Evolution of Chechen Terrorism, 1995-2004', *Central Asian Survey*, 2006 (25), No. 1-2.

40 Kramer, M. (2007: 3). 'The Russian-Chechen Conflict and the Putin-Kadyrov Connection', *Russian Analytical Digest*, 2007, No. 22. Zürcher (op. cit., pp. 99-101): 11,500 Russian soldiers, 53,000 civilians and 7,000 Chechen militants killed, 240,000 refugees. Human rights organizations like Memorial arrive at estimates of 50,000 civilian deaths during the first war and 15,000-25,000 civilians killed or having disappeared during the second war; 350,000 of Chechnya's 800,000 inhabitants took to flight: Lokshina, T. et al. (2005). *The Imposition of a Fake Political Settlement in the Northern Caucasus: The 2003 Presidential Election*, Stuttgart. According to Sergei Maksudov's estimate, a considerably lower number of Chechen civilians were killed (some 20,000), whereas the number of Russians killed (soldiers, Russians living in Chechnya, victims of Chechen terrorist attempts) was relatively higher (also some 20,000): Maksudov, S. (2006: 24; 27). 'Poteri naseleniia Chechni: Po dannym perepisi 2002 goda', *Svobodnaia Mysl'*, 2006, No. 2.

41 Ramzan Kadyrov thought life imprisonment to be insufficient, in fact: Regnum News Agency, 30 January 2009.

42 Kramer, op. cit., p. 3.

43 *International Herald Tribune*, 28 February 2002.

44 Moore, C. and Tumelty, P. (2008: 423). 'Foreign Fighters and the Case of Chechnya: A Critical Assessment', *Studies in Conflict & Terrorism*, 2008 (31), No. 5.

45 Kramer, op. cit., p. 2.

46. Hahn, op. cit., p. 26; Kramer, op. cit., p. 5; Seierstad, A. (2008). *Angel of Grozny: Inside Chechnya*, London.

47. *International Herald Tribune*, 1 February 2009.

48. Kremlin.ru, 14 February 2008.

49. *The Moscow Times*, 13 October 2008.

50. Slider, D. (2008: 195). 'Putin's "Southern Strategy": Dmitriy Kozak and the Dilemma's of Recentralisation', *Post-Soviet Affairs*, 2008 (24), No. 2.

51. C.J. Chivers in *International Herald Tribune*, 1 February 2009.

52. Malashenko, A. (2008: 3). 'Islam and the State in Russia', *Russian Analytical Digest*, 2008, No. 44; *The Moscow Times*, 2 March 2009.
53. *The Guardian*, 23 September 2005; *New Statesman*, 26 September 2005.
54. Ouvaroff, N. (2008: 28). 'The Role of Chechens in the Georgian-South Ossetian Conflict', *Russian Analytical Digest*, 2008, No. 45.

5 Recent Political History of the South Caucasus in the Context of Transition[1]

Françoise Companjen

Introduction

The chain of events since the South Caucasus Republics gained independence in 1991 inspired authors to write about the region using different themes. Some focus on history and nation building,[2] taking the breaking out of the Russian empire as a central theme.[3] Still others focus on nationalism,[4] or on scouting the trail of different colored revolutions.[5] Following the scent of oil in geopolitics[6] is another favorite topic and publications on the August 2008 war in the Caucasus are beginning to appear.[7] In this case I am interested in reflecting on the recent political history of the South Caucasus Republics using transition as a leading concept. This chapter also serves as a general frame for the next chapters all dealing with either Georgia, Azerbaijan and/or Armenia.

After almost twenty years of transition towards democracy and a free market economy, Georgia and Armenia form *hybrid* democracies and are considered to be relatively fragile states. Azerbaijan is a stronger and more economically viable state ruled by an authoritarian regime. Of course one's perspective influences interpretation of democracy. American analysts are less critical of the quality of democracy and more charmed by Georgia' and Azerbaijan's orientation towards the West, than perhaps some of the EU politicians are. These tend to be more critical of the poor human rights situation and the extensive poverty in the South Caucasus. In Europe, certainly after the Russia-Georgia war, the South Caucasus region is often perceived as 'Russia's backyard' generating reluctance to get too involved in this shared neighborhood area. Personally, I would prefer to frame the South Caucasus as 'Europe's front yard' and have the EU develop more instruments for effective involvement.[8]

Although transition in political science and sociology is an older theme[9] the debate on the 'transition paradigm' began anew between 2002 and 2004[10] after a publication by Thomas Carothers in the *Journal of Democracy* wherein he summarized the paradigm's characteristics.[11] Besides having the advantage of being a succinct summary, it also has the advantage that local academics have reflected on it.[12] To a certain extent it has become part of the local discourse.

Several comparative studies on transition in post-communist space have been published in the meantime.[13] In this chapter we summarize the transition paradigm, then give a short overview of the shared recent history of the South Caucasus countries. The main focus is on the major events after independence,[14] but we include the short period of independence between the Russian empire and the Soviet Union from 1918 to 1921. In the discussion and conclusion we probe which facets of the transition 'model' could use more carving out and in which direction. It is argued transition could be traded for institutional transformation.[15] Can the local cultural context be identified as a factor of importance or is 'culture' overestimated at the onset?[16]

The Transition Paradigm as summarized by Carothers

The linkage between transition and full-fledged democracy is based on assumptions considered universal, the reason for which they are labeled as a *paradigm.* The assumptions are that: 1. Any country moving away from dictatorial rule can be considered a country in transition towards democracy; 2. Democratization tends to unfold in a set sequence of stages; 3. Elections have a determinative importance; 4. Structural features such as economic level, political history, institutional legacies, ethnic make-up, and socio-cultural traditions are *not* major factors in either the onset or the outcome of the transition process; 5. Democratization concerns a modification of already functioning states.

Recent Political History of the South Caucasus

The history of the three South Caucasus countries share parallel developments. All three had to survive conquests by foreign empires: the Persian, the Arab, the Ottoman and the Russian.[17] It is remarkable that all three enjoyed a period of independence between 1918-1921 after the Russian Revolutionary year of 1917 and before being incorporated into the Soviet Union. First, they were incorporated as part of a Socialist Federation of Soviet Republics (SFRSs); later, after 1936, as Socialist Soviet Republics (SSRs). All three declared independence in 1991 from the Soviet Union and began the difficult path of transition from a closed society based on socialism and planned economy to becoming open societies with a free market economy and constitutions based on principles of (presidential) democracies. All three constitutions were adopted in 1995.

One difference between the three states is the Christian culture of Armenia (Apostolic) and Georgia (Orthodox) with many affiliations between their mutual aristocratic elites, and the Shi'a Muslim (85 percent) culture of Azerbaijan. Another is the oil economy of Azerbaijan. Georgia has poor relations with Russia since the 1990s, whereas in the case of Azerbaijan, the tensions are focused on Armenia. Armenia has poor relations with Turkey[18] and Azerbaijan, but now enjoys friendly relations with Iran. Russia has been and still is Armenia's ally. After independence Armenia immediately became a member of the Russian led Commonwealth of Independent States (CIS).

The CIS is a loose association of States, an agreement between most of the former Soviet Socialist Republics to coordinate economic and security issues under Russian leadership. CIS participates in the UN peace-keeping forces. Georgia and Azerbaijan procrastinated and only grudgingly joined later. First Azerbaijan in December 1991 and then Georgia in 1992. The CIS harbors a Collective Security Organization (SCO) also under the leadership of Russia. Georgia and Armenia are part of GUAM,[19] a forum formally established in 2001 with Georgia, Ukraine, Armenia and Moldova for development of democracy and economy. Of course, as newly independent states all three countries were introduced into international institutions as the United Nations, the World Bank, The International Development Association, the Organization for Security and Co-operation in Europe, the Council of Europe, and all three are included in the EU-Neighborhood policy now followed up by the EU Eastern Partnership policy.

Finally, another point the three states have in common are territorial conflicts: Georgia vis à vis South Ossetia and Abkhazia;[20] the third autonomous region Adjara joined the central government in Tbilisi after the Rose Revolution. Russia closed its borders to Georgia from 2006 onward with tensions escalating into the August 2008 war. (See chapters 8 and 9). Most recently Russia carefully re-opened travel and trade possibilities with Georgia in early 2010. Armenia and Azerbaijan still have a serious conflict to solve with regard to Nagorno-Karabakh involving Russia and the Minsk Group (co-chairs France and the USA) as mediators. Turkey and Azerbaijan closed their borders to Armenia in 1993 and a ceasefire was signed in 1994. The conflict was frozen with a small first next step taken on November 2nd 2008: the signing of an agreement about procedures (international law and Madrid principles). Following the 'soccer diplomacy' between Turkey and Armenia in 2008/2009, temporary progress was made by signing a protocol to re-open borders between Turkey and Armenia. This protocol, however, has not been not ratified by either party as of spring 2010.

Georgia

Let us begin with a short overview of recent events in Georgia, sometimes referred to as 'the key' to the South Caucasus.[21] After the Russian revolutions in 1917, Menshevik Georgia was an independent republic between 1918-1921. The Bolshevik Ordzhonikidze put an end to this independence when he invaded Georgia with the red army (11th battalion) between February 15 and March 17, 1921. He ultimately managed to annex the whole South Caucasus to the Soviet Union. In 1936, at the height of Stalin's power, constitutional changes were made from Socialist Federation of Soviet Republics (SFSR) to Socialist Soviet Republics (SSR). Abkhazia changed from an SSR to an Autonomous SSR (ASSR), thereby losing the right to sovereignty. The USSR was subjected to programs of Russification.

In the 1970s Eduard Shevardnadze was first secretary of the Communist Party (CP) in Georgia, before he was called to be foreign minister under Gorbachev until the dissolution of the USSR. *Glasnost* and *perestroika* allowing for more openness and participation of the people during the second half of the 1980s, created a social political space for several NGOs to be established around environmental projects ('ecological') sometimes including an alternative political agenda (i.e. Rustaveli Society in Georgia). After the fall of the Berlin Wall, a pro-independence movement took shape under leadership of the dissidents and human activists Merab Kostava and Zviad Gamsakhurdia. Various peaceful anti-Soviet demonstrations were held,[22] such as the one in Georgia on April 9, 1989, when at least twenty people, mostly women, were killed by the Russian army. Gorbachev distanced himself from this incident and had the First Secretary of the CP Jumber Patiashvili replaced by the head of the Georgian KGB. This switching of persons did not help to contain the pro-independence movement. Georgia claimed independence on March 31, 1991.

Zviad Gamsakhurdia was elected as the first president of Georgia in May 1991. He refused to join the Russian led Commonwealth of Independent States (CIS). When South Ossetia wanted to organize its own elections, Gamsakhurdia annulled the autonomous status of South Ossetia and sent a military force. The central Georgian government lost the fight. Losing grip of the very difficult situation, Gamsakhurdia was ousted by militia who invited the former Georgian first Secretary of the Communist Party, Eduard Shevardnadze (by then a retired minister of Russian foreign affairs in Moscow), back to Georgia. Shevardnadze, who could draw on his former nomenklature network, managed to consolidate his position, but he lost Abkhazia and the approximately 240,000 Georgian IDPs who had to flee and still have not been able to return. Shevardnadze called for help from the Russian Federation against Gamsakhurdia who was fighting back from Chechnya and Mingrelia. Russia was prepared to give this help in return for Georgia joining the CIS and allowing Russian military bases on Georgian territory. Gamsakhurdia lost and elections were organized in 1993 with Shevardnadze as the sole candidate. He remained in power, winning the elections of 1995 and 1999, but tripping over the generally acknowledged rigged elections of November 2003.

By law, the speaker of Parliament Nino Burjanadze became president until the formal presidential elections of January 2004. Mikheil Saakashvili won these with flying colors. Between 2004 and 2006 many reforms were made but as tensions with Russia increased after 2006, so did the quality of life decrease, especially for those dependent on export of wine to Russia. Mainly a minority of Georgian and foreign investors pick the fruit of economic aid and development. In spite of great efforts by local NGOs such as the Soco Foundation and other humanitarian aid, approximately 40 percent[23] of the about 4.5 million population lives in poverty. Tensions with Russia escalated in a series of events[24] as negotiations with Georgia and Ukraine on a Membership Action plan (MAP) to join NATO, moved forward. However, a Membership plan was not accepted at the NATO Bucharest top in April 2008. Not so surprisingly,[25] that same summer, a Russian-Georgian war was fought in South Ossetia, whereby Russia, using disproportional force, first occupied buffer zones around South Ossetia and Abkhazia and after the mediation of President Sarkozy (chair of the EU at the time) to retreat from these areas, Russia recognized these regions as independent states.

Although the initial reaction of many Georgians was to support their president in his decision to undertake military action, after the war, having lost both territories along with many lives, the Georgian president had to face a disenchanted population and oppositional forces asking his resignation: the OSCE finally acknowledged that the January 2008 elections had been rigged and should have merited a 'second round', and the president lost good will in Europe. However, contrary to October 2007, perhaps on account of his many advisors, this time he did not touch the people protesting in the streets, even those who had blocked parts of the capital with tents during April and May of 2009. The opposition forces did not manage to work out a viable coalition with a clear alternative program and an alternative leader. People were disappointed in the lack of professionalism of the opposition, in the meantime causing a deep rift and a polarized communication in society. Irakli Alasania, ambassador to the United Nations between September 2006 and December 2008[26] is sometimes named as an alternative leader. He established his own party, the 'Alliance for Georgia'. In 2010 he will probably present himself as a candidate for mayor of Tbilisi against the sitting mayor Givi Ugulava. It is one possible 'route' to more influence, possibly in the form of a future coalition with the ruling party or with opposition parties.

Armenia

Armenia has the most homogeneous population of the former Soviet Republics. Today, about half of the world's 6.5 million Armenians live outside of Armenia forming a large diaspora in the United States and Europe. About a million Armenian lives were lost in 1915 in a war against the Ottoman Empire. It is this massacre that especially the Armenian diaspora with strong lobby's in Washington DC and European capitals wants to have recognized as genocide.[27]

In September 1917, a convention in Tbilisi elected the Armenian National Council which signed an Ottoman-Russian friendship treaty on January 1, 1918. The friendship was short-lived as it was soon followed by two wars with Turkey. In the first, Armenia lost the most Eastern strip of land (Erzinan, Erzurum, Van) to Turkey. The fights continued in September 1918 with more loss of lives and territory. As the terms of defeat were being negotiated, a new pro-Bolshevik government was established in the country. By November 29, 1920, the Soviet army succeeded in ousting the Turks before making peace with them. In 1921 the Bolsheviks and the Turks signed the *Treaty of Kars*. Adjara (later an Autonomous region within the SSR Georgia) was given to Soviet Georgia in exchange for the Kars territory, which included the mount Ararat, holy homeland to the Armenians. Shortly afterwards, in 1922, Armenia was incorporated into the Soviet Union as part of the Socialist Federation of Soviet Republics (SFSRs) but after 1936, as a Socialist, Soviet Republic (SSR).

In view of all these wars, treaties and territorial swaps in the South Caucasus, it is not surprising that the three countries harbor minorities of their neighbors. An Armenian minority exists in the Georgian province of Samtskhe Javakheti (capital Akhaltsikhe)[28] close to the border with Armenia and Turkey. But Armenian minorities also exist in Azerbaijan, notably in Ganja (second largest city of Azerbaijan, previously called Kirovabad) and in the self-proclaimed independent Karabakh enclave with capital Stepanakert (Khankendi in Azeri). Likewise, there is an Azeri minority in Georgia and in Northwestern Iran,[29] which used to be part of Azerbaijan. During the Soviet period deportations took place creating even more patches of minorities. Nagorno-Karabakh was a region (an autonomous *oblast*) of a majority Armenian population on Azerbaijan soil. Besides the question of territorial integrity, the problem is that more than half a million ethnic Azeri had to flee from the Nagorno-Karabakh area.

During the late 1980s – similarly to Georgia and Azerbaijan – Armenia also had its National Movement, which won the first legislative elections taking Armenia into sovereignty (August 23, 1990). Armenia declared its independence on September 21, 1991 through a referendum, but kept cordial relations with Moscow. On October 16, 1991 Levon Ter-Petrosyan, part of the Karabakh Committee of nationalist minded intellectuals, was elected as the first Armenian President. He remained in power until February 1998, when endorsing a negotiation plan about Nagorno-Karabakh forced his resignation. The plan consisted of a withdrawal of the Armenian forces from the occupied territories in Azerbaijan and the preservation of Azerbaijan's territorial integrity with self-governing status of Karabakh. In 1999, as his successor Robert Kocharvan was in power, the political scene was shaken by the assassinations in the Armenian parliament which killed the Prime Minister and six other politicians present at the scene. The reason given was that the corruption (for example with regard to the elections held shortly before helping Kocharvan into power) should stop. The killers received life sentences. President Kocharvan was eventually succeeded by Andranik Margaryan of the Republican Party. After his death in March 2007, Margaryan was succeeded by Serzh Sarkisyan in February 2008.

Nagorno[30]-Karabakh

Nagorno-Karabakh is at present a self-proclaimed independent state, not recognized by the UN or by the International Community. The problem of Karabakh goes back to the time when the South Caucasus was being incorporated into the Soviet Union. In 1920 with little control over Nagor-no-Karabakh by either side, the region was perceived by some to be part of Armenian territory. But in 1921 the young Joseph Stalin, who was working for the 'Kavkas Bureau' in Moscow at the time, assigned Karabakh to Azerbaijan. By 1923 Nagorno-Karabakh was proclaimed an Autonomous *Oblast* of Azerbaijan and so it remained during the Soviet period until unrest grew during *perestroika*. In February of 1988, the Assembly of Na-gorno-Karabakh asked the authorities in Moscow and the president Gor-bachev to be unified with the SSR Armenia. This request was not granted because the Soviet Constitution did not allow for borders to be changed. The request in itself however, was enough to trigger violence between Armenia and Azerbaijan with Azerbaijanis being expelled from Karabakh and pogroms held on Armenians living in the cities of Baku and Sumgait. The Russian army managed to reinstall some order but Moscow's failure to exercise justice spread and intensified the feeling of unrest.

Azerbaijan declared itself independent from the Soviet Union in August 1991, and Armenia did the same in the following month (September 1991). Before the end of 1991 a referendum was held in Karabakh, pro-independence. This independence was formalized on January 6, 1992. Again fights broke out between Armenians and Azerbaijani. Armenians gained the upper hand with assistance of the Russian 336th Rifle Regiment. The Lachin corridor connecting Nagorno-Karabakh to Armenia was also conquered. Massacres took place on both sides, as the important places of Shusha and Khojaly[31] fell, forcing thousands of ethnic Azeri to flee from their homeland.

Although a ceasefire was agreed in 1994, the negotiations which took place since then have not led to tangible results. As Azerbaijan became more important energy-wise with plans for developing pipelines, an oil lobby developed in the west somewhat counterbalancing the influence of the Armenian diaspora. The United States and France joined the Organization of Security and Cooperation in Europe (OSCE)-Minsk group as co-chairs, renewing their commitment to the region. The plan developed in 1997 was agreed to by leaders but was not accepted by the national movement in Armenia, costing Levon Ter- Petrosyan his job.

An agreement was signed a good ten years later on November 2nd 2008, again through mediation of Russia and the co-chairs France and USA of the OSCE Minsk group. Basically it was agreed to intensify their efforts to find a political solution on the basis of international law. According to the Helsinki Final Act, the UN Charter, the Charter of Paris and the OSCE, the occupation of the territory of Azerbaijan and the use of military force to change its borders were violations of international law. Several UN Security Council Resolutions called for withdrawal of the Armenian occupying forces from the occupied territory of Azerbaijan. These resolutions, although not always passed, also recognize the integral right of the population (IDPs) expelled from Nagorno-Karabakh and the occupied corridor, to return to their homes.

The tensions in Azerbaijan with all the Internally Displaced Persons (IDPs) from Karabakh who still hope to return to their homeland, are not over, irrespective of voting behavior in the UN Security Council. Azerbaijan has been doing well economically these past few years, and has built up a substantial army; if negotiations do not amount to any success, it is not unthinkable that the government of Azerbaijan could be tempted into using force to solve the problem of the over half a million IDPs and the 15-20 percent loss of territory, even though Azerbaijan is now abiding by international law. Unfortunately the way of international law has not shown any tangible results so far, and there is a tragic tension between leaders willing to sign an agreement, but not receiving support by the nationalist movement back home. Thus the Armenian president Levon Ter- Petrosyan, willing to endorse an agreement in 1997 was forced into resignation.

Azerbaijan

Azerbaijan proclaimed itself an independent republic in the city of Ganja on May 28, 1918, following the failed attempt to establish a Federal Transcaucasian Republic with Armenia and Georgia. In the capital Baku, however, tensions still existed between communists and Islamists. More precisely, a coalition of Bolsheviks, Mensheviks and Dashnak-Armenian forces, fought against a Turkish-Islamic army (also known as the Baku Commune). This coalition collapsed and was replaced by a British-controlled government known as the Central Caspian Dictatorship in July, 1918. In spite of British forces ultimately helping the Dashnak-Armenians to defend the capital, they lost against an Azeri-Ottoman army on September 15, 1918, only to regain the capital when the Ottoman empire capitulated on October 30, 1918. Azerbaijan was proclaimed a secular republic and its first parliament was opened in the last month of 1918.

Three quarters of a year after the British forces left in August 1919, Azerbaijanis were confronted both with tensions in the Karabakh enclave and with the Bolsheviks. Although the Azeris did put up a fight (April

1920) and lost 20,000 men in the process, equivocally, it must be said that the Bolsheviks did enjoy some support among the local industrial population working in Baku. That very same day, April 28, 1920 a Soviet Socialist Republic (SSR) was formed under Nariman Narimanov. Before the end of the year the same applied for Armenia, and the year after that (1921) for Georgia. Azerbaijan was incorporated into the 'Transcaucasian SFSR' with Armenia and Georgia in March 1922. This lasted until 1936, when under Stalin it was dissolved and the three regions were given the status of SSRs.   Similarly to the North Caucasus where the Soviet authorities tried to eradicate the Arab language and Islamic influence,[32] in Azerbaijan pan-Turkic aspirations or contacts with revolutionary movements in Iran or Turkey were heavily repressed. Anti-Islamic purges took place in the 50s and 60s until Azeri Heydar Aliyev was appointed as the first secretary of the Communist Party of Azerbaijan. He strengthened the ruling position of ethnic Azeris. In 1982 Aliyev joined the politburo in Moscow until Gorbachev forced him to retire because Aliyev, in his view, was opposing the *perestroika* and *glasnost* policies.

As in Georgia and Armenia, NGOs with an implicit political agenda beneath 'ecological' themes[33] emerged in Azerbaijan in the 1980s, further evolving into a nationalist movement, challenging the Soviet system. In Azerbaijan the Popular Front of Azerbaijan (PFA) had this role. Unrest culminated in violent confrontation when Soviet troops killed 132 nationalist demonstrators in Baku on January 20, 1990.[34] Azerbaijan declared its independence from the USSR on August 30, 1991, and joined the Commonwealth of Independent States (CIS) in December 1991. Ayaz Mutalibov won the first presidential elections in Azerbaijan on September 8, 1991 (as the sole running candidate). Fighting over Nagorno-Karabakh, after the fall of the town of Shusha in the Karabakh region, president Mutalibov had to resign. New presidential elections were organized in June 1992.

Elchibey

After Mutalibov's resignation, new presidential elections were held in June 1992. Abulfaz Elchibey, the leader of the previously mentioned Popular Front of Azerbaijan (PFA) and like president Gamsakhurdia of Georgia, a former dissident and political prisoner, was elected president. Akin to Zviad Gamsakhurdia, he was against Azerbaijan's membership of the CIS and was for closer relations with Turkey and for extending links with

Azerbaijanis in Northwestern Iran. However, the unresolved and worsening situation around Karabakh (with Armenians taking more land and more Azeris becoming Internally Displaced Persons) cost Elchibey his job in favor of Heydar Aliyev, who seized power with military support.

The Aliyevs

Similarly to Shevardnadze, also a pensioner who had been First Party Secretary and who first came to power in a non constitutional way, Aliyev was also a pensioner, had been the First Secretary of the CP for Azerbaijan, and came to power through military force until he was elected president about five months later, in October 1993. Aliyev, drawing on his his tribal Nakhchevan network consolidated his position as a dictator and passed the controversial but not condemned elections of October 1998. Both men remained in power well into 2003 in their respective countries. Shevardnadze stepped down after the rigged elections of November 2003 and Aliyev fell ill and was pronounced dead on December 12, 2003.

When Heydar Aliyev fell ill in October, he stepped down and appointed his son Ilham as the party's sole presidential candidate. In a somewhat doubtful election, his son Ilham Aliyev was then elected president on October 15, 2003 with 76 percent of the votes. This time international criticism was given on the quality of elections and Azerbaijan in Human Development Reports has been systematically characterized as less than democratic, in spite of simultaneously being very pro-Western. Ilham Aliyev before succeeding his father, had been a businessman and vice president of the State Oil Company of Azerbaijan (SOCAR). He participated as one of the key figures during the negotiations between the Azerbaijan government and Western oil companies.

Analysis through the grid of the Transition Paradigm

Away from dictatorial rule

The first assumption of the transition paradigm is that any country moving away from dictatorial rule can be considered a country in transition towards democracy. The first problem with this assumption is that especially in Georgia and in Azerbaijan there have been various successive starting points outside of elections. In Georgia: the first president Zviad

Gamsakhurdia was ousted by the militia on January 6, 1992. Then Shevardnadze ruled the roost, first without elections, then was voted in as the sole running candidate, won the elections of 1995 and 1999, until he was ousted by the Rose Revolution in November 2003.

In Azerbaijan: the war about Karabakh created difficulties for elected presidents and the first two Azerbaijani presidents, Mutalibov and Elchibey, lost their positions for it, as did their Armenian counterpart president Ter-Petrosyan. Aliev senior seized power by quickly capitalizing on a military coup before being formally elected. He remained in power for ten years. He appointed his son as Prime Minister, who won the following elections as a sole candidate.

The presidential periods in Armenia have been more equally spread: Levon Ter- Petrosyan (1991-1998) of the Armenian National Movement, followed seven years later by Robert Kocharvan from the Republican Party of Armenia (1998-2003). He was followed by the same party's Serzh Sargsyan in February 2008. But in Armenia we have the killings in the parliament building in 1999.

The second problem with this assumption is that in all cases with different intensity, the style of leadership has turned out to be rather authoritarian. Gamsakhurdia showed traits of megalomania and dictatorship.[35] Shevardnadze and his regime, although allowing for development of civil society, was hindered by corruption, lack of rule of law,[36] and rigged elections. Saakashvili, democratic in name, immediately formalized more power for the president upon election and has not encouraged the development of civil society, although he also achieved a lot in terms of reforms and in modernizing the capital. There is also an initiative to decentralise part of the government to Kutaisi. His re-election in January 2008 is not without doubt.[37] Georgia is now categorized at the lower end of hybrid regimes, as is Armenia. In both countries there are problems with free and fair elections, and problems with freedom of the press. Authoritarianism goes up a notch in Azerbaijan, which is more stable than its South Caucasus neighbors, but it is categorized as an authoritarian regime by Freedom House.

In all three countries, political parties are elite-driven. There is a lack of political culture on basis of party programs, and a lack of debate in Parliament on the basis of arguments. Rather, personal charisma dominates by far, with clan politics and clan rewards as a structural incentive.[38] The first assumption of the transition paradigm that any country moving away from dictatorial rule can be considered a country in transition toward democracy, within a time span of twenty years, does not quite hold yet for the South Caucasus (although there are many positive developments as well), unless one means gray democracies, with irregularities in election procedures, partial to no freedom of the press and regular violations of human rights.

A set of sequence stages

The second assumption of the transition paradigm that democracy tends to unfold in a set sequence of stages is not sustained by the empirical political reality of the South Caucasus countries, but can be retraced to the order in which NGOs were established. 'Following the donor-money' and looking at NGO mission statements, one can see a sequence from environmental NGOs being established during *perestroika* in the context of a pan-European and South Caucasus Green Movement. Then humanitarian aid got started during and after the (civil) wars, especially for the Internally Displaced Persons. Next, with the coming of Donor organizations in the South Caucasus (US AID, Eurasia Foundation, the EU- TACIS- technical programs) projects concerning the writing of new Constitutions and judicial reforms were developed. Then between 1994 and 1996 a myriad of NGOs were established throughout the South Caucasus for strengthening the fairness of elections, for judicial reforms, Human Rights, and for the strengthening of civil society.

Although projects were started to reform the justice department, the resistance to reforms is tenacious and has not been very effective until today. A set of sequent stages implies a kind of evolution where one stage is accomplished, something has been learned with behavior changing structurally, or when institutions are reformed in such a way that undoing these structures is difficult. This is not the case however, not even after the Revolution of Roses. So far the transition shows a very jagged profile without the unfolding of a set sequence of stages. On the contrary, the process has been characterized by (civil) wars and a revolution with partial progress in reforms and with many fall backs. The question is, are these an expression of absence of will,[39] of resistant culture, or of another not yet named factor of influence?

The determinative importance of elections

The political events put into perspective the third assumption of the transition paradigm: the determinative importance of elections. The people during the first Presidential elections in 1991 were so much in favor of a president of their own choice in all three the republics, that the outcome need not be doubted. But the riggings in subsequent elections in all three countries do not suggest that the art of conducting elections freely and fairly has been institutionalized so far. Local and international reports[40] claim serious violations in the South Caucasus countries.[41] On the other hand reform procedures take time, more than the instant democracy rhetoric may suggest.

The local elections were an important spur to general political development. Still, political parties remain weak for largely organizational, financial and cultural reasons, such as the lack of parliamentary and national debate.

The importance of structural features

The fourth assumption of the transition paradigm states that structural features and socio-cultural traditions are *not* major factors in either the onset or the outcome of the transition process. All evidence in the case of the South Caucasus countries suggests otherwise. Three interlinked socio-cultural phenomena and informal structures should be mentioned as factors possibly slowing down democracy: the political clan structure, corruption, and the shadow judicial system (the thieves in law[42]), which 'ruled' in the whole Soviet Union. These 'thieves' were linked to the Georgian Communist Party members in an intricate system of checks and balances. Banish the CP and these informal groups enjoy free reign. Even after a decade of independence and several justice reforms, the thieves in law were thriving as an alternative justice system. This is a structural factor slowing down judicial reforms and the democratization process in various parts of post-Soviet space.

President Saakashvili initially made some serious efforts to tackle all three of these problems with reasonable success. Corruption went down (in police, customs etc.). The thieves in law were locked up or they fled elsewhere. During his state building efforts of tax reforms, customs reforms, building the army and border security, labor relations were modernized and professionalized, young staff members appointed. Nevertheless, as soon as tensions increased after the slamming down on peaceful protesters in November 2007, fraudulent elections of January 2008 and the lost war with Russia in August 2008, the old clan mechanisms are drawn upon, temporarily creating an anti-democratic,[43] polarized fissure in Georgian society.

According to Human Development Reports, Freedom House and the Corruption Perceptions Index, Georgia, Armenia and Azerbaijan respectively take the 67th, 109th and 158th position of the 180 countries on this particular index in 2009. In terms of the Human Development Index, Armenia scores highest (83/197), Georgia (93/197) stands in between and Azerbaijan is situated lowest of the three (97/197) in 2008. In terms of Press Freedom, Freedom House qualified Georgia as 'partly free' in 2009 and Armenia and Azerbaijan as 'not free'.

All three societies are organized rather vertically along the lines of clan structure. The incentive structure for entering politics in all three countries is about the same: entering Parliament and the higher governmental echelons is a way to get access to financial resources (foreign grants, profit from companies and business deals, etc.). Structural factors such as former Soviet practices, the *habitus* of corruption, the political incentive structure and the feeble civil society, apparently play a role in the slowing down of democracy and stability. In short, these features could be summarized as 'political culture'[44] which either needs to be accepted as different with its own merits and rationality as a system, or the political culture would need to be transformed with more horizontal relations between the different parties (coalitions) and with more national involvement through other channels than street occupation.[45]

The fifth factor: Transformation of a functioning state

In view of the fact that the Soviet Union was dissolved due to bankruptcy of the state (corruption, lack of incentive, malfunctioning of the planned economy) and tremendous bureaucracy, the former Union Republics could hardly be seen as properly functioning states. Had the Soviet system functioned well, it would probably not have collapsed the way it did. Breaking out of an empire, a malfunctioning one at that, does require a thorough 're-organization', a re-building of both state and nation. This is a complex process requiring attention by individuals from the state institutions, private and public organizations. In view of the persistent problems with democratization one could wonder which forces are at stake? Are less visible, cultural forces hindering the transition to democracy or are the expectations too high and culturally biased at the onset?

Discussion: Transition and Culture?

Clearly, transition in the South Caucasus during the past two decades has been a capricious and fickle process with false starts, setbacks and surprises. In theoretical terms it has more in common with the multi lineal and differential evolutionary theory of society[46] than to the clear-cut, uni-linear, deterministic transition paradigm. Structural features (economic development, institutional legacies, socio-cultural habits) do play a role in the onset and outcome of the transition process, or after twenty years of development, membership of the Council of Europe, the wish to join NATO (requirement to reform judicial system) Georgia, Azerbaijan and Armenia would have been more democratic, viable states than they are today. Does the economic development come with change in political culture? Do the value orientations more or less shape the development towards democracy and more economic growth? Or are strongly committed individuals needed most, to make a difference?

Theory of economic development and socio-political evolution focuses on such structural features. Some attribute more importance to culture, some more to economy. It is concluded that economic development is to a certain extent predictable towards rational, tolerant, and trusting values; but also that culture is path dependent: value systems are persistent.[47] In other words, if the forces between development and cultural setting are equally strong, the predictable change may fail to occur. In view of the religious diversity in the South Caucasus (Christian, Muslim) it is interesting to note the conclusions from global comparative research between religion and democracy. Norris[48] concludes that the only significant relations between religious beliefs and democracy found, were a negative correlation between Islam and gender equality and a negative correlation between Christian Orthodoxy and democracy.[49] In the context of economic development however, the research by Ross should also be noted. He differentiates types of economic growth and concludes that growth 'based on oil and mineral extraction, [it] discourages women from entering the labor force and tends to exaggerate gender inequalities'. (...) This leaves oil-producing states with atypically strong patriarchal cultures and political institutions.[50] Since the economies of the three South Caucasus countries differ and one of them is strongly based on gas and oil revenues (Azerbaijan), this calls for more comparative research on the relation between economy, culture and political institutions in the South Caucasus.

A quote which can be heard frequently in 2010 in Georgia is, 'everything changes but nothing changes'. Perhaps institutional reform is slow because of the learned disrespect from the Soviet Union for the law. Some scholars argue that ingrained practices of clientelism and corruption have overshadowed formal institutions making it difficult for rule of law (and thus for a stronger democratic state) to grow. How to break out of this vicious circle? Some have suggested teaching 'civics' in schools, others plead for a 'jury system' as a means to encourage rule of law. However it may be, for theorizing effectively, the concept of transition should be worked out in the direction of 'culture and institutional change' and 'how to involve the nation' both in the context of economic activity and in public debate.

Drawing on Leslie White's[51] idea of energy and the evolution of culture: as long many people live in poverty[52] with no surplus energy to spend on anything else but survival, then culture and social self expression will not develop further if the amount of energy to be spent per person does not increase. In 2009 and 2010 the kind of recommendations one can read in Foreign Policy and Security Journals is to involve the whole nation in the process of transition (implying more poverty reduction), not just the elites. Because the aspect of 'effective change' is now being stressed perhaps it is time to refer to focus on transformation.

Finally, the transition paradigm takes a functioning state as a point of departure, whereas states in the South Caucasus virtually collapsed during the 'shock therapy' applied after the dissolution of the Soviet Union. States were weak, state income meager. The relation between statehood, nationhood and democracy should be taken more into consideration when it comes to the South Caucasus. Studies such as that of Gellner give insight into the fact that contrary to western statehood, in the South Caucasus nationhood and statehood do not necessarily coincide.[53] It is therefore not illogical to follow a different strategy of development. It is quite difficult to meet democratic standards in a fragile state struggling with territorial integrity and strongly developed informal contacts.[54] In the West, civil society and democracy generally developed against the State, as a people's counter balance against the State got too strong. The challenge in the South Caucasus states lies in building a stronger state whilst simultaneously allowing civil society to develop in order to stimulate reciprocal relations. This would stimulate change at a collective normative level. And this would be called *transformation* rather than transition.

It takes conscious strategic efforts by individuals and groups of people to work on viable state- infrastructures and to fashion the political and judicial environment towards democratic standards. Without such deeply committed individuals nothing much is bound to happen. Yet, action and interaction are as much a cultural construction as a function of structure. Evidently, the existing social order is embedded in legitimizing ideologies. Possible change and interventions need to be explained or 'disguised' or 'sold' in the accepted ideological, cultural tradition. Thus any activity towards democratization is culturally and ideologically embedded. Also Claessen and Van de Velde in their large comparative work confirm that ideology is more important for socio-political evolution than, for example, war.[55] However, in view of other conclusions on the relation between oil economies and patriarchal cultures and political institutions,[56] more comparative empirical research needs to be done in the South Caucasus on the relation between economy, culture and political institutions.

For a clear analysis and discussion we need to distinguish culture as an all-permeating social and political phenomenon from a thinner layer of pragmatic politics. Pragmatic policy with regard to international relations need not be hindered by a monolithic, essentialist understanding of culture. Politics can supersede cultural differences, justifying to a certain extent the idea of limits to culture. However, the way the politicians communicate, the strategies they choose, the pattern of loyalty exerted, the way they will be perceived by various constituents and the meaning attributed to their actions, will nevertheless be cultural.

Conclusion

Breaking out of the Soviet Union with remnants of policy based on ethnicity tied to territory in various degrees of autonomy for regions within a Union Republic, specifically characterizes the subsequent statehood process. Nationhood and statehood do not synchronize in the same way as happens more or less in a western statehood building process. Structural societal features such as powerful elites, shadow judicial systems, ingrained expectations of corruption by the public, the workings of political clans, weigh on the transition process to democracy and a free market economy. Transition theory for the South Caucasus should take such local cultural and economic (oil) context into account, making the concept of *transformation* more relevant. Transformation implies a normative aspect of change. It implies more involvement of the nation as a whole (fighting poverty and increasing participation), not by bringing politics into the streets,[57] but by developing politics and debate in parliament and in civil society. The lack of trust between authoritarian leaders and the public remains a problem to be worked on. In short, successful state formation depends on the forging of reciprocal connections between the government and the people. Finally, the specific geo-political influence (and sometimes lack of it!) from both the Russian Federation and from the USA, the EU, the OSCE (elections, negotiations) and NATO are forces and voids which give immediate cause for Russian and Western policy makers to reflect on their own contribution to this fascinating region.

Notes

1 I would like to thank Brenda Shaffer for her valuable comments on part of an earlier version of this chapter.
2 King, C. (2008). *The Ghost of Freedom*. Oxford: Oxford University Press; Nikolayenko, O. (2007). *Comparative Politics*. Volume 39, Number 2, January; Fawn, R. (ed. 2003). *Ideology and National Identity in Post-Communist Foreign Policies*, London: Frank Cass; Gellner, E. (1983). *Nations and Nationalism*. NY: Cornell University Press; Jones, S. (1993). 'Georgia: a failed democratic transition'. In: I. Bremmer and R. Taras (eds), *Nation and Politics in the Soviet successor states*. Cambridge: Cambridge University Press; Suny, R. (1988). *The Making of a Georgian Nation*. Bloomington: Indiana University Press; Suny, R. (1993). *Looking toward Ararat. Armenia in Modern History*. Bloomington: Indiana University Press.
3 Razoux, P. (2009). *Histoire de la Géorgie la clé du Caucase*. Perrin; Serrano, S. (2007). *Sortie d'Empire*. CNRS Editions.
4 Jones, S. (2002). 'Georgia from under the Rubble'. In: Barrington, L. (2002). (ed.). *Nationalism after Independence: the Post-Soviet States*. University of Michigan Press. Gellner, E. (1983). ibid. See the Georgian journal *Identity Studies* nr 1, 2009 with articles on nationalism and identity by Gigi Tevsadze, Oliver Reisner, Ghia Nodia, David Darchiashvili and others: https://sites.google.com/a/isystemsinstitute.org/identity-studies/
5 O'Beacháin, D. & A. Polese (2010). (eds) *The Coloured Revolutions in Former Soviet Republics: Success and Failures*. Routledge. Khutsishvili G. (2008). (ed.) *Civil Society and The Rose Revolution*. Tbilisi: Cordaid/ICCN.
6 Cohen, A. (1996). The New 'Great Game': Oil Politics in the Caucasus and Central Asia. Backgrounder 1065. The Heritage Foundation. http://www.heritage.org/research/russiaandeurasia/bg1065.cfm. Publications by Svante Cornell varying from energy, Turkey, Islam, security issues and the August war 2008.
7 Cornell, S. & F. Starr (2009). *The Guns of August 2008: Russia's War in Georgia*, New York: M.E. Sharpe.
8 For example the EU could have observers in the region, now that the OSCE had to withdraw its observers from South Ossetia. The EU could get even more involved in serious negotiations on Karabakh.

9 Rustow (1970), Schmitter (1986) and many others who wrote on 'transitol-
ogy', comparing Mediterranean with Latin American countries, referring
to 'the path' of democracy, or of re-democratisation, sometimes tied to the
study of revolutions (Goldstone 1986) I mention only a few authors who focus on the South Caucasus or who were discussed in the South Caucasus.
Thomas Carothers was one of these authors discussed in Georgia. Carothers,
T. (2002). 'The End of the Transition Paradigm'. In: *Journal of Democracy* July
2002, 13, 1.

10 Fairbanks (2004), Carothers, T. (2007). The 'Sequencing' Fallacy. In: *Journal
of Democracy*, Vol. 18. No. 1. January, 17-27. (2006). *Confronting the Weakest
Link: Aiding Political Parties in New Democracies.* Washington, D.C. Carn-
egie Endowment for International Peace. (2002) ibid. Nodia, G. (2002: 13-19).
The Democratic Path. In: *Journal of Democracy*, Volume 13. No. 3. July. Wol-
lack, K. (2002: 20-25). 'Retaining the Human Dimension' *Journal of Democracy* Volume 13. No. 3. July. Dauderstadt, M., A.Gerrits, G.Markus, (2002).
Troubled Transition: Social Democracy in East Central Europe. Friedrich
Ebert Stiftung Wiardi Beckman Stichting Alfred Mozer Stichting. Dryzek,
J & L. Holmes (2002). *Post-communist democratization; Political discourses
across thirteen countries.* Cambridge: Cambridge University Press.

11 Carothers, T. (2002). 'The End of the Transition Paradigm.' In: *Journal of Democracy*, Volume 13, January.

12 Nodia, G. (2002). Ibid

13 Mc Faul, M. and K. Stoner Weiss (2004: 1-20). *After the Collapse of Communism: Comparative Lessons of Transitions* Cambridge: Cambridge University Press. Stoner Weiss, K. & M. Mc Faul (2005). After the Collapse: The
Comparative Lessons of Post-Communist Transitions. Cambridge University
Press. Mc Faul, M. (2005: 5-19). 'Transitions from Post-communism,' *Journal
of Democracy*, Vol. 16, No.3. July; Steffes, C. (2006). Understanding Post Soviet transitions; Corruption, Collusion and Clientelism. *Euro-Asian Studies.*
General Editor C. Bluth.

14 In view of summarizing the recent history of three countries in one chapter,
I focus on major events and do not delve into 'scandals' and riots which have
taken place in the politics of these three countries during the past two decades.

15 Trenin, D. (2009). 'Russia Reborn.' In: *Foreign Affairs.* Volume 88, no 6. No-
vember/December. Davis, D. (2009: 221-245). Non-State Armed Actors, New
Imagined Communities, and Shifting Patterns of Sovereignty and Insecurity in the Modern World. In: *Contemporary Security Policy.* Volume 30, no
2 August. And more implicitly through discussion of 'normative power' in
Averre, D. (2009: 1689-1713). Competing Rationalities: Russia, the EU and

the 'Shared Neighbourhood'. In: *Europe-Asia Studies*. Volume 61, no 10. December.

16 Shaffer, B. (2006). *The Limits of Culture. Islam and Foreign Policy*. Cambridge, Mass: The MIT Press.

17 See the Introduction and chapters 2, 3, and 4.

18 Most recently serious efforts are made to soften relations ('soccer diplomacy' and the signing of protocols to open Turkish-Armenia border, but the protocols have not been ratified yet).

19 Formerly GUUAM, but Uzbekistan stepped out.

20 The war is delved into in chapters 8 and 9.

21 Razoux, P. (2009). *Histoire de la Géorgie la clé du Caucase*. Perrin.

22 Throughout the South Caucasus. In Azerbaijan an uprising had occurred.

23 Numbers vary from 30 to 50 percent depending on the criteria used.

24 Georgia was accused of harboring Chechen fighters, Russia unilaterally introduced a visa regime for Georgians, Russian diplomats were expelled from Georgia as spies in 2006, Russia closed all its borders for Georgian products (wine) and used gas supplies as a political tool. Air space was violated mutually. An alleged Russian bomb was dropped in tsitelubani, Georgia, on August 7, 2007, without exploding.

25 The build up of tension, the eviction of Russian diplomats, the closing of Russian borders to Georgian products, accumulation of Russian military material at the borders, warnings by president Saakashvili about this, etc.

26 He was also formerly chair of Abkhazia's pro-Georgian government in exile and the Presidents' former envoy of the peace talks between Georgia and Abkhazia, before he was transferred to New York as an ambassador of Georgia to the United Nations.

27 Formulated this way because we need to distinguish the formal foreign policy of the Armenian government from the Armenian diaspora lobby. 15 to 20 countries have recognized the genocide in the meantime.

28 The same province and capital where the Muslim Meskhetians were deported from to Central Asia in 1944.

29 The Azeri Turks are estimated to be about 18-20 million in Iran and are believed to constitute between 16 to 24 percent of the Iranian population. According to Amnesty International: 'Iranian Azeri Turks, who are mainly Shi'a Muslims, are the largest minority in Iran [..] located mainly in the north and north-west of Iran. As Shi'a, they are not subjected to the same kinds of discrimination as minorities of other religions, and are well-integrated into the economy, but there is a growing demand for greater cultural and linguistic rights, including implementation of their constitutional right to education through the medium of Turkish'. *AI index: MDE 13/010/2006*, p. 12.

30 Nagorno is derived from the Russian nagornyi for 'highland': one could also say 'Upper'; Karabakh means 'dark or black garden' in Turkish. The Armenian name for Karabakh is Artsakh.

31 On both sides. According to Human Rights Watch the Khojaly Massacre on February 26, 1992, whereby about two hundred Azeri villagers, women and children were killed by Armenians with help of the Russian 366th Rifle Regiment, is the largest massacre to date in the conflict.

32 See Chapter 4.

33 Companjen (2004) devoted a chapter to environmental NGOs of the eighties and first half of the nineties in Georgia.

34 In Georgia something similar happened on April 9, 1989, and independence was declared in March 1991.

35 The following authors used the following terms to indicate dictatorial tendencies: Dryzek, J. & L. Holmes (2002:148). *Post-communist democratization; Political discourses across thirteen countries.* Cambridge: Cambridge University Press, mentions 'fascist dictator'; Hewitt, G. (1996: 211) 'Abkhazia: a problem of identity and ownership', in J. Wright, S. Goldenberg & R. Schofield (eds), *Transcaucasian Boundaries.* London: UCL. refers to 'incipient dictatorship'.

36 Colloquially called 'syndrome of non-punishment' during interviews in Georgia. Companjen (2004) *Between Tradition and Modernity.* Ph.d. VU Amsterdam.

37 The OSCE first concluded the elections were fair but six months later admitted they were rigged.

38 For clan society in post-Soviet space, 'an informal group of elites whose members promote their mutual political, financial, and strategic interests', see Kryshtanovskaya, O., (1997:14-17). 'Illegal Structures in Russia,' *Trends in Organized Crime.* Volume 3, no. 1, Fall.

39 'Absence of will' is also the title of a DVD made by Mamuka Kuparadze of Studio Re, about Georgia and Abkhazia.

40 The International Society for Fair Elections and Democracy, Freedom House, the Organisation for Security and Cooperation in Europe elections' reports.

41 See Chapter 6.

42 Georgian: *kanonieri kurdebi*; Russian: *vory v zakone.*

43 In the meaning of Parliamentary democracy – political action was taken into the streets.

44 Sumbadze, N. and G. Tarkan Mouravi, (2003). *Democratic Value Orientations & Political Culture in Georgia.* Institute for Policy Studies. http://www.ips.ge.ibid.

45 Nee, V & R. Matthews (2006:411). 'Market transition and Societal Transformation in Reforming State Socialism.' In: *Annual Review Sociology.* Tolz, V.

(1998:1004). 'The soviet state did not encourage horizontal ties between members of society, thus preventing civil society and thereby a viable civic nation from being formed.' 'Forging the Nation: national identity and nation building in post-communist Russia', *Europe-Asia Studies*, Vol. 50, no 6. pp. 993-1022.

46 Carneiro, R.L. (1973). The four faces of Evolution. In: Honigman (ed) *The Handbook of Social and Cultural Anthropology*. Chicago: Rand Mc Nally. (1981). The Chiefdom. In: J.D. Jones RR Kautz (eds) *Transition to Statehood in the New World*. New York: Cambridge University Press.

47 Inglehart, R. (2000). Culture and Democracy. In: L.E. Harrison & S. Huntington (eds), *Culture matters; How values shape human progress*. Basic Books.

48 Norris, P. & R. Inglehart, (2002:16). 'Islamic culture and democracy: Testing the 'Clash of Civilizations' thesis' In: *Comparative Sociology*. Volume 1, 3/4.

49 Norris, P. & R. Inglehart (2002:16) ibid.

50 Ross, M. (2008). Oil, Islam and Women. In: *American Political Science Review* Vol. 102, No. 1 February, p.107.

51 White, L. (1949:367). *The Science of Culture. The Study of Man and Civilization*. New York: Grove Press.

52 Data from the Statistics Department of Georgia (SDSG): 'Incomes of the population, save rare exceptions, have drastically dropped.' 'By the end of 1997, 53.1 per cent of the Georgians lived below the poverty line.' V. Melikidze, 'Georgian Bread Industry During Economic Reform', (Tbilisi, UNDP Discussion Paper Series nr 7, 1998). All statistics show little progress has been made in fighting poverty and also records show that average life expectancy is low, tuberculosis and such poverty diseases are increasing.

53 See also the Georgian Internet Journal *Identity*, wherein Gigi Tevsadze and Oliver Reisner have published on nationalism, and see chapter 7 this volume.

54 According to Estellie Smith (1986:105) those are precisely the characteristics of polities in transition: weak formal structures, strong informal contacts and medium attention for technological development. In: *Development and Decline. The evolution of Sociopolitical Organization*. Massachusetts: Bergin & Garvey.

55 Claessen, H. en P. van de Velde, M. Estellie Smith (eds) (1985: 254). *Development and Decline. The evolution of Sociopolitical Organization*. Massachusetts: Bergin & Garvey.

56 Ross, M. (2008). ibid.

57 See IPS Georgia barometer: comparing public opinion in Georgia before and after the 2008 war with an increase of rally's being mentioned as the way to exert influence on government. www.IPS.ge

6 Authoritarianism and Party Politics in the South Caucasus

Max Bader

Introduction

Political parties in the post-Soviet states of the South Caucasus have been very different types of institutions from their counterparts in western democracies. In Armenia 'no party fulfills the fundamental roles of aggregating the public's interest, offering policy alternatives, or organizing meaningful debate over public concerns.'[1] According to a former country director of the National Democratic Institute in Azerbaijan, a U.S. organization that trains parties in many countries, parties in Azerbaijan 'are a disaster. That assessment includes the ruling party, the opposition parties and the ones created on behalf of the government to placate the West.'[2] In Georgia, parties have been viewed as 'fundamentally different sorts of organizations from their western counterparts.'[3] Evidently then, the study of party politics in the South Caucasus is challenging and demands an unconventional approach.

The two key outcomes that distinguish party politics in the South Caucasus from party politics in western democracies, since 1991, are the impact of *authoritarian practices* and a great degree of *volatility*. The impact of authoritarian practices has been manifest in the creation of political parties, mainly by regime actors, that have distorted the electoral playing field. Volatility in party politics in the South Caucasus has been reflected in a continuously changing supply of parties – in Georgia more so, in Azerbaijan less so – as well as in shifting electoral coalitions and volatility within parties, and is fed by the inherent weakness of most party organizations.

A common conclusion about party politics in all three South Caucasus states is that parties are short of credible roots in society and are essentially driven by elite actors. Considering the combination of a low degree of party system institutionalization and the elite-driven nature of party politics in the post-communist world, it has been suggested that 'much more emphasis should be put on understanding the incentive structures of elites that encourage or discourage stability [of party systems].[4] This article takes up the call of studying the *incentive structures* of the elites who are behind the creation and operation of parties in the South Caucasus, in order to better understand the dynamics of party politics in the region.

Rapid changes in the supply of parties are the clearest indicator of the fluid nature of party politics (volatility) in the Former Soviet Union (FSU). Individual parties, however, have been unstable in more respects. Parties have been subject to far-reaching internal change resulting from defections or the arrival of new leadership. The degree of change could be such that the affected party should be regarded as a different entity. Furthermore, parties often did not compete as independent political forces, but as constituents of larger electoral coalitions, that almost invariably proved to be short-lived. Sometimes, the line between parties and coalitions became difficult to draw, contributing to the low profile of parties as autonomous political forces. Also, parties in some countries, once in parliament, tended to disintegrate into several rivaling factions, from which new parties were sometimes formed. As with electoral coalitions, the distinction between parties and factions could become blurred.

A second key outcome of party politics in the South Caucasus has been the impact of authoritarian practices. Party politics in a less-than-democratic setting should be expected to display a different dynamic from settings in which fair competition can be taken for granted. This straightforward but crucial assumption is insufficiently appreciated in studies of party politics outside of established democracies.[5] In less-than-democratic settings, executive authorities intentionally distort the electoral playing field in order to tighten their grip on power or to extract the rents that are accessible to regime actors by virtue of holding office. Distortion of the playing field is achieved both by checking the opposition and by becoming involved in party-building. Some regimes opt to establish a 'party of power' that towers over other parties in terms of financial and personnel resources and exposure. As will be demonstrated below, regimes may also deploy other types of parties, including satellite parties and spoiler parties, to keep a check on genuine pluralism. Competition between parties in less-than-democratic conditions is often less about policies than about the rules of the political game. Elections may become 'nested games': 'At the same time as incumbents and opponents measure their forces in the electoral arena, they battle over the basic rules that shape the electoral arena.'[6] Moreover, the decisive fault line in electoral competition is that of support for the regime versus opposition to the regime, with little room for political accommodation. Opposition parties will often declare democratic convictions an important motive in their struggle against incumbents, and organize protests against government decisions or election results. In the process, issue-based appeals, which are believed to better structure electoral competition in democracies,[7] are pushed to the background. Finally, the party system configuration under (semi-)authoritarianism mostly lasts only as long as the regime lasts, since regime change often brings about a radical shake-up of the party landscape. Party system change in less-than-democratic settings is therefore mostly conditioned upon the regime's capability of survival.

In the remainder of this chapter I argue just how parties in the South Caucasus have been different from their counterparts in western democracies. In the second section it is argued how institutional arrangements have constrained the leverage of political parties, while the third section discusses the party types which have been products of authoritarian practices and which have been at the forefront of party politics in all three South Caucasus states. Before concluding, the fourth section synthesizes the argument about the role of incentive structures in party politics in the FSU and illustrates that argument by extending Strom's (1990) 'three models of party behavior', originally conceived for advanced democracies, to party politics in Armenia, Azerbaijan, and Georgia.[8]

Parties as vehicles of elite actors

In practically all countries which were once part of the 'third wave of democratization', political parties are subject to a 'standard lament', a range of complaints concerning their functioning.[9] According to this lament, parties lack programmatic distinction, do not genuinely represent people's interests, spring into action only around election time, are leader-centric, and are ill-prepared to take up the responsible task of governing. These defects, unsurprisingly, are also rife across both halves of the post-communist world, including the South Caucasus.

Parties fail to present to voters recognizable programs. In Azerbaijan, 'the differences among [opposition parties] center more on personalities than on political ideology'.[10] As noted, Armenian parties do not fulfill the roles of 'offering policy alternatives' or 'organizing public debate over public concerns',[11] while Georgian parties are said to be characterized by a 'lack of clear ideology, values or vision'.[12]

Unlike the old parties of western democracies, parties in the South Caucasus are an expression of differences between elite actors rather than of societal cleavages. The classic sociological account of party politics explains the origin of parties from these societal cleavages.[13] According to the cleavage hypothesis, social conflict is translated into party alternatives, i.e. different political parties essentially represent different groups in society.[14] The cleavage hypothesis presumes the *ex ante* existence of definable cleavages, e.g. along religious, class, ethnic, or linguistic lines, which split up groups of voters. Together with institutionalist explanations, sociological explanations, of which the cleavage hypothesis is the best-known representative, are dominant in theory on the origin of parties and party systems.[15]

There is little reason to take cues from the cleavage hypothesis with respect to the South Caucasus. At the outset of party politics in the postcommunist world, it was hypothesized that as a result of the 'leninist legacy', no immediately identifiable cleavage structures would be present that could serve as the foundation of strong interest-based parties.[16] Moreover, the South Caucasus states contained a weak, embryonic civil society,[17] a political culture adverse to the development of programmatic parties[18], and lacked meaningful experience with pre-communist multiparty politics, which in some Central and Eastern Europe countries has contributed to structure the return of political competition after 1989. For these reasons, the emergence of broad-based political parties with deep roots in society did not appear likely. Instead, the political party landscape in the South Caucasus would in many ways resemble a tabula rasa on which a wide variety of different players would try their luck to catch the votes of a floating electorate.

Especially in Azerbaijan, and to a lesser extent in Armenia and Georgia as well, political parties coincide with regional clan structures. The ruling Yeni Azerbaijan Party, for instance, is said to represent first and foremost the interests of two clans, while one opposition party is affiliated with a different regionally based clan.[19] In Georgia, some parties are notably stronger in one or two regions, typically those from where the party leaders hail, than in other regions. The lack of 'programmatic linkage' between voters and politicians is balanced by strong 'charismatic linkage'[20] and a dominant position of party leaders within their respective parties. In Azerbaijan, 'the major parties are all dominated by strong personalities unwilling to yield to others'[21],while in Armenia 'the party chairperson is usually the single most important figure'.[22] These party leaders tend to regard their parties as 'projects' that are at their personal disposal and from which certain benefits are sought. In Armenia parties are 'essentially personalistic organizations, instruments for the ambitions of a more or less well-known individual and his clientele'.[23] In Georgia, 'the façade of democracy also covers the country's political parties, while the democratic procedures camouflage the fact that it is the party leaders and the elite who dominate the political scene'.[24]

The leader-centric nature of parties in the South Caucasus is reinforced by voters' preferences. Of Georgian voters more than half admit voting primarily for a party because of its leader, while one quarter thinks a party's program is more important than its leaders.[25] And in Armenia, 'whether in parliamentary, presidential, or local government, ordinary people most often do not consider the ideas or programs of candidates or parties. They usually orient themselves by asking others whom they respect as wise people or those they fear, which are the influential, wealthy, or strong persons in the community'.[26] The relation between political parties and the public at large in Azerbaijan is summed up as follows:

> [A]lmost all of political parties are based on regional affiliation and/ or on personalities of party leaders; effective channels of state-society relations are weak; society at large is disillusioned and apathetic, and elites lack legitimacy among the masses.[27]

Instead of joining existing forces, politicians typically seek to head their personal political vehicles; in Armenia, for instance, this has lead to 'the continued proliferation of unelectable parties and an elitist party system'.[28] Despite insignificant ideological differences and a common interest in toppling the regime, opposition parties rarely manage to combine forces. To the extent that parties cooperate, they do so in the form of electoral coalitions which often fall apart after elections. Fragmentation persists as a consequence of the refusal of party leaders to sacrifice their organizations.

The many parties in the South Caucasus states, with the partial exception of those that are propped up by state resources, tend to be weak and inconsequential. In Armenia, 'most of these [parties] are small clubs rather than organized parties and lack the popular support, organizational structures, and internal resources necessary to win votes and run an government'.[29] Georgian parties similarly are 'more like political clubs with loose organizational structures, small memberships and no real influence',[30] while opposition parties in Azerbaijan are said to be 'disillusioned and weak'[31] and to suffer from 'poor organizational development'.[32]

The limited leverage of parties

Volatility in party supply and volatility within parties, which determine the fluid nature of party politics in the South Caucasus states, hinge on the lack of incentives for political actors to invest in the formation and development of viable parties. The absence of strong enough incentives stems from the limited impact of parties in political life. The limited role of parties, in turn, is largely predicated on the institutional make-up of the political systems of the South Caucasus states. The elements of institutional design that are most widely considered to have an impact on party (system) development, and that will be discussed here, are executive-legislative relations and the electoral system.

The Perils of Presidentialism for Party Development

Since the adoption of their first post-communist constitutions in 1995, the political regimes of the South Caucasus have been primarily either purely presidential (Georgia until 2004) or of the 'highly presidentialized semi-presidential' class (Georgia since 2004, Armenia until 2007, and Azerbaijan throughout). Whether or not executive power was formally shared with a prime minister, both the formal and the actual distribution of the executive has been strongly in favor of the presidency. Only in Armenia since 2007 is there a more balanced distribution of power between president and prime minister. As Elgie[33] points out, highly presidentialized semipresidential regimes 'often suffer the same problems as their purely presidential counterparts', and may even be more 'presidentialized' than some purely presidential regimes, a state of affairs which, with regard to the former Soviet republics, is sometimes captured by the term 'superpresidentialism'.

There is a reasonable consensus that presidential systems are less conducive to democratic consolidation than arrangements with strong legislatures in states moving away from authoritarianism.[34] Among other things, the 'perils of presidentialism' include the personalization of power, the often limited checks on executive authority, the blurring of prerogatives and spheres of accountability of the executive vis-à-vis parliament, and the lack of accountability of presidents due to their fixed terms of office.[35] With regard to political parties specifically, it is argued that there is an 'inverse relationship' between presidentialism and party strength.[36] From the wealth of arguments linking presidentialism to problems with stable, democratic party development, four arguments with particular relevance to the South Caucasus states are summarized here.

First, under presidentialism, the relevance of political parties is diminished as a direct consequence of the way powers are distributed. Most importantly, with the presidency being the main prize of political competition, actors will be inclined to place their bets on securing the presidency.[37] While doing so, they often circumvent parties, especially in places where having party affiliation is considered a liability. Furthermore, while a parliamentary majority, typically consisting of one or more parties, is central in forming the government in parliamentary regimes, it is mostly the president, with or without *ad hoc* approval by a parliamentary majority, who is in charge of forming government cabinets under presidentialism. Particularly in countries where parties are unpopular, presidents prefer nonpartisan, technical cabinets. Making the situation worse, this circumstance prompts careerist politicians who are interested in taking up government posts not to join parties. Lastly, given that parliament is the main platform for parties to manifest themselves, especially when parties are not involved in cabinet formation, the weakness of the legislature reinforces the image of parties as inconsequential organizations.

Second, due to the centrality of the presidency, presidential regimes are more characterized by the 'politics of personality' than are parliamentary regimes, in which parties rather than persons – partisan or not – take center stage.[38] The personalization of politics, where it affects parties, works at the expense of the development of viable party organizations. Most party organizations in the South Caucasus are dominated by 'big men' (rarely women) who personify their parties.[39] Concomitantly, only a few parties have experienced leadership succession.

Following in part from the personalization of politics, parties in presidentialized regimes are less often of the programmatic type and tend to have a stronger electoral focus than in parliamentary regimes. Of the broad categories of programmatic, charismatic, and clientelist parties,[40] the two latter types are found to be more widespread under presidentialism.[41] Although neither charismatic nor clientelist parties necessarily obstruct the consolidation of democracy,[42] the effective interest aggregation and typically larger degree of institutionalization of programmatic parties go together with democratization more readily. Also, and related to the diminished leverage of parties under presidentialism, parties in presidential systems tend to be less cohesive,[43] lending support to the suggestion that parties in presidential systems are differently organized than in parliamentary systems.[44] Finally, executive authorities in presidential regimes may have an interest in checking the development of strong (opposition) parties which potentially pose a challenge to the regime. Especially in a less-than-democratic setting, the regime might be tempted to block parties from becoming too influential, for instance by amending legislation, detaining party leaders, or rigging elections.

Electoral Legislation

The impact of electoral laws on political parties and party systems is extensively studied. After Duverger (1959),[45] a distinction is commonly made between mechanical and psychological effects of electoral laws. While the mechanical working of electoral formulae translates votes into seats in a specific way, the psychological element prompts voters and parties to rethink the possible consequences of their actions and to adapt their voting and electoral strategy to fit anticipated outcomes. As in the relation between strong legislatures and democracy, there is much evidence, from both case-oriented and variable-oriented studies, that proportional representation (PR) is more conducive to democratization than single-member districts (SMDs) in states moving away from authoritarianism.[46]

Georgia and Armenia have had mixed electoral systems, in which a part of parliamentary seats were won in single-member districts, and the rest in a party list vote, since the first parliamentary elections were held in these states after 1991. Azerbaijan equally has had a mixed electoral system until 2002, after which it adopted a purely majoritarian electoral system with SMDs. The main reason why SMDs have a depressing effect on viable party development is straightforward: individuals are elected rather than parties. Especially when parties are unpopular forces candidates in SMD races have weak incentives to join a party, contributing to the limited visibility and significance of parties.

A second reason why SMDs, whether in combination with PR or not, have the ability to stem the development of a pluralist and competitive party landscape lies in its propensity to sustain and strengthen regionalized political bases. In the less-than-democratic conditions of the South Caucasus, however, regimes are reluctant to allow alternative power bases. A more serious threat there is the emergence of one-party dominance.[47] In mixed electoral systems, the party list result for a party of power is often inflated by the outcome of SMD elections. Particularly state-sponsored parties of power, or otherwise parties with larger resources than their competitors, are disproportionately successful in SMD elections.

There are at least two reasons why the mixed electoral system, which 'involves the combination of different electoral formulas (plurality or PR; majority or PR) for an election to a single body'.[48] Massicotte and Blais

(1999) has been detrimental to the development of viable parties in the South Caucasus. The first argument is similar to the one already mentioned in relation to SMD: candidates in the SMD section of the vote often refrain from joining parties. As a result, a large share of MPs is likely to be nonpartisan, a situation which decreases the leverage of parties and can accelerate the creation of unstable factions in parliament, which sometimes draw (former) members from party factions. Second, the SMD section provides an alternative route for parties and individuals into parliament,[49] holding back parties from merging into bigger, more viable forces, and individuals from seeking party affiliation. Individuals with no interest in joining one of the existing parties, as well as parties that see no chance in gaining representation in parliament, independently or for whatever reason, refrain from joining electoral coalition and have the opportunity to try their luck in the SMD section of the ballot.[50] Since small parties – out of strategic calculation – often concentrate much of their effort on winning seats through SMDs, they do not spend as much time and effort on nationwide campaigning, developing a platform and a party organization as they might otherwise.

These arguments make clear that mixed electoral systems in the South Caucasus have not turned out to deliver the 'best of both worlds'[51] of the proportional and majoritarian principles, that has been anticipated by proponents of the mixed system. In the 'best of both worlds' scenario, 'the PR system would channel activity into the parties, and the majoritarian section would create strong incentives to party consolidation'[52]. Instead, the mixed system has in most cases revealed itself to be, in Sartori's (1997) words[53], 'a bastard-producing hybrid that combines their defects'.

Besides SMDs, a second alternative route for small parties and for individuals to gain representation has been provided in the South Caucasus states by the opportunity to form electoral coalitions. The fact that parties often team up with other parties in electoral coalitions has been a major driver of party fragmentation. Parties with no chance of getting into parliament on their own can seize the opportunity to jump on the bandwagon of more prospective parties and by doing so win a small number of seats, despite their lack of an autonomous support base. For these weak parties, winning a few seats is enough of an incentive not to disband their organizations. Furthermore, electoral coalitions work against viable party development by allowing movements (rather than parties) and non-partisan individuals on their lists.

Electoral laws have also had a negative impact on party development when they were frequently amended or replaced. Electoral legislation in the South Caucasus has indeed been subject to several major amendments.[54] Consistent with the hypothesis that electoral laws are typically amended to benefit those who control the legislative process,[55] amendments to electoral legislation in the South Caucasus states have been mostly driven by the intention of regimes to further tilt party competition in their favor. The realization among parties that electoral laws are not fixed and may be subject to amendment in the near future heightens insecurity regarding longer-term prospects, which could induce parties to focus on more immediate goals and put off organizational development. Furthermore, changes in electoral legislation should also be expected to cause shifts in voting behavior, contributing to party system volatility.[56]

The overarching effect of the institutional framework in Armenia, Azerbaijan, and Georgia on party politics has been the diminishing of the 'positions of leverage' of political parties. In brief, parties in the South Caucasus are largely irrelevant, or at best not crucial, in the presidential contest and in government formation; presidentialism and electoral laws encourage a focus on persons rather than on issues in both presidential and parliamentary elections; electoral laws provide alternative routes for non-party actors and weak parties to gain parliamentary representation; and a number of party functions are substituted by electoral coalitions and factions in parliament.

Party building in less-than-democratic settings

The semi-authoritarian and authoritarian regimes that have ruled the South Caucasus states since 1991 have interfered directly in party politics and have themselves become 'entrepreneurs' in political party building. A number of parties, consequently, have been unequivocal products of undemocratic practices. Invariably, these parties have contributed to distort the electoral playing field. The most visible of these parties are the presidential 'parties of power' which dominate party politics in most former Soviet republics.

Parties of power are created at the instigation of the executive branch of government, benefit extensively from state resources, are affiliated with the president – irrespective of whether the president does or does not have a formal role in the party – and, unlike other regime-initiated parties, are created with the purpose of becoming a dominant force in party politics. It is assumed here that the dominant position of a party in the party system is reflected in the control of more than half of the seats in the legislature. Parties of power sometimes fail to get more than half of the vote, such as the Republican Party in Armenia, but still succeed in becoming a dominant force because they attract 'independent' deputies or win most contests in single-member districts.

The key functions that parties of power are designed to fulfill are to amass popular support, primarily in the form of raw votes, and to bind elite actors to the regime. When they are successful in elections, parties of power send a signal of regime strength, which has the dual effect of seemingly conferring legitimacy on the regime and deterring possible contenders from attempting regime change.[57] Binding elite representatives to the regime through a party of power has the effect of curbing the ambitions, which may be against the interests of the regime, of these elites, and of mitigating possible conflict between these elites and the groups that these elites might represent.[58] In order to bind elites to a party of power, the party of power assumes the features of a patronage network; in this patronage network, jobs, economic gains, and other benefits are distributed in return for loyalty to the party and, by extension, the regime.[59] By uniting otherwise disparate elites, deterring potential contenders, and conferring legitimacy, parties of power can make a crucial contribution to regime survival.[60] Because they purposefully benefit from state resources in electoral campaigns, the operation of a party of power is irreconcilable with democracy. State resources, in this context, can range from 'administrative resources' (office, supplies, mobilization of public servants, etc.) to direct monetary transfers from state coffers to the party budget, to the distribution of government jobs and other perks to loyalists.[61] In the rare situation that executive power is split, multiple parties of power may exist simultaneously. During the latter years of the Shevardnadze presidency, for instance, a second party of power, with its base in the region of Adjara, operated throughout Georgia alongside Shevardnadze's central party of power, the Citizens' Union of Georgia.

In addition to a dominant party of power, or instead, more rarely, a dominant party of power, undemocratic regimes may also engage in setting up 'satellite parties'. As parties of power, these are created at the instigation of the executive branch and benefit from state resources. Satellite parties, however, although they do support the government, are less directly associated with the president, and are not supposed to turn into dominant forces. The creation of satellite parties is testimony to the ambition of the regime to keep all or large parts of the party system under control. Regimes that succeed in creating successful satellite parties next to a party of power are among the most effective, but score low on pluralism.

Satellite parties are not always easy to recognize as such because their role in party politics is less obvious than that of parties of power, and because their operation is more similar to that of pluralistic parties. The principal use of satellite parties for the regime is that they appeal to parts of the electorate that, for whatever reason, are not prone to voting for the dominant party of power. If voters are induced to vote for satellite parties, the effect is that a larger part of the electorate ends up giving its vote to parties that are controlled by the authorities. Often, the simultaneous presence of multiple pro-presidential parties, as in Armenia and Azerbaijan, points to the presence of satellite parties. In both Armenia and Azerbaijan, however, the exact relation between the regime and these secondary pro-presidential parties, is unclear.

A subcategory of satellite parties are spoiler parties, which are created with the sole and explicit goal of spoiling the electoral chances of opposition parties. Spoiler parties can fulfill this function, first, by enforcing schisms among the opposition, thereby weakening the genuine opposition, and second, by confusing voters, some of whom as a result may not vote for a genuine opposition party while they normally would have. Often, spoiler parties come in the form of 'clones', copying outward features of existing opposition parties. Such clones have been consciously employed by the regime in Azerbaijan.[62] To spoil the chances of Musavat, for instance, the regime created Modern Musavat, and mimicking the Popular Front, the United Azerbaijan Popular Front was created.[63]

Party building and incentive structures

Parties in the South Caucasus seldom have a societal origin and are typically instigated by elite actors without an immediate constituency. Since these elite actors 'own' their parties entirely, an investigation into the incentive structures of these elite actors should provide insights into the dynamics of party creation and operation in the South Caucasus.

Especially in the initial stage of multiparty politics, party-building in the South Caucasus, as elsewhere in the post-communist world, has involved much 'small-scale political vanity, fanaticism, and whimsy, which have generated a penumbra of tiny "divan" or "taxi" parties'.[64] The persistence of these weak and largely irrelevant parties in some FSU states is not easily explained from an inquiry into the motives of their leaders. It is assumed here, nonetheless, following a key premise in rational choice approaches, that the more relevant political party actors by and large behave purposefully.[65] The principal rationale underlying the activity of these actors boils down to the benefits that they anticipate receiving from electoral success. Borrowing from political economy terminology, they may be thought of as political party 'entrepreneurs'.[66] These entrepreneurs can be divided into those who operate separate from the regime and do not have access to state resources, and those who belong to the inner circle of the regime and therefore do have access to state resources which may be employed in party-building.

Due to the limited leverage, conditioned by elements of institutional design, of political parties in the South Caucasus, non-regime actors have had few compelling incentives to invest in party-building. Incentives to create and sustain viable parties, to the extent that they did exist, moreover, have been offset by a number of other factors that have discouraged political actors to invest in parties. In the South Caucasus states, potential party entrepreneurs may anticipate repression from the authorities when they engage in opposition activity. In effective authoritarian systems, party entrepreneurs may furthermore refrain from party-building because they do not expect to gain electoral success in an uneven playing field. Also, alternative types of organization, such as financial-industrial groups or clan structures based on kinship, may substitute parties with respect to aggregating and defending the interests of elites.[67]

Taken together, a wide range of factors hold back individual actors – likely party entrepreneurs under different conditions – from joining parties or from engaging in party-building: the limited leverage of parties in the overall political process; the poor career prospects in political systems in which executive posts flow to non-partisan actors only; the poor electoral prospects for partisan candidates in single-member constituencies where parties are unpopular; the availability of 'substitute' organizations with more effective mechanisms of interest aggregation; the likelihood of repression; and the limited chance of electoral success in an uneven playing field.

Despite the generally weak incentives to invest in parties for actors not intimately connected to the regime, parties have fulfilled if not the representative, then at least the procedural functions which make parties indispensable in elections with more than one party.[68] A way to picture the incentives that drive party creation and operation in the South Caucasus states is by extending Strøm's 'three models of party behavior'[69] – policy-seeking, vote-seeking, and office-seeking – to the less-than-democratic context of the South Caucasus. According to Wolinetz (2002),[70] 'a policy-seeking party is one which gives primary emphasis to pursuit of policy goals, a vote-seeking party is one whose principal aim is to maximize votes and win elections, while an office-seeking party is primarily interested in securing the benefits of office – getting its leaders into government, enjoying access to patronage, etc.'

Many actual existing parties in the South Caucasus, of course, are 'functional hybrids' which are driven by intricate combinations of different incentives. From the above discussion it should be evident that the regime-initiated parties of power and satellite parties are overwhelmingly vote-seeking. Winning votes both has a direct use (ensuring dominance in the legislature while marginalizing the opposition) and a more indirect use (signaling regime strength, binding elites) for the regime. The regime-initiated parties are by far the most relevant political parties in the three South Caucasus republics. Of the parties that have been created by actors without a direct connection to the regime, many have been primarily interested in winning office, as in Georgia, where [t]he inner logic of most [parties] was not to implement a set of policies for the good of the Georgian people. The main rationale, or 'hidden agenda', for entering Parliament was access to the lucrative resources that could be gained by protecting or lobbying certain business and sectoral interests from within the legislature'.[71]

The office-seeking motives of some parties explain why they are not in direct opposition to the regime, even when they are created by non-regime actors. Parties that are more policy-seeking than either vote-seeking or office-seeking are active in the South Caucasus, but few of them have gained a serious degree of relevance.

The vote-seeking and office-seeking behavior of parties does not per se militate against democracy, as the presence of vote-seeking and office-seeking parties in many western democracies demonstrates. The incentives underlying the office-seeking and vote-seeking behavior of parties in the South Caucasus, however, are indicative of the impact of authoritarian practices in party politics in the region. Given the indirect but positive relation between democratization and the weight that parties give to issue-based programs,[72] the absence of relevant policy-seeking parties in the South Caucasus would be problematic if competition between parties would not be ex ante skewed to the detriment of democratic and programmatic parties. Kitschelt et al. (1999)[73] anticipated that the political legacy from the type of communist rule that was prevalent in the Soviet Union – patrimonial communism – would be more adverse to the emergence of programmatic parties than the types of communist rule in most of Central and Eastern Europe. The reappearance, or continuation, of semi-authoritarian or authoritarian regimes in the region have further constrained the prospects of programmatic parties with roots in society, because the authoritarian regimes had an explicit interest in checking these parties. The impact of the legacy of patrimonial communism on party development in the South Caucasus therefore should be seen in connection with the political trajectory that these states went through after 1991.

Conclusion

Leaving aside more particular outcomes, party politics in the South Caucasus has been characterized by a great degree of contingency and volatility, reflected foremost in party replacement, and by the impact of authoritarian practices. This chapter, starting from the observation that parties in the South Caucasus lack roots in society and are almost entirely elite-driven, has sought to understand these outcomes by analyzing the incentive structures of political party actors. Different types of party actors, divided primarily by their position vis-à-vis ruling forces, are led by different incentives. Actors who do not belong to the inner circle of the regime have insufficient incentives to invest considerably in party-building because the specific design of institutional arrangements, such as executive-legislative relations and electoral legislation, have limited the leverage of parties. The cost of party-building furthermore is elevated by the circumstance that independent party entrepreneurs in an uneven electoral playing field face high hurdles to becoming successful electorally.

Actors from within the regime, or otherwise with powerful connections, on the other hand, create parties which serve either explicitly undemocratic or strictly self-interested purposes. These parties contribute to a distortion of the playing field because they benefit from resources – either state resources or quasi-unlimited private resources – from which many other actors cannot benefit. Often, it is only these parties that are truly relevant in the political life of the South Caucasus states. Regime-initiated parties are primarily interested in maximizing their vote share, while many other parties are interested in assuming office or getting close to office. The dominant models of party behavior in the South Caucasus, then, are vote-seeking and office-seeking; the third model of party behavior – policy-seeking – which is believed to be the most conducive to democratization, is virtually absent among relevant political parties.

Almost no serious scholarly research has been conducted on party politics in the South Caucasus republics. At least three factors help explain this paucity of research. First, parties in the South Caucasus are simply inconsequential relative to a host of other institutions, including, notably, informal ones. Parties are indispensable for fulfilling a number of procedural functions in multiparty elections, but besides this, their leverage in political life, as has been argued above, is highly constrained. Parties are of course not wholly unimportant, especially in cases where a party of power helps prop up a regime, but the key to how these regimes thrive lies elsewhere. Second, the study of party politics in the South Caucasus is complicated by the large extent of volatility: the composition of the party system and the dynamic of electoral competition have often shifted from one election to the next. Finally, concepts developed for the study of party politics in western democracies in general do not travel readily to non-western and especially undemocratic settings. Attempts to measure the performance of party systems in the South Caucasus on common characteristics of party systems, such as their degree of fractionalization and polarization, either fall through or yield contradictory results. Researchers, consequently, have few tools at hand when they study parties and party systems that are starkly different from the familiar image of parties in western democracies. A response to the 'western bias'[74] in political party research should be to study phenomena that are more pertinent to non-western settings and to take cues from other studies of party politics in non-western settings. Considering the elite-driven nature of party politics in the South Caucasus, investigating the incentives of those who are behind the creation and operation of parties is one approach that produces greater insight into the dynamic of party politics in these settings.

Notes

1   Nelson, S. and B. Katulis (2005: vi). *Armenia Political Party Assessment*. Washington, D.C: United States Agency for International Development.
2   Quirk, C. (2007). *Five Myths about the 2008 Presidential Election in Azerbaijan*. http://quirkglobalstrategies.com/blog/?p=60 (accessed December 17, 2008)
3   Wheatley, J. (2005: 158). *Georgia from National Awakening to Rose Revolution*: Delayed Transition in the Former Soviet Union. Aldershot: Ashgate Publishing, Ltd.
4   Tavits, M. (2008: 549). On the Linkage between Electoral Volatility and Party System Instability in Central and Eastern Europe, *European Journal of Political Research* 47 (5).

5   A notable exception is Van de Walle, N. (2003: 297-321). Presidentialism and clientelism in Africa's emerging party systems. *The Journal of Modern African Studies* 41, no. 2.

6   Schedler, A. (2002: 110). 'The Nested Game of Democratization by Elections.' *International Political Science Review/ Revue internationale de science politique* 23, no. 1.

7   Croissant, A. (2002: 346). Electoral Politics in Southeast and East Asia: A Comparative Perspective. Singapore: Friedrich Ebert Stiftung.

8   Strom, K. (1990: 565-598). A Behavioral Theory of Competitive Political Parties. *American Journal of Political Science* 34, no. 2.

9   Carothers, T. (2006: 3-21). *Confronting the Weakest Link: Aiding Political Parties in New Democracies*. Washington, D.C.: Carnegie Endowment for International Peace.

10 Cornell, S. E. (2001: 118-131). Democratization Falters in Azerbaijan. *Journal of Democracy* 12, no. 1.

11 Nelson and Katulis, op cit.

12 Tarkhan-Mouravi, G. (2006: 43). Polticheskie Partii v Gruzii. Zatiunuavsheesia Stanovlenie. *Political Science Quarterly* 1.

13 Lipset, S. M. and S. Rokkan (1967). Cleavage Structures, Party Systems, and Voter Alignments: An Introduction. In *Party Systems and Voter Alignments: Cross-National Perspectives*, Lipset, S. M. and S. Rokkan (eds.). New York: Free Press.

14 Mair, P. (2006). 'Cleavages.' In *Handbook of Party Politics*, Katz, R.S. and W. Crotty (eds.). London: Sage Publications.

15 Mainwaring, S. (1998: 67-81). Party Systems in the Third Wave. *Journal of Democracy* 9, no.3; Ware, A. (1996). *Political Parties and Party Systems*. New York: Oxford University Press.

16 Geddes, B. (1995: 239-274). A Comparative Perspective on the Leninist Legacy in Eastern Europe. *Comparative Political Studies* 28, no. 2.

17 Howard, M. (2003). *The Weakness of Civil Society in Post-Communist Europe*. Cambridge, MA: Cambridge University Press.

18 Kitschelt, H. (2001). Divergent Paths of Postcommunist Democracies. In *Political Parties and Democracy*, L. Diamond and R. Gunther (eds.). Baltimore: The Johns Hopkins University Press.

19 Guliyev, F. (2005: 393-435). Post-Soviet Azerbaijan: Transition to Sultanistic Semiauthoritarianism? An Attempt at Conceptualization. *Demokratizatsiya* 13, no. 3.

20 On different types of linkage between voters and politicians, see Kitschelt, H. (2000: 845-879). Linkages between Citizens and Politicians In Democratic Polities. *Comparative Political Studies* 33, no. 6-7.

21 Ottaway, M. (2003). *Democracy Challenged: The Rise of Semi-Authoritarianism*. Washington, D.C.: Carnegie Endowment for International Peace.

22 Nelson and Katsulis, op. cit., p. v.

23 Astourian, S.H. (2000-2001: 5). *From Ter-Petrosian to Kocharian: Leadership Change in Armenia*. Berkeley Program in Soviet and Post-Soviet Studies Working Paper Series.

24 Dolidze, V. (2005: 49-60). Political Parties and Party Development in Georgia. *Central Asia and the South Caucasus* 6, no. 2.

25 IRI, USAID, Baltic Surveys / The Gallup Organization, IPM. (2007). *Georgian National Voter Study* (February 2007). http://www.iri.org/eurasia/georgia/pdfs/2007-05-09-Georgia-Poll3.pdf (accessed December 15, 2008).

26 Sahakyan, V. and Atanesyan, A. (2006: 347-354). Democratization in Armenia: Some Trends of Political Culture and Behavior. *Demokratizatsiya* 14, no. 3.

27 Huseyinov, T. (2003). Towards Crafting a National Security Doctrine in Azerbaijan. *CACI Analyst* March 26 http://www.cacianalyst.org/?q=node/1008 (accessed December 19, 2008).

28 Nelson and Katsulis, op. cit., p. 18.

29 Ibid., p.15.

30 Dolidze, op. cit., p. 50.

31 Boonstra, J. (2008: 3). *How serious is the EU about supporting democracy and human rights in Azerbaijan?* European Council on Foreign Relations and FRIDE Working Paper.

32 Bunce. V. and S. Wolchik (2007, October 25-26: 37). *Azerbaijan's 2005 Parliamentary Elections: A Failed Attempt at Transition*. Paper prepared for CD-DRL Workshop on External Influences on Democratic Transitions. Stanford University.

33 Elgie, R. (2005: 102). Variations on a Theme. *Journal of Democracy* 16, no.3.

34 Bunce, V. (2000: 703-734). Comparative Democratization: Big and Bounded Generalizations. *Comparative Political Studies* 33, no. 6-7; Frye, T. (1997: 532-552). A Politics of Institutional Choice: Post-Communist Presidencies. *Comparative Political Studies* 30, no. 5.

35 Fish, M. S. (2006: 15-20). Stronger Legislatures, Stronger Democracies. *Journal of Democracy* 17, no. 1; Linz, J. (1990: 51-69). The Perils of Presidentialism. *Journal of Democracy* 1, no. 1.

36 Shugart, M. S. (1998: 1-29). The Inverse Relationship Between Party Strength and Executive Strength: A Theory of Politicians' Constitutional Choices. *British Journal of Political Science* 28, no.1; Shugart, M. S. and Carey, J.M. (1992). *Presidents and Assemblies: Constitutional Design and Electoral Dynamics*. Cambridge, MA: Cambridge University Press.

37 Croissant, A. and Merkel, W. (2001). *Political Party Formation In Presidential and Parliamentary Systems*. University of Heidelberg, Institute for Political Science (mimeo); Van de Walle, op. cit., p. 297-321.

38 Ishiyama, J. T., and R. Kennedy (2001: 1177-1191). Superpresidentialism and Political Party Development in Russia, Ukraine, Armenia and Kyrgyzstan. *Europe-Asia Studies* 53, no. 8; Samuels, D. J. (2002: 461-483). Presidentialized Parties: The Separation of Powers and Party Organization and Behavior. *Comparative Political Studies* 35, no. 4.

39 The term 'big men' is frequently applied in relation to party politics in Africa. Compare Van Cranenburgh, O. (2008: 952-973). 'Big Men' Rule: Presidential Power, Regime Type, and Democracy in 30 African Countries. *Democratization* 15, no. 5 and Van de Walle, op. cit., p. 297-321.

40 Kitschelt, H. (1995). *Party Systems In East Central Europe: Consolidation Or Fluidity?* Centre for the Study of Public Policy, University of Strathclyde.

41 Croissant, A. (2002). Electoral Politics in Southeast and East Asia: A Comparative Perspective. Singapore: Friedrich Ebert Stiftung.

42 Kitschelt observes that 'clientelist democracy has proved durable and has commanded sufficient support to institutionalize and entrench itself for long periods in a variety of polities'. (see, Kitschelt, H. (2000, 872). Linkages between Citizens and Politicians In Democratic Polities. *Comparative Political Studies* 33, no. 6-7); Enyedi suggests that charismatic leadership in parties (at the expense of the visibility of a party program), common to party politics in Central and Eastern Europe, can strengthen party systems (cf. Enyedi, Z. (2006: 230). Party Politics in Post-Communist Transition. In *Handbook of Party Politics*, Katz, R.S. and W. Crotty (eds.). London: Sage Publications).

43 Carey, J. M. (2002, August). *Getting Their Way, or Getting in the Way? Presidents and Party Unity in Legislative Voting*. Paper presented at the annual meeting of the American Political Science Association, Boston; Croissant, op. cit., p. 354; Kitschelt, H. and R. Smyth (2002: 1228-1256). Programmatic Party Cohesion in Emerging Postcommunist Democracies: Russia In Comparative Context. *Comparative Political Studies* 35, no. 10.

44 Samuels, D. J. (2002: 461-483). Presidentialized Parties: The Separation of Powers and Party Organization and Behavior. *Comparative Political Studies* 35, no. 4.

45 Duverger, M. (1959). Political Parties: Their Organisation and Activity In the Modern State, second edition. London: John Wiley.

46 Hoffman, A. L. (2005: 231-242). Political Parties, Electoral Systems and Democracy: A Cross-National Analysis. *European Journal of Political Research* 44, no. 2.; Moser, R.G. (1999: 359-384). Electoral Systems and the Number of Parties in Postcommunist States. *World Politics* 51, no. 3.; Norris, P. (2008).

Driving Democracy: Do Power-Sharing Regimes Work? Cambridge, MA: Cambridge University Press.

47 Birch, S. (2005: 281-301). Single-member district electoral systems and democratic transition. *Electoral Studies* 24, no. 2.

48 Massicotte, L. and Blais, A. (1999: 345). Mixed electoral systems: a conceptual and empirical survey. *Electoral Studies* 18, no. 3.

49 D'Anieri, P. (2007). *Understanding Ukrainian Politics*. Power, Politics, and Institutional Design. Armonk, New York: M.E. Sharpe.

50 Ferrara, F. and Herron, E.S. (2005: 16-31). Going it Alone? Strategic Entry under Mixed Electoral Rules. *American Journal of Political Science* 49, no. 1.

51 Shugart, M. S. and Wattenberg, M.P. (2001). *Mixed-Member Electoral Systems: The Best of Both Worlds?* Oxford: Oxford University Press.

52 D'Anieri, op. cit., p. 159.

53 Sartori, G. (1997: 74-75). Comparative Constitutional Engineering: An Inquiry Into Structures, Incentives, and Outcomes. New York: NYU Press.

54 For a detailed account of changes to electoral legislation in Georgia, see Herron, E.S. and Mirzashvili, I. (2005). 'Georgians Cannot Help Being Original: the Evolution of Election Rules in the Republic of Georgia.' In *The State of Law in the South Caucasus.*, Waters, C. P. M. (ed.). New York: Palgrave Macmillan.

55 Andrews, J. T. and R. W. Jackman (2005: 65-84). Strategic fools: electoral rule choice under extreme uncertainty. *Electoral Studies* 24, no. 1; Colomer, J. M. (2005: 1-21). It's Parties That Choose Electoral Systems (or, Duverger's Laws Upside Down). *Political Studies* 53, no. 1; Ishiyama, J. T. (1997: 95-115). Transitional Electoral Systems in Post-Communist Eastern Europe. *Political Science Quarterly* 112, no. 1.

56 Remmer, K. L. (2008: 5-30). The Politics of Institutional Change. Electoral Reform In Latin America 1978-2002. *Party Politics* 14, no. 1.

57 Geddes, B. (2005). *Why Parties and Elections in Authoritarian Regimes?* Paper prepared for presentation at the annual meeting of the American Political Science Association, Washington DC.

58 Geddes, op. cit.; Gel'man, V. (2008: 913-930). Party Politics In Russia: From Competition to Hierarchy. *Europe-Asia Studies* 60, no. 6.

59 Greene, K. F. (2007). *Creating Competition: Patronage Politics and the PRI's Demise.* The Kellogg Institute WorkIng Papers #345.; Resende, M. and Kraetzschmar, H. (2005). Parties of Power as Roadblocks to Democracy: The Cases of Ukraine and Egypt. In *Democratisation In the European Neighbourhood*, Emerson, M. (ed.). Brussels: Centre for European Policy Studies.

60 Brownlee, J. (2007). *Authoritarianism in an Age of Democratization*: Cambridge, MA: Cambridge University Press; Gandhi, J. and Przeworski, A.

(2007: 1279-1301). Authoritarian Institutions and the Survival of Autocrats. *Comparative Political Studies* 40, no. 11.

61 Greene, op. cit., p. 7-8.

62 Rasizade, A. (2003: 353). Azerbaijan in Transition to the "New Age of Democracy". *Communist and Post-Communist Studies* 36.

63 Bunce and Wolchik, op. cit., p.15.

64 Wilson, A. and S. Birch (2007: 54). Political Parties In Ukraine. Virtual and Representational. In *Political Parties In New Democracies. Trajectories of Development and Implications for Democracy*, Webb, P. and S. White (eds.). Oxford: Oxford University Press.

65 Hershey, M.R. (2006: 75). Political Parties as Mechanisms of Social Choice. In *Handbook of Party Politics*, Katz, R.W.S. and W. Crotty (eds.). London: Sage Publications.

66 Storm, op cit.

67 Hale (2006) provides a comprehensive account of how the existence of substitute organizations to political parties has contributed to the weakness of political parties in Russia. Compare Hale, H. (2006). *Why Not Parties in Russia?: Democracy, Federalism, and the State*. Cambridge, MA: Cambridge University Press.

68 Bartolini and Mair distinguish between representative functions and procedural functions of parties. (Cf. Bartolini, S. and P. Mair. (2001: 332). Challenges to Contemporary Political Parties. In *Political Parties and Democracy. Baltimore: The Johns Hopkins University Press*, Diamond, L. and R. Gunther (eds.). Baltimore: The Johns Hopkins University Press.

69 Storm, op. cit.

70 Wolinetz, S. B. (2002: 149-150). Beyond the Catch-All Party: Approaches to the Study of Parties and Party Organization In Contemporary Democracies. In *Political Parties. Old Concepts and New Challenges*, Gunther, R., J.R. Montero, and J. Linz (eds.). New York.

71 Wheatley, J. (2005: 158). Georgia from National Awakening to Rose Revolution: Delayed Transition in the Former Soviet Union. Aldershot: Ashgate Publishing, Ltd.

72 Croissant, op. cit., 346.

73 Kitschelt, H., Mansfeldova, Z., Markowski, R. and Toka, G.. (1999). *Post-Communist Party Systems: Competition, Representation, and Inter-Party Cooperation*. Cambridge, MA: Cambridge University Press.

74 Erdmann, G. (2004: 63-87). Party research: Western European bias and the 'African labyrinth'. *Democratization* 11, no. 3.

7   Between State and Nation Building:
The Debate about 'Ethnicity' in Georgian Citizens' ID Cards[1]

Oliver Reisner

At any time when you want to start thinking, your thought [...]
already exists as a likeness of thought [...].
There is always a verbal world which generates
Pseudo-questions, pseudo-problems and pseudo-thoughts on its own,
    and it is
practically impossible to distinguish them from true thought.

Merab Mamardashvili[2]

After the war in August 2008 Russia unilaterally recognized the independence of Georgia's separatist regions Abkhazia and South Ossetia. The country is confronted with the specific institutional legacy of Soviet ethno-federalism predetermining ethnic cleavages on the one hand. In parallel the same Soviet system unintentionally created an incentive system for nationalist elites that in 1991, together with national independence, led to nationalist secession of their regional administrative units. In that way it shaped a unique confluence of grievances, perceptions, and opportunities inscribed to a certain historical narrative that developed over the twentieth century.[3]

This chapter deals with one such debate in the Georgian public as a case study for reality perception and value orientation among the people of a transitional society. Based on a close reading of more than one hundred articles and interviews from various print media sources, it inquires about the place of public debates in Georgian society. Is this kind of discourse more public or elite? Is its style imbued with the Soviet heritage or filled with anti-ideological, changing paradigms? Taking the short-term results of this debate into consideration, one may ask, where does the debate lead?

Also different forms of discourse and arguing relate to generational changes: young 'reformers', that came to power after the 'Rose Revolution' as newly appointed ministers, prefer a Western style discourse of democracy, human rights and market economy; by contrast, representatives of the old state elite, the *nomenklatura*, rely on the national discourse which has developed over several decades and became politicized since the late 1980s and after the break-up of the Soviet Union represented the sole source of ideological underpinning for Georgia's independence.[4]

The Debate – a reconstruction

After amendments to the current legislation came into force on 14 January 1999, a heated debate developed in the Georgian media because 'ethnicity' would no longer be indicated on Georgian identity cards and birth certificates. For Guram Sharadze,[5] former Chairman of the Parliamentary Migration Committee, the new law deprived Georgians of the possibility of regulating the country's demographic situation and violated their rights. Georgia, in his words, became a 'test-ground for cosmopolitanism'. Sharadze demanded the suspension of the amendments until the spring parliamentary session and the impeachment of then Minister of Justice Lado Tchanturia as their author, although they had been introduced by former President Shevardnadze himself.[6] Zaza Davitaia, activist of the pro-Zviadist[7] Ilia the Righteous Society and Vice President of the All-Georgian Human Rights Association took it as another anti-Georgian step by the 'factual government of Georgia' aimed at making the Georgians 'tenants' in their own country. The first step, in his opinion, was the law on the unrestricted sale of non-agricultural lands.[8] Shalva Natelashvili, the leader of the Labour Party, also censured the law which removed information on ethnicity from identity cards and birth certificates, and said his party would propose a revision of the law in the spring parliamentary session. In his words, when the Labour Party becomes the parliamentary majority in the next elections in October 1999, they would change the law.[9]

President Shevardnadze called for a reasoned debate on the ethnicity issue in his regular radio interview on 18 January 1999, but he also indicated that he was leaning towards those who favored re-introducing the category. Georgia had its own traditions and it was, in his words, 'not right to follow the West blindly in the matter'.[10] Among them, the World Congress of Georgians declared that, in their opinion, its restoration would help Georgians to 'preserve the function of the historically indigenous nation in Georgia' and 'keep the dominant idea of the Georgian culture' as well as preventing a possible change of the country's name. Seventeen renowned Georgian writers and poets appealed to the President for its restoration, maintaining that otherwise Georgia may lose its name and the country could be overwhelmed by chaos; the Georgian language might no longer be the state language and future generations would be in 'a weaker position when fighting for the existence of Georgia'.[11]

On the other hand, Guram Mamulia, Chairperson of the Repatriation Service and the Parliamentary Migration Committee, argued that Sharadze's campaign against the abolishing of the ethnicity category on Georgian identity cards may impede Georgia's development into a coherent state. He continued by saying that, should the President give way to Sharadze's demands and agree to respective amendments to the law, separatism might increase in the ethnic enclaves of Georgia.[12] In one newspaper's comment, emphasizing Georgian ethnicity as a privileged one, the opposing politicians and public figures were seen to play on 'vile nationalistic instincts' in order to secure their 'cheap popularity' and 'suspicious political careers'. The newspaper also criticized the President for favoring those who wanted to re-introduce the ethnicity category on citizen's identity cards.[13]

The conflict escalated when Guram Sharadze, the initiator of the campaign against the amendments, organized a protest action on 21 January 1999, demanding a ban on the broadcasts of the Georgian branch of Radio Liberty. His anger was caused by a radio review of David Paitchadze, who did not support Sharadze's stand and called it nationalistic. Sharadze even wanted to hit the reporter but missed and hit Paitchadze's colleague, Tamar Chikovani instead.[14]

In his weekly radio interview, President Shevardnadze first expressed his understanding for those who take the nation as the entity of a democratic state. But then he remarked that the ethnic minorities would hardly leave their ethnicity aside, especially those who do not have a state of their own like the Abkhazians.' Once again he sided with 'our writers' and thanked them by saying: 'if a literature does not guard its people, its nation and language, it is not a literature'.[15]

Then Justice Minister Lado Tchanturia defended himself in an interview by asserting that the bulk of Georgian society which protested against the recently adopted law removing the ethnicity category from Georgian citizens' identity cards still lacked skill and vision in managing public affairs. Given the negative public opinion, the law would, in his words, be revised, but this he could only regret. By indicating our ethnicity we turn Georgia into an ethnic zoo, he warned.[16] The NGO 'Liberty Institute' censured Sharadze's campaign at a press conference on 25 January 1999. Its director, Levan Ramishvili, said Sharadze must be charged with the 'persecution of criticism' and be sued for it as he had attempted to hit a reporter from the Tbilisi branch of Radio Liberty and demanded the banning of its broadcasts after the station criticized his position in one of its programs. He remarked that 'pro-Western' Shevardnadze supported Georgian nationalists.[17]

Guram Sharadze's campaign was directed against the Law on the Ownership of Land, some people being absolutely against selling land to non-ethnic Georgians. Koba Davitashvili, a lawyer and a member of the Tbilisi Sakrebulo (city council), argued that in his opinion, a strong anti-reformist movement may emerge soon.[18]

In their appeal to Georgian citizens, the Parliament and the President, as well as the nineteen most active NGOs in Georgia claimed that the ethnicity category on Georgian citizens' identity cards or other papers violated the constitutional principle of equality and may give rise to privileged groups within the population. If the President or the Parliament revised the new law currently in force and restored this category in official papers, the NGOs would appeal to the Constitutional Court.[19] This heated debate continued throughout February, but then ended as abruptly as it began at the beginning of March 1999.

The essential arguments in this polemic debate were already expressed on 9 January by a member of the Georgian bar association, Tsitsino Tskhvediani. She asserted that from a juridical point of view, nothing would be lost by not stating ethnicity on identity cards and nothing would be won by stating it, because Georgia's constitution defends all citizens equally. The constitution twice underlines (in articles 14 and 38) the equality of all citizens in social, economic, cultural and political life regardless of national, ethnic, religious or language affiliation. But Tskhvediani also noted that as Georgians have never been privileged in their country, maybe representatives of other nationalities were *de facto* more privileged than Georgians. The psychologist Mzia Gomelauri showed in her research that the Georgian public understood the homeland as being a territory and a nation inhabiting it.[20]

The demographer Anzor Totadze replied to Sharadze that his main intention was right, but on television he made false claims, because the main intention of his projected bill 'On the registration of civil acts' had been changed. Already at a meeting in 1998, Sharadze demanded the postponement of the next census until citizens' ethnicity was registered in Georgian passports and identity cards. But Totadze insisted on the principle of ethnic identity being included in the census questionnaire instead of the state ascription of ethnicity in personal documents. This would represent an internationally recognized standard in demography, and only in this way could a real picture of Georgia's ethnic diversity be drawn. A census would aim to record the actual situation and not the juridical one as reflected in passports. He confirmed Sharadze's opinion, that for a small nation like the Georgian people in a difficult demographic situation, knowledge about ethnic processes was very important. The state has to know what the ethnic relations within the country are in order to undertake appropriate measures, but the ascription of ethnicity in personal documents is merely a symbolic act. 'It is well known, that insider and foreign malevolent people [avismsurveleebi] are trying to falsify our history, to destroy our united Georgian organism and the country's territorial integrity as well as leading Georgians into confrontation with each other (for example in the Russian census of 1897, the Mingrelians, Svans, Lazes were listed as independent ethnic groups and not as belonging to the Kartvelians).' Totadze asked Sharadze why he had not expressed his criticism in 1998 in parliament while the legislation process was ongoing. According to Totadze, this can only be understood as 'pseudo-patriotism' resulting from personal ambitions and not from the 'national matter' [erovnuli sakme]. Totadze went on to say that nowadays plenty of parties, politicians and opposition forces were only looking out for their personal interests, and instead of doing something, they only move their tongues. If the Georgians proceeded this way, they would lose their independence again.[21] But the new law was unclear regarding the requirements for the registration.[22]

In a populist manner, Sharadze presented the 'Georgians' spiritual and national genocide' as being caused by parliamentarians, plotting against the President and Georgia. He said that this degeneration [gadagvareba] was just the beginning of 'the nations' self-liquidation' as masterminded by 'our enemies'. Denouncing the reformers' act as 'anti-national' he excluded them from the national community. '[T]he loss of ethnicity is the biggest attribute of democracy'[23] he said, linking Western values with anti-national politics. In an authoritarian attitude he underlined his closeness to Shevardnadze and maintained that 'when the President knows about this, he will correct it'. Because of the publicity, Sharadze took the chance to mobilize for his movement 'Georgia First'. Revaz Mishveladze, a well-known writer, was the second most important personality demanding the reintroduction of the ethnicity category. In several articles he rejected the politics of the Georgian government as cosmopolitan and non-national, so that, in his opinion there would be fewer Georgians every day. But 'we need our ethnicity now, facing the twenty-first century with its mixing of cultures and nations'.[24] Sharadze and Mishveladze were supported by Georgia's Writers Union and other cultural institutions and newspapers. It was maintained that after the loss of Abkhazia and the Tskhinvali region,[25] the economy had declined and there was a general wish to see only the Georgian nationality remaining, and this should be defended now. With almost 30 per cent of Georgia's population being ethnically non-Georgian, the proponents of the ethnicity category felt themselves and their co-nationals to be in a state of emergency and they questioned the loyalty of non-Georgians. Some proponents of the ethnicity category impute secessionism to non-Georgians.[26]

In the opinion of their opponents, who were labeled 'reformers', the way to trigger off the secessionist danger is precisely by demanding the state determination of somebody's ethnicity, thus contradicting the constitutional principle of equality for all citizens of Georgia. Young members of the Georgian parliament, the newly appointed Minister of Justice, some critical newspapers and the Prague-based radio station 'Liberty' (run by the US) and many NGOs (with the 'Liberty Institute' in the forefront) were counted as belonging to this group. Lacking broader support among the general public, most of them referred to international standards. Some of them replied in the same crude way by calling proponents of the ethnicity category 'nationalists' or 'fascists'. Other opponents employed irony or cynicism regarding the fruitlessness of their arguments.

This public debate started like an old-fashioned Soviet style campaign with collective letters to newspaper editors and attempts to refute the claims of representatives' with the opposite opinion. While the followers of Guram Sharadze's argument were afraid that the Georgian nation would disintegrate due to the lack of the ethnicity category in official personal documents, the others feared the disintegration of the Georgian state because of its re-introduction. Both sides appealed to President Shevardnadze's ultimate authority. There were lengthy statements of individual opinion, but no real exchange of arguments. Some of the more argumentative contributions from liberal-minded scholars were obscured by the clashes of the main opponents.[27] In the more liberal newspapers there were articles attempting to analyze the debate.[28] However, it is unsurprising that it turned into a personalized debate. It was also hard to find any statements from representatives of Georgia's minority ethnic groups in that debate.

In sum, the striking demand for the ethnicity category to be kept in personal documents and opposition to the adoption of international standards may be interpreted as a call for the continuation of the Soviet practice of positive discrimination or 'affirmative action' to keep the boundaries between different ethnic groups alive. This point might also find adherents among the minority ethnic groups, as President Shevardnadze indicated.[29] There seemed to be no differentiation between ethnic-cultural identity and the citizenship of a state, which is held to be a Soviet legacy by a Georgian scholar of jurisprudence.[30] An essentialist ethnic-cultural definition of the Georgian nation was put above the state, but the state is obliged to maintain this identity by means of passports and other official personal documents.

National identity and citizenship – the Soviet legacy

In international and state law, citizenship describes a juridical relationship between citizens and state polity (community) based on reciprocal rights and obligations. In the age of globalization, former distinctive functions of citizenship are increasingly replaced by a designative function of membership to a political community. This allows for a more differentiated approach to questions of loyalty and national identification.[31] But what connects the status of active citizenship with national affiliation? The reliance on the principle of *ius sanguinis* expresses the historical experience of those people, whose survival in history is not indebted to its organized power, but to its cultural existence and the continuity of ethnic tradition.[32]

While the citizenship regulations in the 'Democratic Republic of Georgia' (1918-1921) were quite liberal,[33] their development in the former Soviet republics followed a special path. Instead of reiterating the common assumption that the Soviet state acted as a nation destroyer, contemporary Western historical and social research has revealed the opposite. In the 1920s, Soviet nationality policy had already established a pyramid of national territorial units, which should have allowed the maximum number of individuals to preserve their nationality without feeling themselves a minority. Collective ethnicity was connected with special territorial-administrative units, whose different status (republics, provinces, and districts) led to a formal ethnic hierarchy. But the ideal Bolshevik concept of national soviets conflicted with the popular notion of national sovereignty. By linking national soviets with the possession of land (then a very scarce resource), it drew national borders so that every village, indeed every individual, had to declare an ethnic allegiance and fight to remain the national majority within its unit. Instead of reconciliation this led to ethnic conflict. The legitimization of an ethnic community depended on the government granting it territory. Nationality, possession of land, and the political control of a territory thus became intertwined.[34]

Apart from putting up borders between communities on ethno-territorial grounds, Soviet nationality policy repeated the same for individuals. In 1932, all Soviet citizens received internal passports that formally defined them in terms of name, time and place of birth, authorized place of residence [*propiska*] and nationality. One's name and *propiska* could be changed, but nationality could not. Individual ethnicity had evolved into a biological category impervious to cultural, linguistic or geographical change. Ascribed by state authorities it seemed to be inherited at birth.[35] By the end of the 1930s Soviet nationality policy abandoned the pursuit of countless nationalities in order to concentrate on a few fully-fledged, fully equipped 'nations'. The compulsory ethnic identification became a tool to favor members of titular nationalities and for the repression of ethnic groups during the Second World War (the deportation of Chechens, Ingush and Germans, discrimination against Jews), effectively determining an individual's fate. All these processes may be summarized as the institutionalization of ethnicity. Opposition to the policy of the central authorities was castigated as 'bourgeois nationalist deviation' or damned as 'rootless cosmopolitanism'.[36] Subordination and compliance was enforced by the threat of installing a new leadership.[37]

After the dissolution of the Transcaucasian Soviet Federal Socialist Republic in 1936 the formation of ethnic identity was structured by the establishing of national republics and a process of cultural construction that favored a national consciousness based on the identification of the nation with a specific territory and state administration in their home republic. The consolidation of the titular national community's hegemony resulted in the historiographic and contemporary 'compartmentalization' of other ethnic groups living within that national republic in the Stalin period, 'one republic – one culture'.[38]

In the post-Stalinist period this principle has been 'de-compartmentalized' into 'one nation – one culture', irrespective of political-administrative and geographic considerations. Dependent on Moscow for funds, the political and cultural entrepreneurs owed their allegiance to 'their own people' and their own national symbols. However, whereas the politicians were structurally constrained within the apparatus, intellectuals were specifically trained and employed to produce national cultures. '[I]n other words, they acted like good patriots – when they were not acting like bad nationalists.'[39] When the Soviet welfare state could no longer afford to fund the production of national cultures and attempted to increase Russian language tuition after the disastrous results of the 1970 census, it became increasingly difficult to distinguish between the two because the national form seemed to have become the content and because nationalism did not seem to have any content other than the cult of form. Therefore many Georgian intellectuals have reduced world perception to the national in Georgian society since the late 1960s, which correlated with a huge expansion of the scientific and cultural staff in their own Republic.[40]

Not only did *glasnost* have an impact on cultural practices under Gorbachev, but also the politics of culture have decisively influenced the culture of politics. By providing a novel framework for the conceptualization of ethnic identity, cultural practices have contributed to the legitimization of an agenda of ethnic rights which include problems of national existence both beyond and within the borders of the republics. The de-compartmentalization of ethnic identity which developed in the realm of culture throughout the post-Stalin period emerged full-blown in social and political activism under Gorbachev. Ethnic politics in the national republics has increasingly revolved around claims for sovereignty and the rights to citizenship in an effort to substantiate demands for more control over local affairs, but also included demands for ethnic rights across republican borders or towards ethnic minorities within them. Moreover, competition over the allocation of scarce resources in the Caucasus has repeatedly led to conflicts between the region's dominant and non-dominant ethnic groups. Where national republican leaderships were intent on 'nationalizing' their ethnic space further, minority ethnic communities quickly learnt the implications of increasingly 'strong republics'. Especially in the Southern Caucasus, the promise of greater autonomy and sovereignty for the republics on ethnic grounds could thus easily be translated into the powerful and even violent domination of titular nations over national communities that are institutionally deprived of the benefits of such newly gained power (for example the Abkhaz in Georgia or the Armenians in Azerbaijans Nagorno-Karabakh region).[41]

When the non-national Soviet state had lost its Soviet meaning, the national non-states became the only possible heirs (except for the Russian Federation).[42] The Soviet era, however, outlawed the creation and development of independent, stable formal institutions, so that such institutions as determining factors for action are not yet available to a sufficient degree. Thus in attempting to define a 'national interest' the only instrument available for this purpose is the 'nature of the outline of hegemonic national identity' as the decisive measure of the success or failure of transformation and creation of the nation. This results in the constant return to Georgia's own history and the use of historical and cultural arguments as a means of conducting political debate, which is so astonishing to Western observers. Because national identity is not conceived of as the subjective identification of individuals, but rather as an objectively binding definition of belonging, this means that those groups which ultimately succeed in implanting their definition of national identity will also determine the interests of the nationalizing state. However, this means that the foundations for the legitimization of a young national state will become an object of domestic political controversy and may thus tend to function in a more disintegrative manner than as an integrative factor.[43] This manifested itself in the overthrow of President Gamsakhurdia in 1991-1992, in the fundamentalist tendencies within the Georgian Orthodox Church and in many other spheres. In this way ethnic political activism has outpaced the state's capacity for innovative political institutionalization.[44]

Georgia's contradictory task – state and nation building

Georgia is currently facing the dual task of building a nation and effecting a transformation away from the Soviet system. In this context, citizenship is not perceived as an institution for state purposes, but has to serve (ethnic-) national affairs. Until recently many Georgians were convinced that ideology in itself should not be discarded, and if communist ideology defended and imposed on the people established concepts and values that were 'convenient' for a definite group of party functionaries, then national ideology would defend and implement national interests, establishing viewpoints and goals beneficial for the whole of the Georgian nation, in exactly the same way. Proponents do not consider the fact that their interests might be unacceptable for non-Georgians and even for many Georgians as well. National ideology represents a system of values, hierarchical in its nature with the homeland at the top.[45] While Zviad Gamsakhurdia spoke of Georgia's 'spiritual mission', this overestimation of its peculiarity is still appropriated by many Georgians.

These assumptions are increasingly contested by representatives of a younger generation, who were trained abroad and for whom being democratic means being pro-Western.[46] Their reformist discourse represents not only a description of intentions, but also functions as a tool in the power play for this 'younger' generation. For these young experts, reform means good prospects of a career. For the representatives of the *nomen-klatura* as well as writers rose under Soviet conditions it means a loss in status and replacement, if they prove unfit for the new conditions. Particularly the *intelligentsia*, as the medium and self-perceived leader of the Georgian nation, has experienced a loss in authority and a challenge to their national ideology by new ideas.[47] The ongoing replacements in the ministries of representatives of the old *nomenklatura* by so-called 'reformers' demonstrates a growing challenge, which is counteracted by a reliance on national ideology.

In adopting the bill on citizenship on 25 March 1993, the Georgian parliament recognized all permanent inhabitants of Georgia at that moment as its citizens without any limitation or required knowledge of the Georgian state language.[48]

On Georgia's route to statehood, the question of the form for the future state has arisen naturally and cannot be reduced to only economic development, geographic factors or historical past. Yet, precisely the euphoric experiences of the Georgian national movement and the ensuing civil war in the winter 1991-1992, the defeat in Abkhazia 1994, the latest war with Russia over the control in the Tskhinvali region (Southern Ossetia) in August 2008, up to the oppositions' uncompromising protests in front of the Parliament from April until July 2009 have unveiled the fiction of Georgian national unity. Even if culturally a nation does indeed exist, this is simply insufficient for establishing a basic political consensus for the society as a whole. A collection of critical essays by young Georgian authors in 1994 expressed the hope that 'suffering leads to comprehension' of the previously inconceivable division of the Georgian people and their defeat by the Abkhazians.[49] They attempted to grasp the causes by undergoing a process of self-critical reflection and not by attributing them solely to external factors (Georgia's geopolitical location and 'demon Russia', etc.); rather the causes were embedded in their own history, culture and mentality as well as by their entanglement in the Soviet system. There is a 'need for a long-run strategy based on a clear vision of Georgia's future' after the 'bittersweet lesson of disillusionment' that independence will solve all the country's problems.[50] This bares witness to a much deeper-seated internal crisis in the transformation of Georgian society, which dates back to the 1970s and continues into the present.[51] This crisis can be summed up as follows: 'Taking leave of the conventions of long-lived morality compels transition to a reflective pattern of justification.'[52] Yet the deficiencies of the Soviet system during the Brezhnev stagnation led to a widespread re-traditionalization in Georgian society.[53]

Any 'modernization' defined as 'growth of the adaptive and self-regulating capacities of a societal system'[54] urgently demands a functional differentiation and separation of the spheres of value (economy, belief, science, society, press etc.) into autonomous areas with their own specific logic. This enables one to arrive at 'segmentary conflict resolutions', which may prevent value conflicts becoming structurally dominant or individual conflicts of interest (most often distribution conflicts) being dramatized into system conflicts.[55]

There are also discussions about new symbolic representations of the state.[56] But if this debate does not concern a broader public, what (hidden) aim does it serve, that the media were not reluctant to give combatants a tribune for their self-presentation? In order to establish the causes of such debates it is necessary to look more closely at Georgia's political culture. Despite two hundred years of Russian hegemony, it must be borne in mind that Georgia as part of the Caucasus has a much longer history of political and cultural integration with the geographically adjoining Middle East, whose influence in social organization as well as in political culture is still decisive. It is therefore necessary to assume a hybrid political culture in the Caucasus, which combines two fundamentally different components: the European notion of a nation-state acquired in the process of Sovietization and the regionally prevailing practice and mentality of primary group identification (as extended family and similarly close personal networks). In this dichotomy, new formal parliamentary institutions are primarily considered disguises for more informal structures as 'clusters of relationships based on networks of relatives, friends, colleagues, acquaintances and neighbors, hierarchically bound together through the on-going exchange of favors and obligations'.[57] Due to their direct access and influence on decision-making, such networks are grouped around powerful individuals such as executive government officials (presidents, heads of key ministries like defense or the interior) or directors of large enterprises. They wield patronage over clusters of adherents, because of their ability to drain available public material resources for these exchanges. So the rivalry of elite networks using political structures of state and society in their competition for these resources has to be considered the fundamental dynamic force in political life. Because these practices of patronage do not fit within the Western state tradition of the 'rule of law', neither transparency in state affairs nor a state monopoly on legitimate violence are going to be enforced. Political parties are mere instruments of this elite competition (as with, for example, the Citizen Union) as are the symbolic language of ethnicity and nation.[58]

In such a context debates normally occur in a more circumscribed fashion, where the participants are aware of the sensitivity of exposing chinks in their armor to their antagonists, because the leaderships have to balance the integrity of their political positions with the aspirations of the population.[59] But the harder the competition between competing elite factions, the stronger the expressions used in the symbolic and political language (condemning each other). The worn-out Marxist vocabulary was replaced by the well-honed and long-practiced language of nationalism in the 1980s, and this became a political tool in denouncing opponents. Donald Rayfield showed this in his analysis of the revival of Georgian expressions from the Stalin era in the late Gamsakhurdia period, concluding: 'What has evolved is a language of discussion which acts outside all recognized intellectual ethics.'[60] Words, having lost their original meanings after 'linguistic alienation' in Soviet society, became mere signs to attract and impress impoverished and disoriented people by extraordinary form and superficial soundness.[61] As exclusive expressions they may find their adherents within Georgia, but 'on the world word market' they have to oppose such terms as 'open' or 'civil' society, 'human rights' and so on.[62]

The proponents of more Western patterns of grasping social reality are confronted with a permanent 'anxiety of influence' of foreign culture on a small nation, which is exaggerated by each attempt to de-ideologize or revise Georgian perceptions of history and culture (e.g. the Georgian Orthodox Church leaving the World Ecumenical Council, McDonalds opening on Rustaveli Avenue, the protest against a planned exhibition of Georgian icons in the US). This may lead to a hopeless attempt at the total obstruction of influence and therefore isolation.[63] Any attempt to implement some ideology of a homogeneous Georgian nation recalls counter-strategies to avoid its ideological adoption by ordinary people which were already developed in Soviet times. Pragmatic as they are, they will 'bend as bulrushes within strong winds.'[64]

However, indigenous and foreign cultures are not as mutually exclusive as they are often presented in public debate; they just represent juxtaposed extremes on a broad and varied continuum where public life may develop itself.

The danger of 'reality crises' and the misdirection of societal development continues to plague Georgia even today, because the economy and other fields like science cannot marshal sufficient autonomy to make decisions according to their own rationality criteria as determined by the institution. Its specific knowledge and its interests are simply not considered in the decision-making process of society as a whole.[65] In the same manner, there is no process by which the specific interests of large sections of the population are incorporated into decision-making processes involving the whole of society. Consequently, motivational structures and living strategies have developed which are essentially immune to ideological demands and thus impervious to political direction. The spheres of the politically controlled public domain and the private sphere which is completely sealed off from the former have drifted further apart and now it appears that they are to be (compulsively) reunited on the basis of a new 'national ideology'.[66] In an effort to offset this trend, schools as well as the media play a key role. They generate loyalty to the state and public morals by instilling a national identity against this trend.[67] The legitimacy of the state community so direly needed is not becoming a reality, because citizens are deprived of any opportunity to participate in this process and a real sharing of interests. Despite the existence of an independent state, Georgian society is in serious danger of becoming 'pathologic',[68] if it does not succeed in developing a universally binding normative order. Desperate calls for 'the iron arm of rule by law', the attempted assassinations of former president Shevardnadze in 1995[69] clearly illustrate how precariously national independence is actually embedded in Georgian society. State building has been concurrent with the process of nation building. The needs of the latter have in many ways complicated the coherence of the former. This represents Georgia's 'trauma of statehood'.[70]

Guram Sharadze, by instigating the debate over ethnic categorization, showed himself and the group he represents as marginalized and because of that in need of appealing directly to the public for support to tie their status to the concern they defend. As suddenly as this conflict appeared in the public eye, it vanished again without any remarkable consequences, switching to a new issue to attract the interest of the public again. This debate may be one of the upheavals of the old *intelligentsia*, an existing remnant layer of Soviet society. The social changes left the former cultural elite without their accustomed role of legitimizing Soviet power or now the Georgian nation. Trying nowadays to 'sell its own forces at free market, turns it [the *intelligentsia*] into a merchant", which makes their former position just more questionable.[71] On the other hand, burgeoning NGOs as Sharadze's former adversaries, still primarily restricted to the capital, have to take the issue seriously. They have to lend the whole debate its plausibility without unpacking the 'rules of the game' and a chance to influence them. Both adversaries are characterized by their relative powerlessness. Because of that they look for support for their issue elsewhere (nation building vs. state building). So this example has demonstrated the limited scope for political development in public debates. While lacking other institutionalized forms of political conflict among different elite factions, these debates in the media are expressions of a hidden, permanent ranking of personal coalitions in a personalized political system.

Notes

1 A very first draft of this paper was presented at an expert meeting organized by the Institute for East European Affairs in co-operation with the Institute of Ethnology of Free University Berlin in 1999. (Koehler, J and C. Zürcher, (eds). (2003). *Potentials of disorder*. Manchester & New York: Manchester University Press). I would like to thank the organizers Christoph Zürcher and Jan Koehler for the opportunity to discuss my argument. Florian Mühlfried, Maria van Ruiten and Francoise Companjen provided valuable comments on later versions of this paper.

2 Mamardashvili, M. (2000: 14-15). *Estetika myshleniya [The Aesthetics of Thought]*. Moscow: Moskovskaya shkola politicheskikh issledovanij [Moscow School of Political Studies].

3 Zürcher, C. (2007: ix). *The Post-Soviet Wars. Rebellion, Ethnic Conflict and Nationhood in the Caucasus*. New York and London: New York Press.

4 Cheterian, V. (2008: 155-215). *War and Peace in the Caucasus. Russia's Troubled Frontier*. London: Hurst & Co.; Reisner, O. (2009: 242-268). Georgia and its new national movement. In: Jahn, E. (ed.): *Nationalism in Late and Post-Communist Europe*. Vol. 2 – *Nationalism in the Nation States*. Baden-Baden: Nomos; Shatirishvili, Z. (2003). 'Old' Intelligentsia and 'New' Intellectuals: The Georgian Experience, in: *Eurozine*, 23.06.2003 at http://www.eurozine.com/articles/2003-06-26-shatirishvili-en.html (13.07.2009). Already in 2003 he did not share the 'new' intellectuals' 'liberal ecstasy' and their eschatological optimism about the 'new world order'.

5 Guram Sharadze (1940-2007) was a philologist and professor of Tbilisi State University closely associated with ex-president Zviad Gamsakhurdia. In 1995 he founded the nationalist movement 'Language, Homeland, Religion'. While criticizing Shevardnadze as an oppositional member of the Parliament of Georgia from 1995 to 2003, in 2003 he joined Shevardnadzes election bloc 'For A New Georgia'. Being a prominent critic of foreign, particularly West-

ern, influence in Georgia, he frequently denounced George Soros's civil society work as well as the liberal minded human rights activists and reformers' initiatives in Georgia. He was killed in May 2007. *Times Online*, 4 June 2007, http://www.timesonline.co.uk/tol/comment/obituaries/article1878519.ece

6   Gudjabidze, G. (1999: 2). *Resonance* No. 9, 14.01.1999.

7   Zviadists are supporters of the first president of the Republic of Georgia, Zviad Gamsakhurdia (1939-1993), who was ousted in January 1992 after less than one year in office as president.

8   Gea news agency. *Akhali Taoba* (New Generation) No. 12, 15.01.1999, p. 2.

9   Gea news agency. *Akhali Taoba* No. 12, 15.01.1999, p. 3.

10 Bransten, J. (1999). Ethnicity Proposal Stirs Debate on Nationality and Citizenship in Georgia, Prague, 22.01.1999 (*RFE/RL*).

11 *Akhali Taoba* No. 17, 25.01.1999, p. 5.

12 Prime-News agency. *Shvidi Dghe* (Seven Days) No. 7, 20.-21.01.1999, p. 1.

13 Koridze, T. (1999). *Droni* (Times) No. 6, 21.-23.01.1999, p. 5.

14 Djokhadze, G. (1999). *Resonance* No. 17, 22.01.1999, p. 1.

15 *sakartvelos resp'ublik'a* (Republic of Georgia) no.21, 26.01.1999, p.2.

16 Samkharadze, N. (1999: 2). *Alia* No. 14, 26.-27.01.1999.

17 Narsia, R. (1999: 2). *Resonance* No. 21, 26.01.1999.

18 Gabedadze, E. (1999: 1). *Shvidi Dghe* No. 10, 27.-28.01.1999.

19 *Shavi Dghe* No. 12, 01.-02.02.1999, p. 3.

20 Dzhaiani, M. (1999). vin gvartmevs samshoblos? vnebebi kartuli p'asp'ort'ebis irgvliv (Who will steal our homeland? Passions concerning Georgian passports). *Droni*, 09.01.1999. English version of 'The Constitution of Georgia' in: *Human Development Report: Georgia 1996*. UNDP, Tbilisi 1996, pp. 137-147.

21 Teimuraz Beridze (head of the State Department for Statistics), Anzor Totadze (demographer) and Tsiala Eliadze (head of the Population Census Committee) convened. See Anzor Totadze, vis stchirdeba aseti t'quilebi ?! bat'on guram sharadzis erti sat'elevizio gamosvlis gamo [Who needs such lies?! About Mr Guram Sharadze's appearance on TV], *akhali sakartvelo* (New Georgia), 21.-27.01.1999, p.11. Cf. ibid., *sakartvelos demograpiuli p'ort'ret'i* [Georgia's demographic portrait]. Samshoblo, Tbilisi 1993.

22 Manana Iashvili, rogor mok'les lasha sharadzes mamastan ertad erovneba [How ethnicity was killed together with Lasha Sharadze's father], *akhali sakartvelo*, 21.-27.01.1999, p.10. The article refers to the death of Guram Sharadzes' son in 1997. Although the death was officially recorded as suicide, Sharadze declared it to have been a political act intended to punish him.

23 Guram Sharadze, shetkmuleba sakartvelosa da p'rezident'is c'inaaghmedg!!! [Conspiracy against Georgia and its president], in: *asavali – dasavali* no. 4 (18.-24.01.1999), pp. 2-3.

24 Revaz Mishveladze, rat'om unda gvec'eros p'asp'ortshi kartuli [Why there has to be written Georgian in our passports], in: *asavali – dasavali*, no.4, 24.01.1999, p. 3; ibid., erovneba „kartveli' daasamares [Bury the ethnicity 'Georgian'], in: *sakartvelo*, 19.-25.01.1999, p. 2, 5 and 7; ibid., khma amovighot, sanam permis gotchebivit dagvnomraven.... [Let us raise our voice until we will be numbered as young pigs on a farm], in: *dro* no.3, 19.-26.01.1999, p. 2.

25 It is also named 'South Ossetia' in Soviet terminology or 'Samachablo' among Georgians. The use of certain place names already indicates certain political claims over the respective territory.

26 See for example the interview with Guram Sharadze, 'jer vibrdzoleb dabadebis motsmobashi erovnebis aghnishvnaze da shemdeg p'iradobis motsmomobaze gadaval' [First I am fighting for the mentioning of nationality in the birth certificates and then continue with the ID's], in *Akhali taoba*, 12.02.1999, p. 5 extracted in French in Thorniké Gordadzé, Claire Mouradian (eds.), *Etats et nations en Transcaucasie. Problèmes politiques et sociaux. Dossiers d'actualité mondiale* N° 827, 17.09.1999, p. 35.

27 Cf. Kartveli eri da kartuli sakhelmtsipos momavali [The Georgian nation and the future of the Georgian state]. Round table organized by *Akhali shvidi dghe* (New Seven Days), 30.01.1998, also extracted in French in Gordadzé and Mouradian, *Etats et nations en Transcaucasie*, pp. 38-42.

28 Teimuraz Koridze, Gurami da misi razmi [Guram and his gang], in *Droni*, 13.02.1999, p.7, also extracted in French in Gordadzé and Mouradian, *Etats et nations en Transcaucasie*, pp. 36-37.

29 *sakartvelos resp'ublik'a* no.21, 26.01.1999, p. 2.

30 Zurab K'ik'nadze, umecreba tu demagogia [Ignorance or demagogy], in: *k'avk'asioni*, 17.-23.02.1999, p. 4.

31 Hailbronner, K. (1999: 5). Ausländerrecht: Europäische Entwicklung und deutsches Recht, in: *Aus Politik und Zeitgeschichte*. Beilage zur Wochenzeitung Das Parlament B 21-22/99, 21.05.1999.

32 Benhabib, S. (1999: 98). *Kulturelle Vielfalt und demokratische Gleichheit. Politische Partizipation im Zeitalter der Globalisierung*. Frankfurt/Main: Suhrkamp. In the Western discussion a possible exit from the dilemma, that a people (*ethnos*) and a political community (*demos*) are not identical, may be a 'transnational citizenship'. Kleger, H. (1995: 85-99). Transnationale Staatsbürgerschaft oder: Läßt sich Staatsbürgerschaft entnationalisieren?, in: *Archiv für Rechts- und Sozialphilosophie*, Beiheft 62, Stuttgart 1995.

33 Decision from the National Council, July 16th, 1918 and the Bill of the Constituent Assembly of Georgia, May 27th, 1920 documented in: Parnaoz Lomashvili, *sakartvelos ist'oria (1918-1985). XI k'lasis sakhelmdzghvanelo. me-*

same gamoc'ema [History of Georgia (1918-1985). Textbook for 11th grade. 3rd ed.] Tbilisi 1997, pp. 22-23.

34 Martin, T. (1999: 538-555). Borders and Ethnic Conflict: The Soviet Experiment in Ethno-Territorial Proliferation, in: *Jahrbücher für Geschichte Osteuropas* 47 (1999); see also Simon, G. (1991) *Nationalism and Policy Toward the Nationalities in the Soviet Union. From Totalitarian Dictatorship to Post-Stalinist Society.* Boulder CO; Hirsch, F. (2005). *Empire of Nations. Ethnographic Knowledge and the Making of the Soviet Union.* Ithaca and London: Cornell University Press: Martin, T. (2001). *The Affirmative Action Empire. Nations and Nationalism in the Soviet Union, 1923-1939.* Ithaca and London: Cornell University Press; Müller, D. (2008). *Sowjetische Nationalitätenpolitik in Transkaukasien 1920-1953* [Soviet Nationality Policy in Transcaucasia 1920-1953]. Berlin: Verlag Dr. Köster.

35 On the 'Passport system', see Zaslavsky, V. (1982). *The Neo-Stalinist State.* Armonk, N.Y. p. 92ff. and ibid., *Das russische Imperium unter Gorbatschow. Seine ethnische Struktur und ihre Zukunft.* Berlin (1991: 13-14).

36 Slezkine, Y. (1994: 444-445; 448). The USSR as a Communal Apartment, or How a Socialist state Promoted Ethnic Particularism, in: *Slavic Review* 53; Simonsen, S.G. (1999: 1070f.). Inheriting the Soviet Policy Toolbox: Russia's Dilemma Over Ascriptive Nationality, in: *Europe-Asia Studies* 51.

37 Suny, R. G. (1994: 259). *The Making of the Georgian Nation.* Second Edition. Indiana University Press, Bloomington and Indianapolis.

38 Saroyan, M. (1997: 135-166). Beyond the Nation State: Culture and Ethnic Politics in Soviet Transcaucasia, in idem: *Minorities, Mullahs, and Modernity: Reshaping Community in the Former Soviet Union.* Edited by Edward W. Walker. Berkeley. (first in *Soviet Union / Union Soviétique* 15 (1988), 2-3 as well as the reprint in Suny, R.G. (ed.). (1996: 401-426). *Transcaucasia, Nationalism, and Social Change. Essays in the History of Armenia, Azerbaijan and Georgia.* Revised edition. Ann Arbor . Saroyan described these processes in the Armenian and Azerbaijani cases, the Georgian-Abkhaz one is covered by Shnirelman, V.A. (2001: 199-350). *The Value of the Past: Myths, Identity and Politics in Caucasia.* Osaka: National Museum of Ethnology. Slezkine, A. (414-452) USSR as a Communal Apartment.

39 Slezkine (450-451). The USSR as a Communal Apartment.

40 Cf. for Georgia: Gerber, J. (1997: 33-113). *Georgien: Nationale Opposition und kommunistische Herrschaft seit 1956.* Baden-Baden: Nomos.

41 Saroyan. (424-426). Beyond the Nation State.

42 Slezkine, The USSR and Ethnic Particularism, p.451f.: 'the tenants of various rooms barricaded their doors and started using the windows, while the befuddled residents of the enormous hall and kitchen stood in the center

scratching the backs of their heads.' There is still no investigation of the inter-action in the development of this national ideology under Soviet conditions, as if there were none. But the production of ideology can not be separated from its social environment.

43 Cf. Jacoby, V. (1998: 17). *Geopolitische Zwangslage und nationale Identität: Die Konturen der innenpolitischen Konflikte in Armenien.* Doctoral the-sis at the Department of Social Sciences of the Johann-Wolfgang-Goethe-Universität Frankfurt/Main.

44 See the detailed analysis of the local tax administration, authorities and police under Shevardnadze around 2000: Christophe, B. (2005). *Metamorphosen des Leviathan in einer post-sozialistischen Gesellschaft. Georgiens Provinz zwi-schen Fassaden der Anarchie und regulativer Allmacht.* Bielefeld: transcript; Hensell, S. (2009: 163-206). Die Willkür des Staates. Herrschaft und Verwal-tung in Osteuropa. Wiesbaden: VS Verlag für Sozialwissenschaften.

45 Berekashvili, T. (1998: 29). National Ideology and Public Interests, in: *p'araleluri t'ekst'ebi / Parallel Texts* no. 2. Tbilisi. A Journal run by the 'Group for Investigation of Contemporary Consciousness' at the Depart-ment of Philosophy and Sociology of the Tbilisi State University chal-lenged the leading national discourse by introducing French philosophy. In an extension of Roland Barthes, the author defines ideology as 'an end-less search for values that are acceptable and topical for the majority of people' (p.33). See also Niedermüller (1994: 21-33). Zeit, Geschichte, Ver-gangenheit; in English: Politics, Culture and Social Symbolism. Some Re-marks on the Anthropology of Eastern European Nationalism, in: *Ethnolo-gia Europaea* 24.

46 Nodia, G. (1995: 107). Georgia's Identity Crises, in: *Journal of Democracy* 6 (1995), no.1.

47 The intelligentsia is characterised by a social scientist as the 'engineers of people's souls', whose leading cultural technology has been substituted for money. Jgerenaia, E. (1998: 79). Utopia and the Field of Sociality (A Socio-logical Essay), in: *p'araleluri t'ekst'ebi / Parallel Texts* no. 2. Tbilisi.

48 Zhorzholiani, G. (1998). Zashchita individual'nykh i kollektivnykh prav natsional'nykh (etnicheskikh) men'shchinstv, in: *1 sametsniero-sazoga-doebrivi k'onperentsia „dghevandeloba da sakhelmdsipoebrivi tsnobierebis p'roblemebi' mokhsenebata k'rebuli (24-25 ap'rili, 1998 c'eli, k. tbilisi)* [The first scientific-public conference 'Present time and problems of state con-sciousness' Volume of presented papers. April 24-25, 1998, Tbilisi], p.201-222, here p.213; Lammich, S. and D. Sulakvelidze. (1996: 361-372). Grund-züge der postkommunistischen Entwicklung des Rechtssystems, in *WGO – MfOR.* On the different situation in the Baltic, see Barrington, L. (1995:

731-763). The Domestic and International Consequences of Citizenship in the Soviet Successor States, in: *Europe-Asia Studies* 47.

49 Group of authors: *tchk'ua vaisagan. statiebi* [From suffering to comprehension. Articles]. Caucasian Institute for Peace, Democracy and Development (CIPDD). Tbilisi 1994. The title is a variation of a play by the Russian playwright Aleksandr Griboedov.

50 Nodia, Georgia's Identity Crisis, pp. 114-115

51 Does Georgia as a substantial part of Transcaucasia belong to Europe and its history? Situated on the geographical border between Europe and Asia it remains a question of self-determination by its peoples, a question of their identities. Social transformations are another extension of changing environments. They are not presented as undermining community life here, but rather in terms of how new elements have been appropriated by the cultural system in place, how people perceived the mutual diffusion of traditional and modern elements in their lives and developed new meanings for themselves or their communities.

52 Eder, K. (1991: 67). *Geschichte als Lernprozeß? Zur Pathogenese politischer Modernität in Deutschland*. Frankfurt/Main. The principle of a generalised reciprocity can be achieved by means of an ethic of (religious or moral) convictions or an ethic of responsibility (Max Weber).

53 Cf. Dragadze, T. (1988). *Rural Families in Soviet Georgia. A Case Study in Ratcha Province*. London and New York.

54 Sterbling, A. (1989: 51). *Eliten, Realitätsdeutung, Modernisierungsprobleme. Aufsätze 1987-1988*. Beiträge aus dem Fachbereich Pädagogik der Universität der Bundeswehr Hamburg 3.

55 Ibid., p. 25.

56 The deputy chairman of the Georgian parliament and famous film director Eldar Shengelaia presented the results of his call for propositions of 'state attributes', according to international norms of heraldry, in an issue of the weekly *p'arlament'is uts'qebani*, (27-28, 5 July 1997, pp. 2-6), see also in the same issue the philosopher Zaza Piralishvili's article, 'For state attributes a state approach is necessary' (*sakhelmts'ipo at'ribut'ik'isadmi sach'iroa sakhelmts'ipoebrivi midgoma*), pp. 47-52.

57 Dudwick, N. (1997: 11; 15). Political Structures in post-communist Armenia: Images and Realities, in K. Dawisha and B. Parrott. (eds.). *Conflict, Cleavage and Change in Central Asia and the Caucasus*. Cambridge. On Georgia see Aves, J. (1996: 11; 15). *Georgia. From Chaos to Stability*. London, The Royal Institute of International Affairs and the only empirical study on this issue: Mars, G. and Y. Altman (1983: 546-560), The Cultural Bases of Soviet Georgia's Second Economy, in: *Soviet Studies* 25.

58 Theisen, S. (1998: 140-158). Mountaineers, Racketeers and the Ideals of Modernity – State-building and Elite-Competition in Caucasia, in: Høiris, O. and S. M. Yürükel (eds.), *Contrasts and Solutions in the Caucasus*. Aarhus, Aarhus University Press. Christophe, *Metamorphosen des Leviathan*, pp. 53-86.

59 Cohen, Conflict and Peace, p. 31. See footnote 70.

60 Rayfield, D. (1992: 273). The Language of Abuse and the Abuse of Language – Polemics in Georgian, in: George Hewitt (ed.): *Caucasian Perspectives*. Unterschleisheim / München. Rayfield is right to state, that if 'Georgian civic thinking is to find sense and an appropriate language, then the best must express their lack of conviction, and this will need not pre-cooked phrases and metaphors, but fresh material. Georgian civic thought should communicate, not anathematise; it needs not a stone language, but a living language where the second person is a collocutor, not a crushed scapegoat, where the first person is a juror, not a prosecutor.' (p. 276)

61 'Society is deprived of the means even to articulate and express its demands because language is monopolized by ideology.' Nodia, G. (1993: 6of.). Nationhood and Self-Recollection: Ways to Democracy after Communism, in: Duncan, P. and Rady, M. (eds.): *Towards a New Community. Culture and Politics in Post-Totalitarian Europe*. Hamburg and Münster.

62 The heads of the NGO 'mamulishvili' [Patriot] proposed to extend the meaning of *kartveli* [Georgian] to all citizens of Georgia and to leave the previous variant only to an ethnic context. Levan Nadareishvili, zneobriv-ganmanatlebluri sakmianoba – erovnuli modzraobis p'rincip'ulad axali et'ap'i [Moral-enlightening activity – a fundamental new stage of the national movement], in: *1 samecniero-sazogadoebrivi k'onperencia 'dghevandeloba da saxelmcipoebrivi cnobierebis p'roblemebi' moxsenebata k'rebuli (24-25 ap'rili, 1998 c'eli, k. tbilisi)* [The first scientific-public conference 'Present time and problems of state consciousness' Volume of presented papers. April 24-25, 1998, Tbilisi], pp. 154-166.

63 Jgerenaia (Utopia, p.83) and Nodia (Nationhood, p.63) called this 'ideological fetishism'. Oliver Reisner, Pamela Jawad, Die Nationalisierung der Religion in der Orthodoxen Apostolischen Kirche Georgiens – Begünstigung oder Hindernis im Demokratisierungsprozess? [The Nationalisation of Religion in the Orthodox Apostolic Church of Georgia – Encouragement or obstacle in the process of democratisation?], in: Mirjam Künkler/Julia Leininger (eds.): Zur Rolle von Religion in Demokratisierungsprozessen [About the Role of Religion in Democratisation Processes] (to be published in 2010).

64 There is also the example of Georgian history teaching in state run secondary schools. Reisner, O. (1998: 409-424). What can and should we learn from Georgian history? in: *International Textbook Research* 20.

65 For Eder (op. cit., p. 11), the connection between the idea of the autonomous subject and forms of egalitarian-discursive nationalisation signifies the 'key to creation of political modernity' and takes place at two levels: 1) Creation of community in the form of an association, for example, involving formal equality of all members, new topics and new manners of speaking and debate and 2) in the legal codification of political activities in the form of regulating the formal chances of access to the political system as well as procedures for involving those persons who will be affected by decisions which have to be made. Benhabib (1999: 80) states as the basic principle of discourse ethics that all those affected by the consequences of their compliance with certain norms should be entitled to decide about their acceptance in a practical discourse according to the interests of every individual. See also Stefes, C.H. (2006). *Understanding Post-Soviet Transitions. Corruption, Collusion and Clientelism*. Houndmills, Basingstoke: Palgrave.

66 Sterbling perceives the obstacles to modernization in eastern European societies as embedded in the fact that in Soviet society the development of elites as a form of societal development along specific socio-cultural and socio-economic interests up to an 'ideologically united elite' was rigidly repressed much in the same manner in which patterns of knowledge, interpretations of reality and criteria of rationality which failed to conform to the dominant ideology as it was officially interpreted were subject to suppression (op. cit., pp. 27f., 38).

67 For an earlier period see Janusz Tomiak in collaboration with Eriksen, K., Kazamias A. and R. Okey (eds.). (1991). *Schooling, Educational Policy and Ethnic Identity*. New York University Press, Dartmouth (Comparative studies on governments and non-dominant ethnic-groups in Europe, 1850-1940, vol. 1); Fletcher, G.P. (1993). *Loyalty. An Essay on the Morality of Relationships*. New York/Oxford: Oxford University Press.

68 'We can speak of pathology if we can establish the fact that a society partially or completely destroys its own structural pre-requisites during the course of its development. The pathological element involved consists of the destruction of any possibility of entering into a debate over which normative order will have collective applicability.' Eder, op. cit., p. 10, original in German, author's translation.

69 This was done because it was assumed that a successful assassination would bring the country as a whole into a state of chaos and clan warfare.

70 Cohen, J. (1999: 29-41). Conflict and Peace in the Caucasus: Obstacles and Opportunities, in *Media and Conflict in the Transcaucasus*. McCormack, G. (ed.). The European Institute for the Media. Düsseldorf; Jones, S.J. (1997: 505-543). Georgia: the trauma of statehood, in Bremmer, I. and Taras, R.

(eds.). *New States, New Politics: Building the Post-Soviet Nations*. Cambridge: Cambridge University Press.

71 Jgerenaia calls the warlord and playwright Jaba Ioseliani the perfect example of 'the last Mohican of the Georgian intelligentsia' (Jgerenaia, Utopia, p.79 and 81).

8   The War in South Ossetia, August 2008: Four Perspectives[1]

Françoise Companjen

The long awaited EU-fact finding mission report lead by the Swiss diplomat Heidi Tagliavini on the August war appeared on September 30th,
2009. The goal of the mission was to 'investigate the origins and the
course of the conflict in Georgia'.[2] It is concluded that although Georgia
started the attack on Tskhinvali, South Ossetia, both parties Georgia and
Russia are to blame for the buildup of tension. Russia is blamed for using
military force to reshape borders, something which had become almost
unthinkable in post-WWII Europe, and for using disproportional force
at that. The report came to focus on the human tragedy involved. About
850 lost their lives; many more were wounded and about 100,000 people
had to flee their homes. The majority of these has been able to return in
the meantime, but between 10,000 and 35,000 thousand people remain
displaced.

There are many different ways in which the war can be framed, from
a local perspective of the different parties involved and what the war is
coming to mean in 'the West'. Was it an expression of nineteenth-century
Russian 'empire mentality', a come-back from the humiliating experience
of the Soviet Union falling apart, in a new twenty-first century jacket? Was
it a big power exercising influence in its own 'backyard'? Or was it a case
of 'David and Goliath', a small power fighting to maintain its territorial
integrity against a giant? Or was it a small power more or less falling into a
Russian trap, whether or not encouraged by American conservative hawks,
just before the American elections? Is it a build-up of ethnic tensions or a
case of unfortunate coincidences: an add-up of structural incentives, personal ambition and the presence of weapons, as some claim?[3] Where does
one then place the 250,000 Internally Displaced Persons (IDPs) in Georgia, in this sense-making process? Interpreting and assessing what this
war means for the foreign policy of various countries and their strategic
relations is still going on in various think tanks over the world.[4]

In this short contribution we focus on the background information needed to understand why there is a territorial problem in the first

place and where the 250,000 IDPs came from. Since knowledge is always knowledge from a certain position embedded in a cultural context and world view, we provide the reader with the perspectives on the war and its background by four major players in the field (Russia, Georgia, South Ossetia and Abkhazia). Obviously these frames are generalized summaries since any nation is composed of various constitutive forces and groups of people with their own interpretation of events, their own political clan affiliations. Still, some facts can be highlighted and some principles explained. First of all it needs to be understood that by law of the last Soviet Constitution (1977) the SSR Georgia included the Autonomous Socialist Soviet Republics (ASSRs) Abkhazia and Adjara, and the Autonomous *Oblast* (AO) South Ossetia. After the fights in 1991 with South Ossetia and 1992/1993 with Abkhazia, these disputes were not resolved but 'frozen'.

The Russian perspective

The Russians have had to sorrowfully see the Soviet Union fall apart in what looks like a definite end to 500 years of Russian Empire of which the last decades as a superpower offered an alternative to capitalism. At the very end of the 1980s, millions of Russian citizens suddenly found themselves on foreign territory in Eastern Europe, in the Caucasus and in Central Asia. In Georgia for example, about six percent of the population was Russian and in Abkhazia about fourteen percent. The Abkhaz coast, although formally Georgian territory, was in the 'life world' of Russian people 'their Riviera'. An important Russian military base is located there, as are many *dachas* (summer houses) of Russian generals.

With regard to South Ossetia and Abkhazia, Russia felt it was justified to support the autonomy of these regions. From a Russian perspective the Federation is taking responsibility for the local people in South Ossetia and Abkhazia by handing them Russian passports because this gives these people a legal right to pensions and other possible social benefits. The local people preferred a Russian passport to a Georgian one because until recently it was much easier to travel through Europe with a Russian passport. Contrary to Abkhazia, South Ossetia is of slight strategic importance to Russia.

Russia-Georgia

From a Russian perspective, Moscow has protected Georgia throughout history by incorporating Georgia first in the Czarist empire and later into the Soviet Union, thereby helping feudal Georgia to modernize. Georgia could show some gratitude for the education received by Russia.[5] Since Georgian intelligentsia often followed their education in St Petersburg until the Russian Revolution, Georgian minds were formed in part by Russian education. These students are sometimes referred to as the *tergdaleulebi*: meaning in Georgian, 'those who have drunk from the River Terek'.[6] From a Georgian perspective this meant 'having crossed the River Terek'. Prince Ilia Chavchavadze (1837-1907) was the most influential of these educators, helping the Georgian people into a sense of national awakening. Notions of the Southern Enlightenment (Diderot) reached Georgia through Russia: Catherine the Great had given support to Diderot even if she thought the ideas were not practical ('anything is possible on paper, but I have to use human skin'). Other ideas reached Georgia (and Armenia) through Lord Byron who wrote a critique on Russian culture and progress. But it is not only culturally, but politically that should there be gratitude to Russia.

The civil war of 1992/1993 was ended thanks to Russian intervention in the person of Yeltsin. The Russian Federation is sorry to see President Saakashvili follow such a pro-Western, pro-NATO course and that he has delivered 2,000 men for the second Iraq war.[7] With the Baku-Tbilisi-Ceyhan oil and gas pipeline, Georgia moreover annoyingly interferes with Russia's already fading monopoly[8] of oil and gas deliveries to Eastern and Western Europe.

March 2008

The recognition of Kosovo by the West has been of influence on the Russian strategy in the Caucasus: Moscow decided to answer to this recognition by discussing the recognition of South Ossetia and Abkhazia, as early as March 2008. The earlier talks (annulled by President Obama) of placing a rocket shield in Poland and the Czech Republic, and negotiations of possibly including Ukraine and Georgia in NATO in the future, challenged Russia to re-evaluate its own position and borders. The postponing of a Membership Action Plan for NATO of Ukraine and Georgia at the Bucharest top in April 2008, also may have been interpreted by the Russians as a 'now or never' reason to recognize Abkhazia and South Ossetia because once Georgia would really be involved in NATO, any kind of fight would be too dangerous. The Winter Olympics at Sochi in 2014 require stability and control along the Black Sea Coast favoring a short-term solution. Finally, it was not sure whether the lease of Sevastopol harbor would be prolonged by Ukraine, a reason for Russia to look for other ports[9] on the Black Sea coast. In the meantime the lease has been prolonged.

The war August 2008

The Russian Federation prefers the term 'peace enforcement' to 'war'. Russia does not deny that mistakes were made, but claims these were not valid reasons for Georgia to ignore the ceasefire and begin an attack on Tskhinvali, South Ossetia. From a Russian perspective the truce was violated and many unnecessary civil casualties were caused. The Russians also do not deny that the 58th army found itself close to the entry of the Roki tunnel (connecting North and South Ossetia), however the movements were simple routine shifts. The Russian point of view is that when the Georgian army entered Tskhinvali, the peacekeepers had no other choice but to move to peace enforcement to protect innocent citizens against Georgian aggression. Horror stories on alleged cruel behavior by Georgian soldiers towards the inhabitants were spread. Russian peace-enforcing troops needed to prevent a 'genocide' from happening. The Russians compare their role to that of the US Americans in Serbia.

The Georgian perspective

Of the three autonomous regions of Georgia, Abkhazia and South Ossetia had claimed independence and Adjara has complied with the central authority in Tbilisi in 2004. Georgia has had to deal with about 240,000[10] Internally Displaced Persons (IDPs) since the civil war 1992/1993; and about another 10,000 IDPs from South Ossetia after the war in August 2008.

The civil war

According to the Soviet Constitution of 1977, Georgia had the right to separate itself from the Soviet Union, but the three autonomous regions did not have the right to split off from Georgia. Georgia did exactly that in two steps: first on March 31, 1991 in a referendum for independence from the Soviet Union, and on May 26th, 1991 in the first post-Soviet presidential elections in an independent Georgian Republic. Zviad Gamsakhurdia, appealing to anti-communist feelings and nationalistic aspirations, won the first Georgian presidential elections with 87 percent of the vote. When South-Ossetia announced its own elections in December 1991, the Georgian president canceled the autonomy of South Ossetia and sent troops there, a military intervention which he lost. A month later, Gamsakhurdia was ousted from Georgia by militia who invited the ex-foreign minister of the Soviet Union and First Secretary of the Communist Party in Georgia, Eduard Shevardnadze, back from Moscow to restore order in Georgia. Gamsakhurdia, however, fought back from exile.

In July 1992, the leader of Abkhazia Ardzinba wrote a letter to Shevardnadze announcing that Abkhazia wanted to return to the Constitution of 1925 when Abkhazia was an SSR in a joined federation with the SSR Georgia. About a month later (14-16 august), Georgian troops were shot in Abkhazia when they crossed the Georgian-Abkhazian border unannounced looking for kidnappers (a frequent activity in those days).[11] The Georgians shot back and the fight escalated. In spite of the Abkhaz being outnumbered by a majority of Georgians, the Abkhaz won the war with help and intervention of Russia and voluntary fighters. When about 250,000 ethnic Georgians had to flee Abkhazia, some sources considered this to be 'ethnic cleansing'. From a Georgian perspective it looked as if Abkhazia wanted to split itself off, using violence if necessary.

To end this war against both Abkhazian troops and against Gamsakhurdia fighting back, Shevardnadze decided to ask for help from the Russians and make a deal with president Yeltsin. All former Soviet Republics (such as Ukraine, Moldova, Armenia, Azerbaijan, and the central Asian republics) had joined the Commonwealth of Independent States (CIS), a commonwealth under leadership and economic-political influence of the Russian Federation, except for Georgia. Georgia would now become a CIS-member, Russia would get military bases in Georgia for a certain amount of time and with about 2,000 to 3,000 CIS-troops form a peacekeeping mission under the auspices of the UN and of the OSCE. In exchange, the pro-Gamsakhurdian troops would be defeated. The territorial dispute was called 'frozen' to at least avoid further violence and to allow for negotiations. Shevardnadze remained in power until the Revolution of Roses in November 2003.

From a Georgian perspective, Tbilisi offered various far-reaching proposals to Abkhazia and almost came to an agreement had it not been for the Russian Federation exercising power behind the scenes. For Tbilisi the return of the IDPs was a major point of negotiation.[12]

Georgia-Russia

After the Rose Revolution, president Michael Saakashvili made a radical choice for the USA, NATO and the EU when he was elected president in January 2004. He wanted to build a state modeled after the West. He hoped through a NATO membership to restore the territorial integrity of Georgia, his first and foremost electoral promise. Through NATO he hoped to somehow counterbalance the influence of the Russian Federation on these territorial issues, all the more so that the UN had not achieved much progress in ten years time.

The tensions increased especially between 2006-2008, first of all when Russian diplomats were rather ostentatiously expelled from Georgia on the pretext of being spies. Russia's answer was to boycott Georgian wine and other products on the pretext that the products did not meet certain health standards. Russia also handed out many Russian passports both in Abkhazia and in South Ossetia, thereby violating international law agreements. An (alleged) Russian bomb was dropped in Tsitelubani, Georgia on August 7, 2007, but did not explode. Air space was mutually violated. In view of the fact that the CIS peacekeeping forces consisted mainly of Russian soldiers, from a Georgian perspective the peacekeeping force was biased and this was unacceptable to Georgia.

The war of August 2008

At the end of July and beginning of August 2008 there were some incidental fights between Georgian and South Ossetian soldiers. These hostilities formed the basis for a truce arranged by the Russian peacekeepers. This truce was broken when President Saakashvili ordered his army to block the Roki tunnel connecting North and South Ossetia. The president had received information that the Russian 58th army had collected itself there. To meet this goal the Georgian army had to fight its way through the South Ossetian capital Tskhinvali in the direction of the tunnel to protect what was Georgian territory by international law standards.

It took much longer than expected to reach the tunnel. Moreover the Russians were quick to respond with air attacks both on the Georgian troops moving northwards as on other military targets in Georgia 'proper'. In short, the Georgian troops never arrived at the Roki tunnel in time, caused quite some indiscriminate civil damage on the way, and were damaged themselves by Russian air attacks. Russia occupied territories around both Abkhazia and South Ossetia.

The South Ossetian perspective

South Ossetia used to house about 60,000 inhabitants, one third of which was Georgian. The area was characterized by a mixture of Georgian and South Ossetian villages with people living there coming from mixed marriages many of which were assimilated into Georgian culture. The border areas east and west were largely under the control of Tbilisi. From 2006 onwards South Ossetia had two governments: one from the separatist government with Kokoiky, and one true to Tbilisi with Sanakov, located in Kurta. The South Ossetians, akin to the North Ossetians in language, race and culture (descendants from the Alans), at various moments have indicated a desire to merge with North Ossetia, which is part of the Russian Federation. Also, during the Russian revolution South Ossetians felt closer to Bolshevik Moscow than to Menshevik Tbilisi. As an Autonomous *Oblast* they were entitled to their own language and culture, but not to sovereignty.

The civil war

When the leaders from South Ossetia wanted to have their own elections in December 1991, the Georgian president Gamsakhurdia retrieved the autonomous status of this region and sent Georgian troops: thousands of people were killed, many South Ossetians fled to North Ossetia, and the Georgians lost this military intervention. The fighting ended formally in July 1992 under the guidance of president Yeltsin. A peacekeeping operation was started under the responsibility of the OSCE with troops from CIS countries; in practice those were mainly Russian soldiers. In 1993 and 1994, after the election of new South Ossetian leaders, they repeated their wish to join North Ossetia.

The South Ossetes have survived with small-scale farming and the black market. There is little employment. The central government in Tbilisi had the large *ergneti* market close down in an effort to restructure its own economy and ban the black market. South Ossetians were pushed into the arms of Russia (passports, financial security) and North Ossetia even more. In 2006 a referendum was held among the people of South Ossetia. A majority wished for association with North Ossetia. However, the results of this referendum have not been recognized by any international organization.

The war of August 2008

The South Ossetes claim that the Georgian army ravished Tskhinvali, not making much distinction between civil and military targets. South Ossetians from a Georgian background claim that Ossetian soldiers attacked mainly people from Georgian villages, thereby committing 'ethnic cleansing'. Especially the South Ossetians and North Caucasian voluntary militia plundered.

In the first few days after the war in August, the people expressed their wish to connect with North Ossetia but the president Edward Kokoiky had to retrieve this wish and exchange it for independence. Russia would not be able to claim it had enforced peace. If South Ossetia joined North Ossetia it would look like ordinary military annexation by Russia. Russia has recognized South Ossetia as an independent state, but the vast majority of the international community has not.

The Abkazian perspective

The population of Abkhazia counted 525,061 inhabitants according to the 1989 census: 17.8 percent Abkhaz, 45.7 percent Georgians, ca. 14 percent Russians and a few more Armenians. By 2003, the population was diminished by half: most of the Georgian part had fled in September 1993. In 2009 there are 30,000 to 55,000 ethnic Georgians in Abkhazia especially in the Gali region. The exact number is hard to tell because at least 10,000 mainly elderly ethnic Georgians are seasonal workers, farming in the Gali region, but spending the winter months back across the border close to Zugdidi. Between the civil war 1992-1993 and the August war of 2008, the central Georgian authorities still had control over 'Upper' Abkhazia, an area around the Kodori valley. The same applies to the region around Gali, a small town in southern Abkhazia close to the Georgian city of Zugdidi.

Abkhazia: from SSR to ASSR

As early as November 1917, just after the October Russian Revolution, Abkhazia accepted its own Constitution. Abkhazian leadership had friendly ties with the government in Moscow based on Bolshevik sympathies. When the Red Army led by Ordzhonikidze betrayed and occupied the independent Republic Georgia in February 1921, the Abkhaz leaders asked Lenin for an SSR status and received it. There was a problem however, because the SSR status was granted as a 'treaty republic' together with the SSR Georgia. Georgia and Abkhazia were condemned to each other. In 1931, Stalin changed the Abkhaz SSR status into an ASSR status. Consequently, Abkhazia lost its right to sovereignty. The Georgian language was declared the official language and ethnic Georgians were encouraged to live there. The many mixed marriages date from this period, as do the migration of Russians and Armenians to Abkhazia.

The Civil War

The Abkhaz deny any kind of separation through violence. From their perspective they were still negotiating with Tbilisi about their status, when the then Georgian minister of Defense Kitovani crossed the border close to Zugdidi without prior announcement. Allegedly he was looking for a kidnapped minister with eleven staff members. The Abkhaz only then opened fire when they found these people illegally present on Abkhaz territory. Moreover they refer to a 'cultural genocide' by the Georgian army because their national archives and cultural monuments were specifically targeted during the civil war which followed.

Abkhazia declared itself independent not straight after the war in 1993 but only in 1999, after the population had chosen for an independent state in a referendum held on October 3rd of 1999. The Abkhaz want recognition of their independence before they let any IDPs return to Abkhazia. One of the discouraging factors is they would be a minority again in their own country if all the IDPs were to return. In spite of a lot of good work done by various NGOs[13] getting people to talk with each other again, resentment and fear remain after the atrocities committed to each other as fellow citizens and neighbors.

March 2008

In March 2008, Georgia published a peace proposal much akin to the previous one in 2006. The document provides unlimited autonomy for Abkhazia (right to an own Constitution, government and laws, except for foreign policy and sovereignty) but is slightly less advantageous than the 2006 proposal. The previous proposal suggested a Federal State which Abkhazia would be part of with an Abkhazian vice president and Abkhaz as one of the formal languages of Georgia. Abkhazia came close to accepting both the 2006 and 2008 proposals, but a treaty was not signed.[14]

Although Abkhazia was not directly involved in the war, peace enforcer Russia occupied buffer zones around Abkhazia. Many people fled from that region increasing the number of IDPs. With help from the Russian air force, Abkhazia was also able to reclaim the last bits of territory (Kodori valley and the Gali region) from the central authority in Tbilisi. Russia recognized Abkhazia as an independent state. Contrary to South Ossetia, Abkhazian infrastructure has not been damaged. With the Winter Olympics planned in 2014 right across the Abkhaz border at the Russian Sochi, there are quite a number of financial interests along the coastline in that region.

Conclusion

The independent EU-report concludes that although Georgia struck first, Russia reacted with disproportional force and that both parties carry responsibility in the escalation towards the war. Russia has recognized the independence of South Ossetia and of Abkhazia, but the UN has asked the international community not to recognize these states and so far most of the international community has not.[15] Georgia considers Abkhazia and South Ossetia as occupied territory by Russia.

From this case we can see the old Soviet party politics and fissure between Bolsheviks and Menshevik continuing into the war. The ethnic-territorial basis laid by Soviet governance as we have seen in previous chapters, also lies at the foundation of this conflict since 250 ethnic Georgians had to flee from Abkhazia.

Some may think Russia brought stability to this region by force. The war however did not solve any problems, thereby not enhancing sustainable stability. Most of all, a solution from the 250,000 IDPs who have had to leave their homes and possessions in Abkhazia and have now been living in rather poor conditions in Georgia for almost two decades, has not been found yet.

In due course Abkhazia will probably want real independence instead of being incorporated into the Russian Federation which is now informally the case. South Ossetia is hardly a viable state and will want and need to join North Ossetia, which is part of the Russian Federation. Should this happen the August military action will have been more than a 'peace enforcing' war: Russia will have fought a war and gained land from it. Chechnya, far from stabilized, now has legitimate reason to claim independence from the Russian Federation and demand recognition as well.

Finally, all this sets a doubtful example for Azerbaijan with regard to Nagorno-Karabakh which is still an unresolved conflict. Azerbaijan, with the oil revenues of the past years, has built up an army and it still has more than half a million IDPs[16] who would like to return to their homeland. In short, it would be better to really solve this problem (and the others) by very intensive cooperation by all involved, with more commitment from the EU.

Notes

1 An exchange of ideas between Charlotte Hille and myself on a different, mainly pre-war draft (with thanks to Bert Bomert of Cicam Nijmegen for his comments) evolved into two separately written post-war short articles in Dutch for *Atlantisch Perspectief* Vol. 33, 2009. Chapter 8 of this book is partly based on *AP* Vol. 33 nr. 2, 2009. See also Chapter 9 by Charlotte Hille, first endnote.

2 Independent International Fact Finding Mission Report (September 30th, 2009). Volume 1, page 5. Visited several times from October 2009 to February 2010. http://www.scribd.com/doc/20441575/Independent-International-Fact-Finding-Mission-on-the-Conflict-in-Georgia-Volume-I. See also IPS barometer on local public opinions before and after the war.

3 [3] King, C. (2008:212). *The Ghost of Freedom. A History of the Caucasus*. Oxford: Oxford University Press. 'In the Caucasus the real story of the late twentieth century is not about deep-rooted sentiments of ethnicity or ancient grievances but about the ways in which personal ambition, structural incentives, and the simple presence of sufficient quantities of guns led to bloody conflict.'

4 See: Cornell, S. & F. Starr (2009). *The Guns of August 2008: Russia's War in Georgia*, New York: M.E. Sharpe. Or see Asmus, R. (2010:02). *A little War*

that shook the World. Georgia Russia and the future of the West. Palgrave Mc Millan. In this book he claims Dick Cheney was for more military support of Georgia against Russia, contrary to Steve Hadley who was against a military confrontation between the USA and the second nuclear power in the world. See also Pertti Joeniemmi (2010). The Georgian Russian Conflict. A Turning-point? In: *DIIS Workingpaper.* http://www.diis.dk/graphics/Publications/WP2010/WP2010-02_Georgian_Russian_Conflict.pdf; see also, for example, IPS website for more publications on the war: www.IPS.ge

5   See Bruce Grant's latest book (2009). *The Captive and the Gift: Cultural Histories of Sovereignty in Russia and the Caucasus.* Cornell University Press. The *mission civilisatrice* of the Russian empire and the 'logic of sovereign rule' (Grant) expecting gratitude from the colonized areas, are worked out in this book.

6   See Reisner, O. (2010). Travelling between two worlds – the Tergdaleulebi, their identity conflict and national life. In: *Identity Studies* nr 1: https://sites.google.com/a/isystemsinstitute.org/identity-studies/oliver-reisner

7   These men were called back during the August war but many of them have now been sent to help the Allied forces in Afghanistan.

8   China is competing rapidly eastward. See Trenin, D. (2009: 69). *Foreign Affairs.* 'By 2009, however, many of Moscow's plans for energy dominance had unraveled.' November/December 2009.

9   Some analysts advise shifting weight and importance to the port of Vladivostok with China on the rise. Perhaps even turn this port into a second capital. Other studies show a shift in Russian identity from Western towards Asian.

10   Numbers are approximate and some 10,000 mainly elderly were season workers commuting between Zugdidi and the Gali region , staying in Gali in summer and fall for harvesting and returning to Zugdidi in winter.

11   UN Human Development Report, (1995: 9). The report mentions 'several officials being abducted to Abkhazia'. Hewitt,G. (1996: 217). 'Abkhazia: a problem of identity and ownership'. In: J. Wright, S. Goldenberg & R. Schofield (eds), *Transcaucasian Boundaries.* London: UCL. Hewitt questions whether the ministers, A. Kavsadze and R. Gventsadze, were detained on Abkhazian soil with supposedly Abkhazian approval. Besides, according to the Keesings Historisch Archief, March (1993:161), Gventsadze was released on August 14, the day Shevardnadze mobilized Georgian troops.

12   See Chapter 9 for more detail.

13   The London based Conciliation Resources for example. Or Tbilisi based NGO Studio Re (documentary's by Mamuka Kuparadze). Or Paata Zakhareishvili, Centre for Development and Cooperation, who as an expert on this conflict is involved in various NGOs, Human Rights Committees, and in

publishing (with Arda Inal-Ipa and Paula Garb) a Dialogue series: *Aspects of the Abkhaz-Georgian Conflict.*

14 Sometimes the Russians are blamed for influence behind the negotiation scenes. Sometimes it is pointed out that the central government in Tbilisi made questionable moves such as transferring the trusted Georgian former envoy for peace talks with Abkhazia at a crucial moment in 2006. Or not meeting the Abkhazian representatives who had come to Tbilisi to negotiate. See also the documentary 'The Absence of Will' by Studio Re, Georgia.

15 Along with Nicaragua, Venezuela, Hamas, a Micronesian republic Nauru, Transnistria, South Ossetia, although perhaps not all in ratified form.

16 A UN report cites a little over 600,000 IDPs but other publications cite even higher numbers.

9 The Recognition of Abkhazia and South Ossetia: A New Era in International Law[1]

Charlotte Hille

Summary

With the recognition of Abkhazia and South Ossetia by the Russian Federation and Nicaragua, a new phase in the conflict between these republics and Georgia started. This chapter aims to analyze what chances and consequences the recognition brings seen from an international legal perspective. Since the negotiation process between the parties plays an important role in creating solutions for still pending conflicts, the mediation efforts by the UN are analyzed to see why it is so difficult to find common ground regarding the international legal status of Abkhazia and South Ossetia.

Events of August 2008

During the night of 7 August, 2008 Georgian forces attacked Russian peacekeepers in the South Ossetian capital Tchinval. A Russian military reaction was swift. Under the pretext of protecting its citizens in South Ossetia, many of which held Russian passports, Russian forces entered South Ossetia. The mandate of the Russian peacekeepers was upgraded to peace enforcing, according to Russian Minister of Foreign Affairs Sergei Lavrov.[2] The events in South Ossetia also resulted in combined Russian-Abkhazian military activity in and along the border with Georgia at the Kodori Gorge. The Abkhazians feared Georgian military activity in and along the border of their territory. The military operation, performed by the Pskov regiment from South Russia, was successful.[3] Georgian troops were removed from South Ossetian territory.

Recognition by Russia

As a result of the fighting, Russia took political steps. Meetings between the Russian President Medvedev and his Abkhazian and South Ossetian counterparts Bagapsh and Kokoity took place. On 26 August, 2008 this resulted in the formal recognition by Russia of Abkhazia and South Ossetia as independent states.[4] Medvedev followed the rationale of Western European states in the case of Kosovo, many of which formally recognized Kosovo as an independence state after February 2008. Recognition was granted notwithstanding Serbia's claim to territorial integrity. Resolution 1244 of the UN Security Council remained valid, respecting Serbia's territorial integrity. This means that Kosovo was recognized while at the same time there was a legally binding document in force demanding (implicitly) not to recognize.

The recognition of South Ossetia and Abkhazia by the Russian Federation was by no means a surprise. Already in 2006 Putin had warned he was prepared to recognize Abkhazia and South Ossetia if Western European states and the US would recognize Kosovo.[5] The argument that Kosovo was a special case, where the international community had prepared it in the past nine years for greater autonomy as part of its international administration, was not impressive.[6] Marti Ahtisaari, the Finnish Special Envoy of the UN Secretary General to Kosovo, concluded in a report sent to the Security Council in March 2007 that there was no other option but independence for Kosovo, which should be reached with an initial period of supervision by the international community. Ahtisaari's argument was that independence was the only option to realize a politically stable and economically viable state.[7] An additional argument for independence was that the uncertainty about the future of Kosovo threatened democratic development and ethnic reconciliation. The international presence would be necessary both in the field of overseeing minority rights, the rule of law, decentralization and the protection of religious rights.[8]

According to Ahtisaari 'A return of Serbian rule over Kosovo would not be acceptance [sic] to the overwhelming majority of the people of Kosovo. Belgrade could not regain its authority without provoking violent opposition. Autonomy within the borders of Serbia – however notional such autonomy may be – is simply not tenable.'[9]

Therefore, according to Ahtisaari, this was not a precedent, but a case on its own. It seems however as if the West, by recognizing Kosovo, has deliberately taken the risk that Abkhazia and South Ossetia would be recognized by Russia, and possibly by other States.

Prelude towards recognition

The outbreak of hostilities in South Ossetia was not a sudden eruption of the conflict. Analysts had had information on the buildup of Georgian military presence in the border area of South Ossetia since summer 2004, when newly elected Georgian president Saakashvili visited South Ossetia.[10] In 2006, Georgian troops were stationed in the Kodori gorge along the border with Abkhazia. The pretext was the fight against a Georgian warlord, Emzar Kvitsiani, who defied Georgian rule, and the restoration of constitutional order.[11] In both cases there were incidental cross border incidents.

In 2007, the Georgian government decided to move the governments in exile of Abkhazia and South Ossetia. These governments included Georgian citizens who had fled Abkhazia and South Ossetia during the conflicts in the 1990s and got their support from Internally Displaced Persons (IDPs), but had not much support in South Ossetia and Abkhazia proper. The governments in exile were moved to the border area of Abkhazia and South Ossetia.[12] This could potentially have resulted in cross border incidents.

Frozen conflicts

The conflict over the status of South Ossetia and Abkhazia has its background in the international legal principles that peoples and minorities in states have the right to self-determination. The outside borders of the state shall not be changed without its consent, which is called the right to territorial integrity. The right to self-determination of peoples and minorities, whether ethnic, religious or cultural, is mostly regarded as working internally (within the state), which means that minorities and peoples in a state have the right to freely speak their languages (and therefore have their own newspapers, radio and television, and language education), the right to freely profess their religion and the right to live and express their own culture.[13] The external working of the right to self-determination, also called secession, can create problems when the metropolitan state does not approve of the secession, since it infringes upon the right to territorial integrity. The clash between these two principles has not yet been solved, resulting in several cases of *de facto* states, which are not accepted by the international community which adheres to the borders of the metropolitan state. In principle international law takes a neutral position towards secession, but practice shows that *de facto* states are mostly not recognized by other states if the metropolitan state does not approve of the secession. This is different if there are longstanding serious human rights violations or genocide against a people, living in this state but not in neighboring states, and this people does not get internal self-determination.[14] Pieter Kooijmans, former judge at the International

Court of Justice, takes the position that realization of secession through the use of military violence is forbidden.[15] In practice we see that a successful secession may in the end lead to recognition by the international community.[16] In the case of Abkhazia and South Ossetia, the conflicts originate from the rise of nationalist feelings at the beginning of the 1990s among Georgians, Abkhazians and South Ossetians.

The negotiations since 1992 have concentrated on finding an acceptable solution guaranteeing the rights of all parties to the conflict. With the recognition of Abkhazia and South Ossetia by Russia and Nicaragua, a new phase in the search for a solution of the conflict between these republics and Georgia has arisen.

In casu there are several conflicting concepts: the right to self-determination of Abkhazians and South Ossetians versus the right to territorial integrity of Georgia. A difference of opinion exists concerning: the amount of autonomy of minorities and peoples within, or outside Georgia with a link to Georgia; the wish of (part of) a people, the Ossetians, to join with their brethren in North Ossetia, which is situated in the Russian Federation[17]; the wish of a people, the Abkhazians, living in their titular nation, to form an independent state. In principle, peoples have a right to a state. That means that if a people in a multi-people or multi-ethnic state over a prolonged period of time asks for internal self-determination and does not get this, there is a stronger case when the people secedes from the metropolitan state. Recognition will be easier accepted.[18]

The recognition of Abkhazia and South Ossetia by the Russian Federation is a unilateral act. In principle, states have to be cautious to recognize new states, since premature recognition may result in loss of face, and recognition is a onetime act, which will not be reversed.[19] Therefore, with the recognition of Abkhazia and South Ossetia, they are states in the sense of the Montevideo Convention, and according to the four criteria of state building: territory, population, government and recognition. There are no rules in international law which state how many states have to recognize before the state will be taken seriously, which means that two recognitions are sufficient to speak of a recognized state. There are no rules in international law on how big a state should be, how many inhabitants it should have or whether it is economically viable.[20] Therefore, Abkhazia and South Ossetia are now independent states, while many states and international organizations as the UN, NATO, OSCE, EU, Council of Europe still recognize the *status quo ante*, and stress their respect for Georgian territorial integrity. This is based on UN Security Council resolutions stressing the territorial integrity of Georgia.

James Crawford, a specialist in state building, differentiates between collective non-recognition for legal reasons and collective non-recognition for political reasons. The latter is purely discretionary, while the former is a prevention of the consolidation of unlawful situations. Non-recognition is obligatory if demanded by UN Security Council Resolution.[21]

In order to understand the events of August 2008, it is necessary to look at the background of this conflict and the developments which led to the period of 'frozen conflict' between Georgia, Abkhazia and South Ossetia.

Negotiations since 1992

Following the independence of Georgia, internal armed conflicts with South Ossetia and Abkhazia broke out. After the cease fire agreements with South Ossetia (Dagomys Agreement of 1994) and Abkhazia (1993) negotiations started. These were marked by disagreements. South Ossetia had lost its Autonomous Oblast (AO) status in 1990 when Georgian president Zviad Gamsakhurdia lifted South Ossetian autonomy following Ossetian demands for union republic status. Abkhazia, which had kept its Autonomous Socialist Soviet Republic (ASSR) status, referred to its status as a treaty-SSR in the period from 1921 to 1931 in Georgia, and wanted extensive autonomy.[22] An important document in the Abkhazian-Georgian conflict was the adoption of UN resolution 937 in 1994. All parties pledged to work towards a return of the (Georgian) refugees and internally displaced persons to Abkhazia, and an extending of the mandate of UNOMIG.[23] When time went on, and different proposals concerning federal, confederal or unitary status of Georgia had been discussed, as well as the position of Abkhazia in these proposals, an impasse was reached. A similar pattern developed in the conflict with South Ossetia, where the issue of alignment with North Ossetia was not debatable for Georgia, and a return of AO status was not on the agenda.[24] After some years of negotiations all possible positions had been taken by the parties, and the conflict became 'frozen'. There was negative peace (no fighting), but no positive peace (peace accord). Both parties had reached a position where it could possibly be detrimental to push for a resolution of the conflict. In the best scenario for Georgia, it could recapture Abkhazian and South Ossetian territory, but at the expense of fighting, and losing face in the international arena. In the case of Abkhazia and South Ossetia, they now factually had independence, though they were boycotted, and resolution of the conflict might imply losing some of this independence.

The status as 'frozen conflict' also resulted from the tactics of the negotiators. As time went on, the momentum for a breakthrough was lost. There were spoilers both in and outside the delegations. Doves were replaced by hawks, there was sporadic fighting along the borders of the conflicting parties, and rhetoric was used as other means of continuing the fight. As time went on, and new special representatives of the UN Secretary-General were appointed in the case of the Georgian-Abkhaz negotiations to report on the situation and mediate, parties had to build confidence in the mediator, and once again the willingness to work towards a compromise diminished. Parties dug themselves in, and the peace proposals were often reformulations of earlier versions, to which the other party could only say no.[25]

It is questionable whether one could really speak of a 'frozen conflict' since negotiations, sporadic fighting, and developments in international politics continued.[26]

Apart from the attempts at negotiating by the OSCE in the Georgian-South Ossetian conflict, which were conducted under the supervision of the Joint Control Commission, consisting of Russia, Georgia and South Ossetia, and the UN as well in the case of the Abkhazian-Georgian conflict, there were also attempts by the Harvard Project on Negotiation (PON), and the Institute of Strategic Studies in London, to try to create a favorable situation for negotiations in either track one or track two of the negotiations.[27] While negotiations continued both in track one (at state level) and track two, president Michael Saakashvili, who was elected president in 2004, prepared his republic for better relations with the West. Having studied in the US, he had the sympathy of the US public and politics. His marriage to Sandra Roelofs, of Dutch origin, made him popular in the Netherlands. After Michael Saakashvili brought Ajaria back under central authority, and threatened former president Aslan Abashidze of Ajaria into exile in the Russian Federation, he tried to lure South Ossetia back into Georgia. This attempt failed, since the situation was very different from the situation in Ajaria. While the population in Ajaria is ethnically Georgian, professing the Muslim faith, the population of Ajaria was also tired of the growing corruption in the republic, which was linked to the policy of president Abashidze. In South Ossetia the population had survived a war with Georgia only twelve years earlier. The Ossetians belong to another people, speaking another language, Ossetian. The Russian presence in South Ossetia in 2004 was already considerable. This made president Saakashvili decide not to attack. What he did do was close the market on the border between Georgia and South

Ossetia, and take measures against smuggling across the Russian-South Ossetian border.[28] This was a blow to the black market in South Ossetia, and had consequences for the economy. It was under such circumstances that South Ossetians and Abkhazians who had to renew their passport, and who did not want to apply for a Georgian passport, decided to apply for a Russian passport. South Ossetia and Abkhazia could not issue passports of their own, since these were not regarded as legitimate travel documents across the border, because the entities were not recognized as states. A Russian passport furthermore gave right to retirement pay, an extra incentive to opt for a Russian passport. This possibility existed since a law from 1991 gave the opportunity to opt for a Russian passport even if living in other republics, which were formerly part of the Soviet Union.[29] Therefore, it is no wonder that many opted for a Russian passport. Georgia objected, but did not go to the International Court of Justice, which might have been expected in such a situation, since the Russian Federation quite obviously interfered in the internal affairs of Georgia (Article 2(4) of the UN Charter).

In the end, the conflicts over the status of Abkhazia and South Ossetia were not only frozen conflicts, but even worse, forgotten conflicts, with little international attention.[30] The fighting in August 2008 did two things: the conflict became violent, and it placed these 'forgotten' conflicts back on the international political agenda, thus creating new possibilities to negotiate a settlement. The role of Russia in this process has become considerable, though Russia has been a party to this conflict since the beginning of the 1990s, when president Ardzinba of Abkhazia complained that the ceasefire agreement with Georgia, signed under the supervision of Russia, did not leave any room for an input by the Abkhazian president.[31]

Negotiations in Geneva

The ceasefire agreement of French president Sarkozy, who was also presiding the European Union at the moment, formulated that new negotiations would take place between Russia and Georgia. The negotiations are taking place under mediation by the UN, OSCE, and EU. Important parties such as the US are also present, though they do not participate in the peace talks.

The first round of negotiations was to take place in October 2008. At the opening of the negotiations major problems erupted on who would be present at the negotiations.[32] Georgia declared it would negotiate with Russia, but not with the Abkhazian and South Ossetian delegations, which were also in Geneva. Russia considered it necessary to include the Abkhazian and South Ossetian delegations, since they were part of the conflict, and moreover, they were now independent states which had to be present at the international negotiations as aspects of their position were discussed. The South Ossetian and Abkhazian delegations also expected to be taken seriously as they were now recognized states, and the position of Russian military directly affected their interests. The Russian, South Ossetian and Abkhazian delegations threatened to return home if the South Ossetian and Abkhazian delegations were not admitted. Since no solution on the correct negotiation partners could be obtained, the meeting was immediately postponed until November.

Mid-November 2008 a second round of negotiations started. The mediators found a way to incorporate the relevant parties in the process. Georgia allowed participation of delegations from the Abkhazian and South Ossetian government, and asked that delegations from the (Georgian) Abkhazian and South Ossetian government in exile also be present. Instead of official meetings, the different groups met informally in working groups, thereby giving Georgia the idea that the Abkhazian and South Ossetian delegations had lower status. One has to keep in mind that peace negotiations do not imply recognition of a party as an independent state. So for Georgia this was rather part of her strategy, than a risk of recognizing Abkhazia and South Ossetia.

No tangible results were reported during the December round of negotiations. However, there was some progress concerning confidence building, which was regarded as a positive sign.[33]

During the negotiations in February 2009, a partial breakthrough was reached in the group which negotiated on the issue of security. All parties concerned would have weekly contact on security issues, there would be extra contact when security risks would emerge. Some journalists stated that these are for the moment mere words, and their significance in practice has to be proven.[34] However, the fact that parties agree on regular contact with regard to security is also to be seen as an intention to observe a longer term ceasefire and towards normalization of relations. In the group which negotiates a return of refugees and Internally Displaced Persons (IDPs) no progress was made.

Are Abkhazia and South Ossetia taken seriously, if the negotiations start with respect for Georgian territorial integrity?

The negotiations at Geneva can be regarded as asymmetrical. It is clear that the position of Russia and Georgia is stronger than the position of Abkhazia and South Ossetia. This is not only underlined by the fact that the latter have until now only been recognized by two states, Russia and Nicaragua, but also by the fact that the mediators, the UN, OSCE and EU have pledged adherence to the principle of Georgian territorial integrity. This might bring into question the neutrality of the mediators. Though from an international legal point of view there can be an argument to follow this line, *in casu* Russian military support in Abkhazia and South Ossetia is therefore automatically regarded as interference in internal affairs of Georgia, even if the governments ask for Russian military support, and the two newly recognized states are regarded as still being part of Georgia. Though mediators are supposed to be impartial, this once again underlines the fact that mediators in the international arena often are not.[35]

Another problem is that this position diminishes the scope of maneuver of South Ossetia and Abkhazia in the negotiation process. It will be more complicated to create and keep trust of all parties in the mediation process. How can Abkhazian and South Ossetian negotiators have trust in mediators who *a priori* take the side of Georgia? And what will happen if the mediation efforts of the OSCE (which initially mediated in the South Ossetian-Georgian conflict) and the UN (which initially mediated in the Abkhazian-Georgian conflict) with the EU (which joined in resolving this conflict in August 2008 when French president Sarkozy brokered a cease-fire between Russia and Georgia) fail in their efforts? This might result in a new situation where the international community will 'forget' the conflict (by not paying attention to it), and no resolution of the question of security, return of refugees and position of Russia in this matter will be reached. It furthermore will diminish the credibility of the international organizations.

New developments in international law, the chances created by Kosovo

The recognition of Abkhazia, South Ossetia and Kosovo creates opportunities to rethink state building and consider new concepts of internal and external sovereignty, common state ideas, federal and confederal options.

The development of relations with *de facto* states and states which are recognized by a minority of states means that boycotts against entities which seek external self-determination could be reconsidered, and that conflict prevention methods should be used at a much earlier stage when minorities feel at risk. How international law on this topic will develop still depends on the willingness of states. It is however clear that with the recognition of Kosovo by some 54 Western states a precedent has been created, which has been used by Vladimir Putin in the cases of Abkhazia and South Ossetia. Though all parties manipulate international law to their own advantage (after all, UN Security Council resolution 1244, which respects territorial integrity of Serbia for Kosovo, is still in power, as well as UN Security Council resolutions respecting Georgia's territorial integrity) so all newly independent three states cannot become members of the UN, due to binding UN Security Council resolutions on this matter.

It is necessary to take the situation of *de facto* states serious in international relations. One option to solve conflict between the state and the *de facto* independent entity is to mediate in a more robust way, in order to avoid a stalemate like we saw in Georgia's conflicts with Abkhazia and South Ossetia in the past ten years. On the other hand, if parties are not willing to come to terms, force will not help. In such a scenario, the *status quo* will be as it was before the recognition, the only difference being the increased relations between Russia, Abkhazia and South Ossetia.

Other aspects which might be reinterpreted are the constitutive and declaratory theories with regard to *de facto* republics. According to the declaratory theory, it is sufficient for an entity to qualify as a state when the requirements of the Montevideo Convention (1933) are met: the entity has a territory, with a population living in it, and it has an (effective) government. Those who adhere to the constitutive theory stress that one can only speak of a state once other states have shown a willingness to engage into relations with that state. For those lawyers recognition is the most important criteria regarding state building. The group which adheres to the declaratory theory, which considers an entity a state when it meets the first three criteria of a state, and consider that such an entity has rights and duties in international law, is growing.[36]

In finding a solution to the status of *de facto* entities, one can also opt for playing with the concept of internal and external sovereignty. Sovereignty, according to James Crawford, is 'the plenary competence that States prima facie possess'.[37] Independence is used to denote the prerequisite for statehood. There are different sorts of sovereignty to be discerned. Internal sovereignty means sovereignty over specific fields of politics and law in the state.[38] External sovereignty includes the right to sign treaties. This sovereignty normally belongs to the central government, but there are examples where parts of a federal state got limited external sovereignty.[39] The right to represent the state normally remains with the central authorities. As with several types of state (unitary state, federal state, confederal state), different levels of sovereignty or autonomy can be attributed to decentral authorities or *de facto* entity.

The issues of (cultural) autonomy and sovereignty have been on the agenda since the end of the First World War: In the Aaland case, which was brought before the League of Nations for arbitration at the beginning of the 1920s, the question was whether the population of the islands, which were 90% Swedish, would be allowed to align with Sweden. During the nineteenth century the islands had changed hands several times between Sweden and Finland. Since 1809 the islands formed part of Finland (which at the time formed part of the Russian Empire). In December 1917 the islands declared independence from Finland, fearing anti-Swedish sentiments from the Finnish governments. This question resembles the dilemma of the South Ossetians. Based on international law (sea law) the islands were in an arbitral award by the League of Nations considered part of Finland, but with extensive language and cultural rights for the Swedish population.

The fear of losing cultural and ethnic rights, and the fear of assimilation is similar in the case of Abkhazia and South Ossetia. What is different is that the population of the Aaland Islands never declared independence, something the governments of Abkhazia and South Ossetia did, after consulting the population in a referendum.

In the case concerning the question whether Quebec had the right to secede from Canada, the Supreme Court of Canada ruled that though the French-speaking Quebecois have the right to internal self-determination, such as the right to speak their language, they did not have the right to external self-determination, since this would only apply in cases where no internal self-determination is being realized by the central authorities. Furthermore, though the Quebecois speak another language, this does not qualify them as a distinct people, and therefore they do not have the right to external self-determination on these grounds.

The Canadian Supreme Court ruled in this case:

'Although there is no right, under the Constitution or at international law, to unilateral secession ... this does not rule out the possibility of an unconstitutional declaration of secession leading to a de facto secession. The ultimate success of such a secession would be dependent on recognition by the international community, which is likely to consider the legality and legitimacy of secession having regard to, amongst other facts, the conduct of Quebec and Canada, in determining whether to grant or withhold recognition.'[40]

James Crawford, a specialist in state building, refers to the eminent international lawyer Hersh Lauterpacht, stating: 'The position is that secession is neither legal nor illegal in international law, but a legally neutral act the consequences of which are regulated internationally.' As Lauterpacht pointed out: '[i]nternational law does not condemn rebellion or secession aiming at the acquisition of independence.'[41] This position was affirmed by the International Law Commission in its discussion of the principle of non-recognition of territorial acquisition by illegal force. Article 11 of the Draft Declaration on Rights and Duties of States, which embodied that principle, was amended by limiting it to acquisition 'by another State' so as to deal with the case of secession.[42]

The quest for independence of Abkhazia and South Ossetia resembles the case of Quebec in the sense that both entities speak different languages, which they were allowed to use by the central Georgian authorities in the pre-conflict phase. The case does differ from Abkhazia since the authentic population of Abkhazia forms a distinct people living in a defined territory, while the Ossetian people is divided over two territories.

Conclusion

The recognition of Abkhazia and South Ossetia has resulted in different developments: from a political point of view, the Russian Federation has legalized a factual situation by recognizing *de facto* states, conform the recognition of Kosovo. From a legal point of view, the recognition gives a new impetus for *de facto* entities to aspire *de iure* statehood, while it may have created a breakthrough in thinking about states and independence. The fact that the UN, OSCE, Council of Europe and EU underline their respect for Georgian territorial integrity will slow down further recognitions by states. The possibilities of recognition by Georgia of Abkhazia and South Ossetia is nihil in the foreseeable future. Several possibilities to include Abkhazia and South Ossetia in Georgia, in a federal or confederal state, or in a common state, are further away with the independence of Abkhazia and South Ossetia.

Notes

1 Part of an earlier version of this chapter was published in *Atlantisch Perspectief. Vol. 33, No. 1, 2009*. The legal analysis can also be found in Hille,C.M.L. (2010). *State Building and Conflict Resolution in the Caucasus.* Leiden: Brill.

2 http://www.un.int/russia/new/MainRoot/docs/warfare/statement090808en. htm, accessed 31 March 2009.

3 http://www.cdi.org/russia/johnson/2008-156-4.cfm, accessed 31 March 2009.

4 http://www.rferl.org/content/Russia_Recognizes_Abkhazia_South_Ossetia/1193932.html

5 On the one hand, Putin endorsed Serbia's territorial integrity and urged a 'solution mutually acceptable to Kovoso leaders and Belgrade'. On the other hand, Putin clearly implied that Russia would officially recognize the secessionist territories in the post-Soviet conflicts if the United States and other Western governments recognize Kosovo's secession from Serbia, Jamestown, 2 February 2006, http://www.jamestown.org and www.rferl.org/content/Article/1077075.html, accessed 22 January 2009.

6 UN envoy on Kosovo's status says 'independence is the only option'. http://www.un.org/apps/news/story.asp?NewsID=22013&Cr=kosovo&Cr1=, accessed 20 March 2009.

7 UN envoy on Kosovo's status says 'independence is the only option'. http://www.un.org/apps/news/story.asp?NewsID=22013&Cr=kosovo&Cr1=, accessed 20 March 2009.

8 Ibid.

9 Ibid.

10 http://www.eurasianet.org/departments/insight/articles/eavo71204.shtml, accessed 31 March 2009; http://www.crisisgroup.org/home/index.cfm?l=1&id=3380, accessed 31 March 2009; http://www.globalsecurity.org/military/library/news/2005/07/mil-050728-rferlo3.htm, accessed 31 March 2009.

11 Liz Fuller, 'Georgia: Troops Deployed to Rein in Militia,' http://www.rferl.org/content/article/1070114.html, and http://www.kommersant.com/p-9225/r_500/Unpredictable_Results_in_Kodori_Gorge/. However, Ghia Nodia did not see a reason for a military invasion, though he mentions the risk of a spill over effect of the Georgian military operation in the Kodori gorge to Abkhazia, http://www.eurasianhome.org/xml/t/expert.xml?lang=en&nic=expert&pid=740, all accessed 30 March 2009.

12 http://www.caucaz.com/home_eng/depeches.php?idp=1486, http://www.unhcr.org/refworld/country,,FREEHOU,,GEO,4562d8cf2,487ca1e91a,0.html, and accessed 31 March 2009.

13 Article 27 International Covenant on Civil and Political Rights.

14 Raic, D. (2002: 332). *Statehood and the Law of Self-Determination.* The Hague: Kluwer Law International. Crawford, J. (2006:415). *The Creation of States in International Law.* Oxford: Oxford University Press.

15 Kooijmans, P. (2002:24). *Internationaal Publiekrecht in Vogelvlucht.* Deventer: Kluwer.

16 An example is Bangladesh, which against international legal rules was recognised after it seceded from Pakistan in 1971.

17 Shortly after declaring independence, Kokoity was stated saying: 'Yes, we will be part of the Russian Federation,' South Ossetian President Eduard Kokoity told reporters in the Russian resort of Sochi on the Black Sea. 'We will do it according to the norms of international law.' http://www.rferl.org/content/Kokoity_Says_South_Ossetia_Will_Become_Part_Of_Russia/1198058.html, accessed 31 March 2009, http://www.timesonline.co.uk/tol/news/world/europe/article4732541.ece, accessed 31 March 2009.

18 Raic, D. (2002: 366-372). *Statehood and the Law of Self-Determination.* The Hague: Kluwer Law International.

19 Kooijmans, P. (2002:25). *Internationaal Publiekrecht in Vogelvlucht,* Dordrecht: Kluwer. Malanczuk, P. (1997: 85). *Akehurst's Introduction to International Law.* London: Routledge. Crawford, J. (2006: 416). Ibid.

20 Kooijmans, P. (2002: 20-21). ibid. Duursma, J. (1996:117-118). *Fragmentation and the International Relations of Micro-States.* Cambridge: Cambridge University Press.

21 Crawford, J. (2006: 157-158). ibid.

22 In the Lykhny declaration, adopted by the Abkhazian Forum in 1989, a group Abkhazians aimed at SSR status separated from the Georgian SSR. They referred to the SSR status Abkhazia held from 1921 to 1931. Lynch, D. (2004:28). *Engaging Eurasia's Separatist States.* Washington: United States Institute of Peace Press. An SSR is a Socialist Soviet Republic. An Autonomous Socialist Soviet Republic has lower status, and will be part of an SSR, see Lynch, D. (2004: 27). ibid.

23 UN resolution S/RES/937 (1994).

24 The Georgians call it Samachablo region, named after the Georgian noble family who ruled over the territory which is called South Ossetia in former days, see also on the negotiations under Saakashvili in 2004-2005 http://www.jamestown.org/single/?no_cache=1&tx_ttnews%5Btt_news%5D=30643, accessed 31 March 2009.

25 Chester Crocker explains how conflicts become intractable (a feature which applies to the Georgian-Abkhazian and the Georgian-South Ossetian conflict) in: Crocker, C. (2004). *Taming Intractable Conflicts: Mediation in the Hardest Cases.* Washington: United States Institute of Peace Press.

26 SC/6671, 7 May 1999.

27 Track two negotiations concentrate on negotiations at the NGO level, aimed at strengthening civil society and prepare the population for reconciliation and resolving of the conflict.

28 http://www.civil.ge/eng/article.php?id=7734, accessed 31 March 2009.

29 http://www.un.int/russia/new/MainRoot/docs/warfare/statement090808en. htm, accessed 31 March 2009.

30 Crocker, C. , F.O Hampson, P. Aal (eds), (2004: 49-52). *Intractable Conflicts, Mediating in the Hardest Cases.* Washington: United States Institute of Peace Press. The authors describe various forms of forgotten conflicts. *In casu* the Georgian-Abkhazian and Georgian-South Ossetian conflict could fall in the sub category 'neglected conflicts'.

31 http://www.circassianworld.com/croniclewar.html, accessed 31 March 2009 and C. Crocker, ibid.

32 Hille, C. (2009: 26). 'Onderhandelingen in de Kaukasus'. *Atlantisch Perspectief.* No. 1.

33 www.wtop.com/?nid=104&sid=1553526, accessed 22 January 2009.

34 http://www.europeanforum.net/news/568, and http://www.rferl.org/archive/ The_Caucasus/3/963/963.html, accessed 31 March 2009.

35 See also C. Crocker, F.O Hampson, P. Aal (eds), (2004: 23). ibid.

36 Duursma, J. (1996: 111). ibid.

37 Crawford, J. (2006:89). *The Creation of States in International Law.* Oxford: Oxford University Press.

38 Kreijen, G. (2003) *State Failure, Sovereignty and Effectiveness: legal lessons from the decolonization of Sub-Saharan Africa*, doctoral dissertation, Leiden. Kreijen discusses the definitions of sovereignty and the way the concept is used in cases of weak and failing states. This discussion also applies in the relations between *de facto* states and the metropolitan state, since the loss of territory of the metropolitan state implies that the state is weak.

39 Tatarstan got limited external sovereignty in the Russian Federation at the beginning of the 1990s, just like Ukraine and Belarus had limited external sovereignty in the Soviet Union, and could participate in activities at the UN.

40 *Reference re Secession of Quebec,* (1998), SCJ No 61, para 155, ILR 537, 595.

41 *Recognition*, 8: and (1928) AJ 105, 128.

42 ILC Yearbook (1949: 112-13). 9, 1. In: Crawford, J. (2006: 390). ibid.

10 Freedom of Speech in the Caucasus: Watch-dog Needed in Armenia and Azerbaijan

Lia Versteegh

Introduction

In the light of the adoption of Recommendation 1247 of 1994 on the expansion of the Council of Europe, it was decided that 'in view of their cultural links with Europe, Armenia and Azerbaijan would have the possibility of applying for membership provided they clearly indicate their will to be considered as part of Europe'.[1] In January 2001, the Republic of Azerbaijan and the Republic of Armenia became members of the Council of Europe. Only two decades ago they were still part of the former Communist bloc, with an authoritarian political structure, modeled on that of the USSR. In joining the Council they became members of democratically-accountable countries, in accordance with the system of the Council of Europe. One of the requirements of this system is the adherence to the Treaty of the European Convention for the Protection of Human Rights,[2] which aims to protect individuals against arbitrary actions of national public authorities.

The protection of human rights is included in the national constitutions of both countries. However, according to recent monitoring reports, they seem to have great difficulty in fulfilling their commitments to the Council of Europe. Although Armenia and Azerbaijan have been members of the Convention since 2001, there is still a great deal of criticism about the way their public authorities interfere with the right to free expression, one of the most important liberties, as it is one of the conditions for critical analysis of violations of other human rights. Freedom of expression has been guaranteed in Article 10 of the Convention.

The aim of this paper is to give insight into the obligations of national authorities to guarantee freedom of expression in accordance with Article 10 of the Convention, and to demonstrate the rights of the victims of violations in proceedings before the Court of Human Rights. To that purpose I would like to exhibit the working of Article 10 ECHR, and to demonstrate complaints stating the lack of commitment from the national authorities of Armenia and Azerbaijan to the Convention and lastly, to reveal the position of the individual victim in Armenia and Azerbaijan in Court Law in cases concerning the freedom of speech.

The European Convention on Human Rights[3]

The European Convention of Human Rights was originally drawn up by the Council of Europe in response to the atrocities of the Second World War. The main aim was to protect humanity against violations of human rights. Another goal was to build a legal framework against communism. Norms and values were set to provide guidelines for democratic states and societies. The result was a Convention principally built on civil and political rights. The aim of the Council of Europe, as written in the Statutes of the Convention, was 'to achieve a greater unity between Member States for the purpose of safeguarding and realizing the ideals and principles which are their common heritage'.[4] To achieve this purpose the Member States were required to 'accept the principles of the rule of law and of the enjoyment by all persons within its jurisdiction of human rights and fundamental freedoms'. Both Armenia and Azerbaijan have constitutions acknowledging these fundamental principles.[5]

The institutional framework of the Council consists of organs. There is a Committee of Ministers, the Parliamentary Assembly and the European Court of Human Rights (ECHR).

The Parliamentary Assembly consists of 626 members, elected by their national parliaments and based on the density of a country's population. The work of the Parliamentary Assembly is carried out by specialized committees, which address various issues, such as human rights.[6] This organ provides the Member States with Recommendations on a domestic situation. The Committee of Ministers is the decision-making body of the Council of Europe, consisting of the foreign affairs ministers of each Member State. The Committee formats answers to Europe-wide questions, and is charged with the task of supervising the execution of judgments[7] and thus these actions of the committee are relevant for the purposes of this article.

The Court of Justice is the instance charged with legal procedures. It handles both the admissibility and the applicable rights. It acknowledges two important legal rights: the obligatory right for the individuals to submit applications to the Court and the mandatory jurisdiction of the Court.[8] The Court is authorized with binding final judgments. It seeks to find answers on legal questions relating to interpretations of the ECHR of Member States (Art. 47 ECHR) in a reasoned opinion.[9]

Since there is no legal obligation to insert the text of the Convention into domestic laws, the implementation of the Convention has become a matter of legal technique. However, States are obliged 'to ensure that their domestic legislation is compatible with the Convention and, if need to be, to make any necessary adjustments to this end'.[10]

According to Article 1 of the Convention, States are liable for violation of it, for instance if national laws are incompatible with the Convention or if public authorities act against the ECHR.

Article 10 of the Convention: Freedom of Speech

Rights of the Convention

The rights that the Convention confers upon the citizens of the contracting States deal with obligations of the State. The duties that correlate to human rights can be divided in different categories: the first category refers to certain limits of state power and are known as 'freedoms from' guaranteed by the State. Non-intervention of the State is the main characteristic of these rights. They are called political and civil rights. The second group of rights deals with economic, social and cultural rights. They are referred to as 'freedoms' but in fact they require State involvement and active State action. Contrary to the first group of rights this group cannot exist without the intervention of the State and it includes rights such as the right to education, social welfare, economic equality, and cultural heritage.[11]

For the purposes of this article we concentrate on Article 10 that guarantees freedom of expression and reads as follows:

1   Everyone has the right to freedom of expression. These rights shall include freedom to hold opinions and to receive and impart information and ideas without interference by public authority and regardless of frontiers. This Article shall not prevent States from requiring licences of broadcasting, television or cinema enterprises.

2   The exercise of these freedoms, since it carries with it duties and responsibilities, may be subject to such formalities, conditions, restrictions or penalties as are prescribed by law and are necessary in a democratic society, in the interests of national security, territorial integrity or public safety, for the prevention of disorder or crime, for the

protection of health or morals, for the protection of the reputation or rights of others, for preventing the disclosure of information received in confidence, or for maintaining the authority and impartiality of the judiciary.

In order to understand more clearly the way in which the Court rules, a technical description of this article's functions follows. As we can see, Article 10 consists of two parts.[12] The first paragraph sets out a right that is qualified in the second paragraph of the article by a list of limitations. Implicit among these is the intervention of authorities to protect rights under certain prescribed conditions. When a State seeks to rely on a limitation to protect those rights which come under Part 1, there could be a breach to a personal individual right. To find out whether a breach exists, the Court follows a three-part examination. Firstly, it determines whether the interference is in accordance with, or prescribed by, law; secondly, it looks to see whether the aim of the limitation is legitimate in the specific circumstances; and finally it questions whether the restriction is necessary in a democratic society. Central to this determination is the proportionality of the interference in securing the legitimate aim. Any interference of authorities with the rights named in these articles has to be in accordance 'with the law' or 'prescribed by law'. These references mean that interference with Convention rights has to be based on national law and should be foreseeable in national law. Nationals are given the right to know the substance of their legal rights. However, the law does have not to be statutory. For instance, a law that interferes with a political and civic right could consist of the rules of a Veterinary Surgeons' Council[13] that also need to be formulated precisely enough to make the rights of the citizen clear.

Restrictions on the Freedom of Speech

What are possible restrictions on the freedom of speech? In relation to restrictions, there are a variety of requirements mentioned in the second paragraph of Article 10. This deals with the question of whether intervention by authorities is necessary in a democratic society. This includes in both articles the implication that any action taken by authorities is in response to a pressing social need and that the interference with protected rights is the minimum action possible in meeting the requirements of a pressing social need. As said before, the limitations should be 'provided by law', and 'necessary in a democratic society' to serve a legitimate purpose. The latter requirement is called the 'test of proportionality'. According to this test the Court is expected to balance the severity of the restriction placed on the person against the common interests of society, the public interest. The formulation of this has been given by the Court in the Silver case in which the Court states that 'The Contracting States enjoy a certain but not unlimited margin of appreciation in the matter of the imposition of restrictions, but it is the Court to give the final ruling on whether they are compatible with the Convention; the phrase "necessary in a democratic society" means that, to be compatible with the Convention, the interference must, inter alia, correspond to a "pressing social need" and be "proportionate to the legitimate aim pursued".'[14] This is called the Margin of Appreciation of the State. Let us now consider the scope of this Margin of Appreciation, as related to the freedom of speech.

The Scope of the Margin of Appreciation

In its rulings the Court of Human Rights has provided the contours for the Margin of Appreciation. These are best known from case law in which the Court has stated: 'Freedom of expression constitutes one of the essential foundations of a (democratic) society, one of the basic conditions for its progress and for the development of every man. Subject to paragraph 2 of Article 10, it is applicable not only to information or ideas that are favorably received or regarded as inoffensive, but also to those that offend, shock or disturb the state or any sector of the population. Such are the demands of that pluralism, tolerance and broadmindedness without which there is no democratic society.'[15] In the first place it is up to national authorities to make pluralism, tolerance and broadmindedness acceptable through means of free speech. They are, by reason of their direct and continuous contact with vital forces in their countries, 'in a better position than the international judge to give an opinion on the exact content of these requirements as well as on the "necessity" of a "restriction" or "penalty" intended to meet them.'[16] The Court has a supervisory function which obliges it to pay the utmost attention to the principles that characterize a 'democratic society'.[17] However, the Court has never explicitly discussed the extent of the concept 'democratic society'. It implies all kind of values, such as pluralism, tolerance, broadmindedness, equality, liberty and self-fulfillment, together with the rights named in the Convention.[18] As indicated by the Court, the national authority is the principle public body that must balance all the interests at stake.

Various forms of freedom of expression can be distinguished. They range from political speech to criticism of the judiciary, hate speech, to matters concerning public morality. The first type of expression, called political speech, has to do with the functioning of democracy itself. As it forms one of the basic elements of a democratic society, the Court of Human Rights affords less protection to politicians than to citizens who use their right of free speech and are blamed for criticizing officials. When journalists published articles criticizing the former Austrian Chancellor, the Court stated that, 'The limits of acceptable criticism are accordingly wider as regards a politician as such than as regards a private individual. Unlike the latter, the former inevitably and knowingly lays himself open to close scrutiny of his every word and deed by both journalists and the public at large, and must consequently display a greater degree of tolerance...'[19]

The margin of tolerance should be much wider when free political debate is the subject of discussion. The Court noted that 'the limits of permissible criticism are wider with regard to the Government, by virtue of its dominant position, than in relation to a private citizen, or even a politician.'[20] The 'criticism of the judiciary' is another form of freedom, which has granted a wide margin of appreciation to national authorities. The background to this attitude is the intent to maintain confidence in the judiciary. *The Sunday Times*-case made it clear that the 'notion of the authority of the judiciary is objective.' [21]

The third type, 'hate speech', is a phenomenon that comes under the protection of freedom of speech, although the Court is inclined to hold restrictions on this type of speech. Historical experience of societies is of importance for their attitude towards hate speech.[22] On the point of freedom of expression and public morals the court emphasizes 'the nature and requirements of morals vary from one country to another, from one region to another'.[23] The Court acknowledges that there is no uniform concept of public morality to justify expressions that 'shock' or 'disturb' or 'offend'.[24] But the court also held that 'as a matter of principle it may be considered necessary in certain democratic societies to sanction or even prevent improper attacks on objects of religious veneration, provided always that any "formality", "condition", "restriction" or "penalty" imposed be proportionate to the legitimate aim pursued...'[25]

This article focuses on the political meaning of freedom of speech, to which in the case law of the Court more protection is afforded than to artistic expression. In order to balance the interests at stake the Court uses the doctrine of the margin of appreciation. The Court is also forced to use this doctrine, due to the diversity of legal and cultural traditions among the Member States that incorporate the European Convention.[26] Armenia and Azerbaijan are examples of cultural and legal diversity. This raises queries concerning the participation of these countries in the European Convention of human rights and the meaning of political freedom of expression in these countries.

Participation of Armenia and Azerbaijan in the European Convention

What is the position of Armenia and Azerbaijan concerning Article 10 of the European Convention? Azerbaijan and Armenia joined the Council on 1 January 2001; Azerbaijan was allocated six seats in the Parliamentary Assembly; Armenia, four.

On entering the European Convention the leaders of the two countries, Kocharyan of Armenia and Aliyev of Azerbaijan, pledged their commitment to the Council's ideals. Kocharayan, acknowledging that his country still had a long way to go, said:

> With its full accession to the Council of Europe, Armenia is registering a considerable degree of progress in democracy-building. We realize that we are still in the middle of this road. Meanwhile, Armenia is committed to full and timely observance of its post-accession obligations.

Aliyev also admitted to the large amount of work that had to be done to build a democracy in his country by saying:

> The process of implementing reforms and democratic changes is a work in progress. Reforms will be implemented, not because of the reforms in themselves and not because anybody wants us to implement them. This must be done in a well-thought-out way and must be understood and accepted by our society.[27]

Coupled to the signing of the Convention for both countries was the acceptance of numerous conditions, such as signing and ratifying the European Convention for the Prevention of Torture and Inhuman or Degrading Treatment or Punishment and its Protocols, the Council of Europe's

Framework Convention for the Protection of National Minorities, the European Charter for Regional or Minority Languages, the European Charter of Local Self-Government, the European Social Charter, the Criminal Law Convention on Corruption and the Civil Law Convention on Corruption and many more laws and protocols, such as the Code of Criminal Procedure, the law on the Ombudsman and an agreement on the release of 'political prisoners'; to guarantee freedom of expression and the independence of the media and journalists they had to agree to re-examine and amend the law on the media, to turn the national television channel into a public channel, managed by an independent administrative board and to cooperate fully in the setting up of a monitoring committee and to cooperate in the monitoring process. Also, the judiciary became part of the signing and ratification process, including promises to re-examine and amend the law on the bar, the re-examination and amendment of the procedures for appointing judges and accepting the rule of law. A huge number of measures, laws and new instruments had to be accepted and had to become implemented in the national systems of Armenia and Azerbaijan.

When discussing Azerbaijan's application for membership in its Opinion No. 222, the Parliamentary Assembly stated that Azerbaijan was moving towards a democratic, pluralist society in which 'human rights and the rule of law are respected, and, in accordance with Article 4 of the Statute of the Council of Europe, is able and willing to continue the democratic reforms initiated in order to bring its entire legislation and practice into conformity with the principles and standards of the Council of Europe'.[28] More or less the same was said by the Committee of Ministers about the admittance of both countries. It stressed the need of implementation of substantial democratic reforms.

A motive for the Council to answer to the application could be found in the consideration of the Parliamentary Assembly that the accession of both Azerbaijan and Armenia could help to establish the climate for a solution to the Nagorno-Karabakh conflict.[29]

After joining the Convention, the unstable political systems of both countries were monitored on a regular basis by the Parliamentary Assembly. The reports of the Parliamentary Assembly show the difficulties the newly acceded members have in finding their way to become democratic societies in terms of the European Convention

Reports on Violation of Freedom of Expression in Armenia and Azerbaijan

Azerbaijan

In 2002, the Resolution 1272 of the Parliamentary Assembly indicated some encouraging results but also stressed the importance of the rules of a fair hearing and asked for the review of the cases of alleged political prisoners;[30] in the 2004 Resolution it was said that many of the political prisoners had been convicted, even when the presiding judge acknowledged that there was no criminal evidence.[31] In Resolution 1398 of 2004 on the Functioning of Democratic Institutions in Azerbaijan, the Assembly noted that, despite the requests made in an earlier resolution in 2004, some political and alleged political prisoners were in jail and people still ran the risk of being arrested for political reasons. More expressly, the Assembly stated that 'the freedom of expression is not guaranteed in practice and journalists are increasingly engaging in self-censorship...' and with regard to the media, the Assembly notes that 'the independent media in Azerbaijan should be able to resume their activities without being constantly threatened or harassed'.[32] In 2005, the ad hoc committee set up to observe parliamentary elections in Azerbaijan said that – although the election law stipulated that political parties are entitled to free broadcast time – the possibilities for candidates who did not belong to a certain political bloc or party, to present their views on politics were restricted. The State-funded broadcaster AzTV showed news in favor of the ruling party and gave no attention to the opposition, failing to meet its legal requirements.[33]

Complaints about political prisoners still continued. The Recommendation of 2005 stated that the Committee of Ministers urged the Azerbaijani authorities to find a speedy and permanent solution to the issue of political prisoners. Examples were given of serious dysfunctions in the justice system in Azerbaijan and the shortcomings of its criminal legislation. Presumed political prisoners should be sentenced in accordance with the requirements of a fair trial, as laid down in the Convention and case-law of the Court.[34] Independent journalism and free press were threatened: 'Intimidation, physical violence, and even murder or reporters and editors have become commonplace.'[35]

Azerbaijan currently has the highest number of arrested journalists among all 56 Member States of the Organization for Security and Cooperation in Europe (OSCE). Recently a newspaper publisher and editor-in-chief was sentenced to two-plus years prison for slander. Only by the intervention of local journalists, human rights activists and American and British diplomats, had the closure been stopped.[36] A further illustration of the seriousness of the situation is that of approximately 50 journalists putting pressure on the media.[37]

More recently in 2008, it was reported that four journalists 'facing national security charges are freed on bail' for the sum of 50 million *toumen* (45,000 euros) but they were still charged with 'conspiracy' and 'offence against national security'.[38] Yet another reported incident was: 'Press freedom activist hospitalised since being mistreated in Baku police station.'[39] And there are many more negative reports, such as the one under the heading of 'Assaults continue on Azerbaijani reporter,' of May 2008, on the physical assaults on Agil Khalik, a reporter for the opposition daily, Azadlyg;[40] the Amnesty International Report 2008 states that 'Freedoms of expression and assembly continue to be widely restricted' and that police not only use excessive force to prevent journalists from reporting or filming, but also torture or other ill-treatment is being used by law enforcement officials. Even deportation and extradition are routine. [41]

Evidently, at the level of public authority, there is still a lack of compliance with commitment to freedom of speech.

Armenia

In 2004, the Parliamentary Assembly presented a written query to the Committee of Ministers, stating that Armenia 'is continuing systematically and manifestly its unlawful activities' and asked: 'What measures can be taken by the Committee of Ministers to implement the requirements of the Statute and cease the membership of Armenia which is violating the Parliamentary Assembly principles of this Organisation?'[42]

A report on the 2007 parliamentary elections in Armenia confirmed this question, stating that 'none of the elections organised in Armenia since its independence were considered to be conducted in line with the Council of Europe standards for democratic elections'. The Parliamentary elections on 12 May 2007 were different, as Armenia demonstrated 'its political will to organise genuinely democratic elections'.[43] This time the public media adhered to the legal provisions for equal access to free airtime for political parties involved in the elections. However, it is remarkable that the media still showed partiality in favor of the ruling parties and reporting on opposition parties was significantly limited.

Only a year later, in its Resolution 1609 (2008) on the functioning of democratic institutions in Armenia, the Assembly Parliamentary reiterated that there was a clear lack of public confidence in the electoral process, a lack of impartiality in the election administration, and a lack of transparency in the vote count. And 'despite successful legislative reforms, the courts still lack the necessary independence'. Further it stated: 'Even though there is a pluralistic and independent print media, the current level of control by the authorities of the electronic media and their regulatory bodies, as well as the absence of a truly independent and pluralist public broadcaster, impede the creation of a pluralistic media environment and further exacerbate the lack of public trust in the political system.'[44] It was indicated 'that progress has been insufficient, despite the political will expressed by the Armenian authorities to address the requirements laid out in that resolution'. Therefore, the Assembly addressed concrete demands to the Armenian authorities: it decided to consider the possibility of suspending the voting rights of the members of the Armenian parliamentary delegation to the Assembly at its January 2009 part-session, if the requirements laid down in Resolution 1609 (2008) were not met by that time.[45] A remarkable standpoint, perhaps, but understandable, taking into consideration the facts of limitations on press and media freedom. Most physical attacks took place at election-related rallies or during government functions which the media was trying to cover. In the same category are the attack on the Editor-in-Chief of the opposition newspaper Iskakan Iravuk by unidentified assailants and his subsequent hospitalization and the criminal charges filed by the police against two opposition editors in October 2008. Both were charged with inciting violence by attending an opposition rally.[46]

These examples demonstrate that incidents of interference with the freedom of expression are not exceptional. In order to restrict forms of unnecessary interference, the Parliamentary Assembly of the Council of Europe presented a document on freedom of the press and the working conditions of journalists in conflict zones in 2005.[47] This document makes clear that serious violations of the freedom of the media occur, including cases of physical aggression towards journalists. Aggression used consists of threats and imprisonments, carried out in such a way that 'Reporting on corruption, financial abuses, drug trafficking and terrorism could still be a potential life hazard for journalists everywhere in Europe.'[48] This, while freedom of expression and information in the media are seen as an essential requirement for democracy. More recently, in 2008, national parliaments were invited by the Assembly to analyze their media situation on a regular basis and to compare the national system with other systems in order to find shortcomings.[49]

To encourage the freedom of expression, the Council of Europe has set clear standards on media freedom: journalists should not be imprisoned and panel law against incitement to hatred or for the protection of public order or national security must respect the right to freedom of expression. Journalists should set up their own professional codes of conduct and disclose to their readers any political and financial interest. The Assembly has declared that state officials should not be protected against criticism and insults to any greater extent than ordinary people and that political parties and candidates must have fair and equal access to the media. Also, the media should be free to disseminate their program content in the language of their choice. Next to these requirements, transparency is seen as a valued requirement in the context of media ownership and influence.[50]

In some states the authorities are more inclined to confer rights upon citizens and groups. In those states it is less necessary to monitor the authorities than in others where there is an ongoing struggle to prevent national authorities and institutions from contravening freedom of expression. Political pressure is put on states with a lesser evident democratic system that cannot guarantee freedom of expression to their citizens. However, the obligations of a state cannot be enforced by legal measures.

One of the constructive parts of the European Convention is the fact it acknowledges claims of individuals. The Court is able to receive complaints when all efforts to settle it on a national level have been taken and national remedies have been exhausted. This obligation can cause a variety of difficulties for the individual, for example, financial and psychological challenges. Even greater problems can arise if the judiciary is not considered impartial, in repressive political systems. Nevertheless, proceedings brought before the Court may end in a solution which could not be obtained at national level, as the Court follows a fixed way of reasoning by applying Article 10.

Case-law of the Court of Human Rights

At first sight it is striking that only a few cases against Armenia and Azerbaijan have been brought before the European Court of Human Rights on the topic of freedom of expression. Six cases have been lodged against the Republic of Armenia on the subject of Article 10; seven cases have been lodged against the Republic of Azerbaijan. In the majority of these cases the court ruled non-applicability because of the non-entering into force of the treaties between those countries and the European Convention.[51] There were only two condemnations, one against Armenia and one against Azerbaijan, which will be described in detail as follows.

The first case to be considered is that of Mahmudov and Agazade versus the Republic of Azerbaijan. The applicants were two Azerbaijani nationals, Mr Rovshan Asgar oglu Mahmudov and Mr Yashar Vaqif oglu Agazade. They stated that their conviction for publishing an allegedly defamatory article had constituted a violation of their freedom of expression. According to Para 6 of the verdict the facts are the following: 'The first applicant was the acting chief editor of the *Müxalifet* newspaper. The second applicant was a journalist working for the same newspaper. According to facts in the judgement, in its issue of 12-18 April 2003, the newspaper published an article named 'Grain Mafia in Azerbaijan' under the by-line of Samir Sharif, a pseudonym of the second applicant. The article was accompanied by a picture of J.A., who was a member of the National Academy of Sciences, a well-known expert in agriculture and a member of the Milli Mejlis (Parliament). The article spoke mainly about a number of problems in the country's agricultural sector. It also appeared to imply, amongst other things, that J.A. was in charge of the breeding of certain experimental crops in "experimental" fields in several agricultural districts. J.A.'s name was printed in full in the article itself.' The article deals with subjects such as corruption and the dismissal of certain government officials for reasons which remain obscure. It also accuses President Aliyev of nepotism and it pointed a finger at the country's agricultural policy in which thousands of hectares of fertile land had been turned into experimental zones for 'valuable sorts' of grains. A special group of people monopolized the grain-growing industry. It accuses the agriculture mafia that hold fertile land hostage, under the label of 'state land fund'. It blames this mafia for selling equipment to the peasant at a much too high cost, which leads to an increase of the personal wealth of their gang.

On 23 April 2003, J.A. filed a criminal complaint with the Yasamal District Court. He claimed that the newspaper article was offensive to him and that the article implied that he was in close contact with certain alleged criminal circles. He felt himself accused of serious crimes such as abuse of state funds; he accused the first applicant of failing to prevent this. Both applicants denied the accusations. The Yasamal District Court convicted the applicants of defamation and insult under Articles 147.1 and 148 of the Criminal Code. The Court noted that the applicants' denial of the fact that the article had anything to do with J.A. was without grounds, because the text of the article clearly mentioned J.A.'s name in full. The court's verdict was a total five-month imprisonment under the Articles mentioned before. However, at the same time, Section 2.3 of the Milli Mejlis (Parliament) Resolution on Amnesty in Connection with the Anniversary of the Victory over Fascism in World War II, dated 6 May 2003, was applied and the court excused them from serving their sentences. Even so, the applicants appealed. The Court of Appeal upheld the Yasamal District Court's judgment. So did the Supreme Court. Applicants then went to the Court of Human Rights, alleging that there had been an unjustified interference with their right to freedom of expression.

The Court had to answer the question whether the interference was 'prescribed by law' and pursued the legitimate aim of protecting the reputation and rights of others and if it was 'necessary in a democratic society'. To that purpose the Court considered that the applicants' conviction by the national courts amounted to 'interference' with their right to freedom of expression. Was the interference justified? The conviction was based on the criminal code and that was meant to protect the 'reputation of rights of others', namely J.A. The interference was accordingly 'prescribed by law' and had a legitimate aim under Article 10 par. 2 of the Convention. But was the conviction, in the eyes of the Court, also 'necessary in a democratic society?' In its deliberation the Court put stress on some general principles. 'In cases such as the present one, concerning the press, the national margin of appreciation is circumscribed by the interest of the democratic society in ensuring and maintaining a free press. Similarly, that interest will weigh heavily in the balance in determining, as must be done under paragraph 2 of Article 10, whether the restriction was proportionate to the legitimate aim pursued.' The Court's opinion on this point was that the press fulfils a 'public watchdog' function and that the duty of the press is 'to impart information and ideas on political issues and on matters of general interest' and the subject of agriculture concerned a matter of public interest.[52] Regarding J.A.'s complaint that he was indicated as 'a certain known person' the Court stated again that a public figure, such as a politician, should be more open to criticism than a private individual. Only the words 'mafia' used in the title and the words 'experimental fields' were considered defamatory in their context.[53]

Finally, in judging whether there was a 'pressing social need', the Court stated that one should distinguish between facts and value judgments. The latter are difficult to prove but they should have a firm basis. The Court considered that the expression 'mafia' was deliberately false information within the meaning of Article 47.1 of the Criminal Code but that this expression was not directly used in reference to J.A.; the Court under-lined that journalistic freedom covers a certain degree of provocation. On the other hand, the Court observed that the phrase about 'experimental fields' was a statement of fact. The Court illustrated this presumption by quoting the various sentences of monopolist activity by J.A.[54] However, in this connection, the Court reached the conclusion that applicants refused to support their assertions with any evidence, that the given facts were generally-known facts and also that the fact of 'directly accusing specific individuals by mentioning their names and positions' placed the appli-cants in the position to prove their statements. The assertions of the ap-plicants were considered to be without sufficient factual basis and for that reason the interference of the authorities was considered relevant. The question of the proportionality of the sanction implied the duty of the media was to fulfill their role of alerting the public of misuse of public power. As the fear of being sentenced to imprisonment could have a chill-ing effect on the journalistic freedom of expression, the given sentences were found too severe. Therefore the Court concluded that, 'although in-terference with the applicants' right to freedom of expression may have been justified, the criminal sanction imposed was disproportionate to the legitimate aim pursued by the applicants' conviction for insult and defa-mation'.[55] The domestic courts went beyond the 'necessary' in restricting the applicants' freedom of expression. In its final judgment of 18 Decem-ber 2008, the Council declared that there had been a violation of Article 10 of the Convention.

Next is the case of Meltex ltd and Mesrop Movsesyan versus Armenia. This case was lodged with the Court by a limited company, Meltex Ltd, and its chairman, Mr Mesrop Movsesyabn, the applicants of the case. The background facts are: Mr Mesrop became involved in TV broadcasting in January 1991 when he established a television company, which should have been the first independent television company in Armenia, the so-called A1 + Television Company. A license for broadcasting gave permis-sion to A1+ Television Company to broadcast during an assigned period. While broadcasting, A1+ received much criticism from public officials regarding the contents of its programs. For example, during the run-up to the presidential elections, A1+ refused to limit its emissions to pro-gov-ernmental materials. Consequently State broadcasting activity was post-poned in May 1995. After that Mr Mesrop established and registered A1+ as an independent broadcasting company outside State control, which became structured as the original television company A1+. In 1996, it was granted a license by the Ministry of Communication giving it permission to install a transmitter in Yerevan and to broadcast. Later, A1+ established a network of nine privately-licensed regional television companies.[56] In 2000-2001, legislative changes were introduced in the spheres of television and radio broadcasting. A new licensing and monitoring system would improve control over private television and radio companies. A1+'s license was replaced with a new one granted just for a couple of months. In the meantime, a National Television and Radio Commission Act was introduced, calling for tenders for various broadcasting frequencies. A1+ applied for a tender for band 37. There were several other applications and, since A1+'s request was refused by the National Television and Radio Commission (NTRC), A1+ ceased to broadcast and started legal proceedings against NTRC, claiming the annulment of the refusal. The national court dismissed A1+'s claims.

In May 2003, the NTRC put out another call for tenders for band 25 and, in October 2002, it announced a new call for tenders for five other bands. All tenders were refused to A1+ and subsequently A1+ lodged two applications with the Commercial court, complaining about the function of NTRC in respect to the tenders. More specifically, it complained about the lack of any notification of the reasons behind refusal of tenders. The Commercial court distinguished between cases in which licenses had been awarded on the basis of the results of a tender process and other cases. In the case in question, the decision of NTRC not to grant a license was considered as based on competition. The court concluded that A1+ had been informed in a timely and lawful manner about the decisions concerning the tender process.[57] In appeal the Court of Cassation dismissed the appeals as unfounded and A1+ complained to the European Court of Human Rights about the license refusals, stating that they amounted to a violation of its freedom of expression.

Firstly, the European Court of Human Rights discussed whether there had been interference with the applicant company's freedom to impart information and ideas. The Court reasoned from the types of license and could not discern clear reasons for refusal. It states that there was interference because NTRC effectively refused to grant A1+ a license, which hindered A1+ in its freedom to impart information and ideas. Although States are allowed to regulate the freedom of expression by means of a licensing system, any interference should be founded on domestic law and refer to the law in question. In the opinion of the court, it would be contrary to the rule of law when an executive could have unlimited discretion in deciding on a request. The law should indicate the limitations of executive's discretion in order to offer protection to the individual against arbitrariness. Although the National Broadcasting Act defined criteria on which the NTRC could base its refusal, the Act did not prescribe that the licensing authority give reasons for its refusal, which led to A1+ not being made aware of the reasons behind the denial. The Court concluded that the licensing procedure did not offer 'adequate protection against arbitrary interferences by a public authority with the fundamental right to freedom of expression' by which the interference did not meet the requirements of the Convention. The violation of Article 10 was sustained but the claimed pecuniary damage because of lost anticipated income was refused because of lack of causal link between the alleged violation of Article 10 and the pecuniary damage claimed.[58] The aims of the interference had to be justified according to the third sentence of paragraph 1 of Article 10. In the view of the court it was obvious that the NTRS's letters that announced the results of the competition had not given grounds for the refusal. Therefore it was impossible for A1+ to know whether it met the license criteria. Lack of openness and transparency and adherence to the law made NTRC in breach of Article 10.

The above case law clearly demonstrates the importance of having access to the Court. However, even more essential is the enforceability of human rights. According to article 53 of the Convention, parties are officially committed to abide by the decisions of the Court in any case to which they are part. Nevertheless, a Member State that is unwilling to cooperate cannot effectively be forced to accept a Court decision in cases to which it is a party. This means that material enforcement on a Member State cannot be guaranteed. Only political force can be brought to bear on a Member State for being an undemocratic state.

Final Part

The Convention for the Protection of Human Rights and Fundamental Freedoms promotes the values of human rights as common values for all citizens of the Member States of the Convention. These values became, as political and normative elements, binding components for individuals in the original western European Member States. In contrast, the two countries, Armenia and Azerbaijan, were part of the Soviet system. Unlike Western European countries, they had no background of living with political and civil rights and freedoms when they joined the Convention. They are still countries in transition. In my opinion, this is the perspective from which we should look at the circumstances around violations of freedom of speech in these countries. However, they still remain contract in parties to the Convention and, as such, subdued to the legal system of the Convention. There is no doubt that the norms and values of the European convention should be sustained. To that purpose the Parliamentary Assembly and the Committee of Ministers of the Council are able to signal difficulties and dysfunctions of the domestic legal human rights systems. Their warnings and recommendations to national governments are especially needed for as long as the danger of these countries sliding back to a pre-accession situation is still there.

The international authorities of the Council of Europe have a shared responsibility, together with national public authorities, with regard to guaranteeing human rights protection. One of the essential features of the Convention system is the compulsory right of the individual position. The enormous number of complaints in the media about violation of Article 10 in Armenia and Azerbaijan, is shocking. But even more astonishing is the fact that so few individuals lodge complaints at the Court of Justice. Domestic judiciary procedures, or the lack of an efficacious legal aid system may be the cause. Although it is difficult to identify hard and fast rules governing the doctrine of freedom of speech,[59] the facts presented in this article are clear enough to start proceedings before the Court of Human Rights.

Member States in breach of contract of their obligations, are a clear demonstration of the extent to which their domestic legislation is in accordance with the requirements of the European Convention, or of the lengths to which national authorities are inclined to go in order to protect the validity of democratic rights in their country.

Continuing discussion with these Member States on the issues of adjustment of their state systems, as well as systematic monitoring of the judiciary, are needed. They form a minimum guarantee for improvement in the development of Armenia and Azerbaijan into entirely democratic, functioning members of the Convention.

Notes

1   Parliamentary Assembly of the Council of Europe (1993). The Parliamentary Assembly considers the political and human situations in the applying countries regularly and gives opinion about the application for membership.
2   Convention for the Protection of Human Rights and Fundamental Freedoms of 4 November 1950, entered into force on 3 September 1953.

3　The description of the position of the European Convention of Human Rights has been derived from the working paper of Versteegh, C.R.M. (2008) *Human Rights Enforceability under the European Union's Reform Treaty as an Incentive for Member States. The case of Hungary*. Working Papers European Studies. Amsterdam.

4　Article 1 (a) Statute of the Council of Europe, the Constitution of the Convention.

5　See: http://confinder.richmond.edu/ under Armenia and under Azerbaijan

6　Also other issues are dealt with such as social, health and family affairs, economic affairs and development and equal opportunities for men and women.

7　Article 46 (2) of the Convention provides: 'The final judgement of the Court shall be transmitted to the Committee of Ministers, which shall supervise its execution'.

8　Article 34 of the Protocol 11 that entitles any person, NGO or group of individuals claiming to be the victim of a violation to bring the case directly before the Court without restriction.

9　Ovey, C. & White, R. (2006: 11-12), *The European Convention on Human Rights*. Oxford: University Press. There is a strict framing of the conditions of advisory opinion. That is why this procedure has not been used yet. On the contrary the advisory opinion procedure under the Inter-American Convention on Human Rights has proved to be fruitful.

10　Court of Justice, Case 9 June 1958, 214/56, De Becker versus Belgium.

11　Cassese, A. (1986: 310-311), *International law in a divided world*, Oxford: Clarendon.

12　Articles 8, 9 and 11 of the Convention consist of the same system.

13　European Court of Human Rights, Judgement of 23 March 1985, Barthold versus Germany; Series A, No 90; (1985) 7 EHRR 383.

14　European Court of Human Rights, Judgement of 25 March 1983, Silver versus United Kingdom, Series A, No 61; (1983) 5 EHRR 347, Para 97 of the judgement.

15　European Court of Human Rights, Judgement of 7 December 1976, Handyside versus United Kingdom, Series A, No 24; (1979-1980) 1 EHRR 737, par. 48.

16　European Court of Human Rights (7 December 1976: para 48). Ibid.

17　European Court of Human Rights (7 December 1976: para 26) Ibid.

18　Ovey & White (2006: 233). Ibid.

19　European Court of Justice, Judgement of 8 July 1986, Lingens versus Austria, nr. 9815/82, Para 42.

20　European Court of Human Rights. Judgement of 23 April 1992, Castells versus Spain, nr. 11798/85, Para 46.

21 European Court of Human Rights. Judgement of 26 April 1979. *The Sunday Times* versus United Kingdom, No 6538/74, Para 59.

22 Bakricioglu, O. (2007: 726 note 78). 'The application of the Margin of Appreciation Doctrine on Freedom of Expression and Public Morality Cases.' In: *German Law Journal*, no. 7, compares the European system to the system in the United States where hate speech is regarded as a price society has to accept to pay freedom of expression.

23 European Court of Human Rights. Judgement of 14 May 1988, Muller & Others versus Switzerland, nr. 10737/84, Para 16.

24 European Court of Human Rights (7 December 1976). Ibid. The Court did not take into account the fact the book was published in several other states, including Belgium, France, Germany, Greece, Italy and Sweden.

25 European Court of Human Rights. Judgment of 20 September 1994. Otto-Preminger-Institute versus Austria, nr.13470/87, Para 49.

26 Bakriciogly (2007: 730-731). Ibid, shows the inconsistent application of the doctrine and the uncertainties critics are not always able to deal with.

27 Radio Free Europe, 25 January 2001. See: www.rferl.org/content/article/1095594.html (visited 27 March 2009).

28 Parliamentary Assembly of the Council of Europe. Opinion No. 222 (2000). Assembly debate on 28 June 2000. See Doc. 8748, *Report of the Political Affairs Committee*, Reporter: Mr Baumel, and Doc. 8757, Opinion of the Committee on Legal Affairs and Human Rights, reporter: Mr Clerfayt. Text adopted at the same date.

29 The Nagorno-Karabakh conflict is about the area Nagorno – Karabakh formally a part of Azerbaijan, but de facto self-declared independent and mostly populated by Armenians. See Chapter 5.

30 Parliamentary Assembly. Resolution 1272 (2002) 1, *Political prisoners in Azerbaijan*, nr, 8-12.

31 Parliamentary Assembly. Resolution 1359 (2004) 1, *Political prisoners in Azerbaijan*, nr. 13.

32 Resolution 1398 (2004, nr, 7 – 9). Implementation of Resolution 1358 (2004) on the functioning of democratic institutions in Azerbaijan.

33 Elections in Azerbaijan 2005, Ad hoc committee to observe the parliamentary elections in Azerbaijan. 6 November 2005. Reporter: Mr Leo Platvoet (Netherlands/UEL). Nr. VI.

34 Parliamentary Assembly. Recommendation 1711 (2005). Follow-up to Resolution 1359 (2004) on political prisoners in Azerbaijan, nr. 5.

35 Report: CIS countries are the 'world's most dangerous places for journalists', 25 June 2007. UNHCR Ref World. See: http://www.unhcr.org/refworld/docid/46c58ef021.html (visited 25 March 2009).

36 Eurasia Net, 'Azerbaijan tops the charts for number of imprisoned journalists', 22 May 2007. Online: http://www.unhcr.org/refworld/docid/46f258a544.html (visited 25 March 2009).

37 Radio Free Europe (14 June 2007). 'Police break up journalists' demonstration in Baku'. http://www.unhcr.org/refword/docid/469f5b8a1e.html (visited 25 March 2009).

38 Reporters Without Borders, 10 November 2008, 'Four journalists facing national security charge are freed on bail', 10 November 2008 Online: http://www.unhcr.org/refworld/docid/49193c15.html (visited 25 March 2009)

39 Reporters Without Borders,(20 June 2008). 'Press freedom activist hospitalised since being mistreated in Baku police station', 20 June 2008. Online: http://www.unhcr.org/refworld/docid/485f4c0216.html (visited 25 March 2009).

40 Committee to Protect Journalists (20 March 2009) 'Assaults continue on Azerbaijani reporter'. Online: http://www.unhcr.org/refworld/docid/48358a9136.html (visited 25 March 2009).

41 Amnesty International, 'Amnesty International Report 2008'- Azerbaijan, 28 May 2008. On line: http://www.unhcr.org/refworld/docid/483e27793.html (visited 25 March 2009).

42 Parliamentary Assembly (4 October 2004). Doc. 10308, 'Cessation of the membership of the Republic of Armenia in the Council of Europe'. Written question no 455 to the Committee of Ministers.

43 Council of Europe, Ad hoc committee to observe the parliamentary elections in Armenia (12 May 2007) Leo Platvoet (The Netherlands, UEL), No.10.

44 Parliamentary Assembly (2008). Resolution 1609 on 'Functioning of democratic institutions in Armenia', nr. 6. See: http://assembly.coe.int/Main.asp?link=/Documents/AdoptedText/ta08/ERES1609.htm visited April 2009.

45 Parliamentary Assembly (2008). Resolution 1620 on the adoption of Resolution 1609.

46 Freedom House, Freedom of the Press 2008 – Armenia, 29 April 2008. http://www.unhcr.org/refworld/docid/4871f5ebc.html visited 2 April 2009.

47 Parliamentary Assembly (15 November 2005). Doc. 10742 'Freedom of the press and the working conditions of journalists in conflict zones'. Recommendation 1702 (2005).

48 Parliamentary Assembly (30 September 1999). Doc. 8557 on 'Freedom of expression in Europe'. Motion for a Recommendation, nr. 1-4.

49 Parliamentary Assembly (7 July 2008). Doc. 11683 on 'Indicators for media in a democracy'. Report Committee on Culture, Science and Education. Nr. 3-8.

50 Parliamentary Assembly (2008, nr. 8) Doc. 11683. Ibid. The requirements are more or less literally taken from this report.

51 http://cmiskp.echr.coe.int/tkp197/portal.asp?sessionId=21145421& (visited 2 April 2009).

52 European Court of Human Rights, Judgement of 18 December 2008. Case of Mahmudov and Agazade versus Azerbaijan. Application no. 35877/04, Para. 37-38.

53 European Court of Human Rights, (18 December 2008: para 39 – 40). Ibid.

54 Reporters Without Borders (2008: para 41 – 43) Ibid.

55 Reporters Without Borders (2008: Para 53). Ibid.

56 European Court of Human Rights, Judgment of 17 June 2008, Case of Meltex Ltd and Mesrop Movsesyan versus Armenia, Application No. 32283/04, Final 17/9/2008, Para 5- 9 more or less literally.

57 Parliamentary Assembly Resolution 1609 (2008: Para 10 – 50). Ibid.

58 Parliamentary Assembly Resolution 1609 (2008: para 77 – 100). Ibid.

59 Bakircioglu, (2007: 722). Ibid. She states that merely general principles can be withdrawn from the case law of the Convention.

Eva Navarro Martínez

Introduction

Under the same moon: a meeting with artist Luba Mirjadova
(Baku, 2007)

Under the gypsy moon
things are looking at her
and she can not look them back.

These are the verses that inspired the last painting of Assyrian artist Javad
Mirjavadov (1923-1992). His wife, the painter and poet Luvob Mirjavadova, showed me the painting in her house in Baku, Azerbaijan, in April
of 2007. I was traveling there with a group of artists, art teachers and students taking part in a research project organized by the art school, Gerrit
Rietveld Academie in Amsterdam. The trip to Azerbaijan and Armenia
was the colophon of a series of conferences and research seminars held at
the school by artists and scholars from Caucasus or specialists on those
countries. The aim of our trip was to make contact with art institutions
and artists of the region and, eventually, to establish links between them
and Dutch or European art organizations for future projects.

I was brought to Luba's house by a young and brilliant photographer,
Rena Effendi, of whose work I will talk later. Luvob Mirjavadova lives in
one of the old parts of Baku, on the top of a hill, where tracks of Soviet
occupation are still visible in the kind of architecture. This part of the city
is composed of small and beautiful streets, which time has rendered dirty
and broken. Some of the houses are partially or completely collapsed, and
the ruins of some of them remain still in the streets, as dead elephants,
waiting to be replaced by the monstrous skyscrapers that are forming the
new landscape of the Baku.

Luba receives us very warmly. She is more than sixty years old but she
is full of energy when she talks and moves. Her clothes are marked with

paint; she has been working before our visit. Her house is her studio; or her studio is her house. We come in; the space is full of canvases, everywhere, and poems, written in Cyrillic, filling the little free spaces: on small pieces of walls, on the doors, on the furniture... My impression is that of having entered, literally, in a live work of art, a labyrinth of words and colors. I really feel like Alice in Wonderland, trapped in space and time. Among the canvases, an old gas kitchen is waiting to be brought to the trash. 'It almost killed me! – she says – it broke down and the whole house began smelling of gas... It almost killed me! It's from the Soviet time', she adds and we laugh. It is only an old gas kitchen, but here, among the poetry and paintings it looks like another piece of art: 'It is like a work of pop-art', I say, making her laugh loudly. She adds: 'a work of Soviet pop-art!' We all laugh again. I take photos of everything. The whole house is a work of art. She is also.

The kitchen, which is her atelier, smells of saffron, 'Iranian saffron', she explains, 'because the Spanish one, which is my favorite, is hard to find here', she says. She is cooking rice with lamb and saffron – for both of us, because she expects me to eat with her. It is almost lunchtime and she just asks if I like rice and lamb. She offers me a glass of wine. I am moved by the hospitality and kindness of this woman, by her great personality, and by the art surrounding me. Rena must go, but I will stay here to see her work. That is the reason I went there. Luba moves a lot, and I follow her from one part of the house to the other; she moves as we talk. She asks me about my trip and she tells me about her life, about her husband, and their lives as artists in the Soviet era. She is very critical about that period and also about the current government and the political and economic situation in Azerbaijan – 'they are still the same people... Almost nothing is changed; the oil magnates are destroying the city, building those horrible monsters of skyscrapers and taking all the money...' And then her critique moves on to religion, to Islam and, especially, to Islamic fundamentalism. Her work clearly reflects her 'ideological' principles, as we will see later.

She brings me to a room. It is a big room full of canvases and drawings by her and her husband. Some of the pictures are two meters high. There is nothing else in that space – only canvases and drawings, of herself and Javad, filling all the space. The light comes in through the one small window in the room, but this can't be reached since a big haze of canvases is placed before it.

'Are you from Granada?' – she asks – 'like Federico García Lorca... Beautiful!' She has never been there but she loved it. She seems to know a lot of Spanish artists and writers; also American and European. One could easily think that for a 'non-conformist' artist, Lorca is indeed a referent, since, after his murder by Franco's militaries, he became a kind of symbol of the repressed artists and civilians. So it is strange to find Lorca's coetaneous artists who take him, his figure and his work, as a symbol of 'anti-repression' and liberal political ideas. Lorca is, primarily, a good example of the struggle (through writing and art) of the individual against the established (and repressive) moralism and norms; he is an example of the struggle for freedom of expression and also for the artist who, above all, remains fair to his or her (personal and artistic) ideals and principles. People who know his work well can appreciate this, and so did Javad Mirjavadov. 'You are from Granada and you know Lorca's poetry, then you must recognize this... Look...' Luba asks me and then she takes my hand, places me in front of a picture and recites in English: 'under the gypsy moon, things are looking at her, but she can not look them back'. I am in front of a very strange picture. Choreography of green, white, blue and little bit of red forms a strange and primitive figure situated in the center of the painting, taking almost all the canvas's space. It is difficult to react to this painting and, actually, difficult to describe now what I was experiencing. 'I can't believe this, Luba, I don't know what to say.' I can't believe I am hearing Lorca's *Sleepwalking romance* (this is the poem's title) thousands of kilometers away from Granada. I am impressed by this work, by Luba's emotional words as she reads the verses, written in Cyrillic in the back of the canvas, as she tells me this was the last work of Javad Mirjavadov, painted a couple of days before dying. He was very ill as consequence of a brain attack and from that moment his work had become irrational, almost primitive; he had even covered some of his canvases with black paint and re-painted them again, but in a totally different style: closer to ancient and primitive paintings which had been a referent throughout his life. Indeed, this last work unites the irrationalism and the mystery of painting with the 'duende' (the soul) of Lorca's poetry and the Andalusian tradition; this painting unites different times, different cultures and different artistic traditions. Illness had devastated Javad's brain, but it had left him these verses, as the only table to cross to the 'other side'.

This was in April of 2007, and this is just one of the meetings I had with the Armenian and Azerbaijani artist. I had met some Azirian artists before coming to Luba's studio, one being the writer Ali Akbar, who would be my link to discovering other artists and writers in Yerevan. My trip from Azerbaijan to Armenia (through Iran, due to the conflict) made it possible for me to know, personally, the work of artists and writers from both countries and from different generations, and hear their positions and concerns as artists regarding their political, social and economic contexts. In the following pages I will come back to them and their cultural activities, in the context of national and international culture as well as in the context of some South Caucasus political and social transformations in the last decades.

The reason I begin this paper via this anecdotal yet crucial meeting with Rena Effendi, Luba and the work of Javad Mirjavadov, is in order to introduce, first of all, at least three generations of Azerbaijani artists, and secondly, to present some of the main themes to be developed in the following pages. These are: memory and time as themes in Caucasian art; tradition and modernity in the work of art; and the 'historical' tension between the artist as an individual defending a total freedom of creativity and the work of art, against any system or official culture. All of these themes will be analyzed alongside the social, political and cultural context of the Caucasus in the last decades of the twentieth century and the beginning of this millennium.

This paper will take a walk through some artists' work, which, as well as being original, controversial and individualist, reflects (more or less conscientiously) some ancient elements of South Caucasus cultural baggage, while at the time forming a bridge to coetaneous West(European) cultural artistic phenomena.

Through invisible paths: South Caucasian modern art beyond time and space

Before approaching Armenian and Azerbaijani art, I would like start making some comments regarding the character of a work of art in general and its role beyond the artistic world. Critical discussions on questions of 'pure art' or 'art for the sake of art' against art as a 'social value' or 'engaged art' have been held for more than two centuries;[1] but it was probably at the turn of the twentieth century, and, mainly due to the Avant-garde, that this discussion became stronger. Although the 'radical' artistic positions of the twentieth century artist made it possible to release art and culture, in general, from its social, political, ideological, etc., dependence or service, my starting point is that no work of art can be studied or completely understood without taking into account the context in which this work was created. This is, for example, the axial of the sociology of culture (from Bajtin, to Adorno, Barthes, Scarpit, etc.) and cultural studies (Stuart Hall, Raymond Williams, et al.). A cultural reading of art attempts to study it taking into account the social, historical, ideological, etc., structures behind cultural and artistic practices. Contextual components are not necessarily present 'a priori' in a work of art, but they can be found in it, due to its inner nature as 'product of its time.'[2]

We can extrapolate Barthes' statement that a writer's work always reflects the time in which it was written to the whole cultural field. This is what the empirical sociology of literature calls (Schmits, Scarpit) *mediations*.[3] But, at the same time, I agree with other twentieth-century critics and artists that art is not the mere illustration of life (though it can be) but rather a recreation of it, and also the idea that a work of art can only be 'devoted' to what Spanish philosopher Ortega y Gassed (1925) called 'the aesthetic pleasure' it can produce in the person who can appreciate its inner beauty, free from any social component.[4] The Azerbaijani art critic Dilara Vahabova, starts from this assertion in the introduction to the exhibition *The known as unknown held* by Yeni Qalereya (New Gallery) in Baku in 2005.[5] The exhibition tried to offer a 'representative panoramic' of Azerbaijanian art in the last half of the twentieth century. Art, Vahabova says, 'is a completely autonomous sphere of activity that exists under the immanent laws and obtains an exclusively specific language of expression. The plastic, line, color...'[6] The exhibition showed artists from both sides 'of the barricade,' that is to say, artists who 'collaborated with the state of power' during the Soviet system and those known as 'hardline non-conformists,' who rejected any form of restriction, ignoring the established rules and principles in their creative activity. This strong division between official and non-conformist artists seems to be the general line to describe artistic activity in Caucasus, in concrete in Azerbaijan, during the Soviet system, as seen in several articles and exhibitions dedicated to that time.[7] However, despite this strong division, they have, as Vahabova points out, a common characteristic, which, actually, is inherent to the nature of creativity: Time and History. According to her, those are 'unyielding phenomena,' which made it possible to unite into the whole the 'left and the right, the conformists and non-conformists, the archaists and innovators, here and now, at the present point at the present time,' no matter what style or trend this or that artist works in. 'For it's impossible to lie in art, and, in this respect, an art object of any epoch is the most real, most truthful document of its time.'[8] Indeed, the art historian is alluding here to the Barthesian idea that a work of art can't lie about its time and spatial circumstances.[9] Time – as Duration and History – is a decisive factor, she argues. It is time that unites people of many nationalities, ages and talents.[10] I consider this to be a very important statement, since it makes it possible to establish bridges not only within Caucasian art itself (due to a common history), but also with other European countries, as we will see in the following pages. Time, as the inner condition of any cultural activity, allows us to draw lines in both vertical and horizontal directions: vertical ones, through chronology and history; and horizontal ones, through (geographical) space, beyond 'local' and national borders. Artist and art critic Teymur Daimi traces both lines when he describes the trends and activities of Azerbaijani contemporary art. Regarding time, he affirms 'the modern culture of each country feeds on the invisible spiritual emanations of the historical past of the nation inhabiting that country.' And he adds, 'I think I am not mistaken if I say that the primeval art of Gobustan, carpet art and miniature painting generally appear to be the powerful cross-linking energetic basis on which Azerbaijani visual art of the twentieth century has been formed.'[11] Besides this, he establishes connections between Azerbaijani artists, their close environment, and the international cultural world. When he refers to art during the Soviet period, he distinguishes, as Vahabova did, between those artists directly influenced by the social realism and (quite aware) of being integrated in the established system, and those 'non-conformists,' who (also consciously) denied the socialist establishment and took as their artistic reference the Western European avant-garde.

However, artists are not always aware of the connections their works establishes with space and time, which is justified by Daimi through Derrida's concept of the 'psycho-semantic phenomenon.' According to the French philosopher, this phenomenon occurs when works of an author are actualized, not on the levels of surface meaning and those the author wants to attract attention to and, therefore, consciously emphasizes, but those meanings which unconsciously appear in the text in spite of or even contrary to the author's will. This is a level going beyond any ideological intention. And in this vein, the art professor Dickran Kouymjian writes, regarding Armenian artists, that they: 'whether creating in the homeland or the diaspora, are in the last analysis artists. As such they bring to their creativity, consciously or unconsciously, the legacy of heredity and environment that is each person's lot in the acting out of his or her life.'[12] So, the artist's individualism, tradition and context are encountered elements in a work of art, and we need to take this into account when we want to study it. I shall try to do this in my approach to some Armenian and Azerian artists' work.

Exile, memory and art as replacement

Throughout the twentieth century, Armenia and Azerbaijan have 'shared' some historical and political events, such as for example, some decades of Soviet occupation and later a conflict between both countries, which is still ongoing. Through this history, their inhabitants have suffered diasporas and exile, military conflicts and genocides, drastic economic, social and religious changes. Also, since ancient times, both countries have crossed spaces of different folkhoods and cultures, which have legated theirs cultural tracks.[13] All of these phenomena have undoubtedly influenced art and cultural production. In periods of conflicts or in the decades of Soviet occupation, artists of both countries had to make their work in exile, in prison, or in very difficult and even oppressive circumstances. Their work, when it was recognized (mostly abroad or after their deaths) is an alternative production to the official art promoted by the Soviet system. These artists, even if they sometimes didn't create in their own countries or if their work was not (or rarely) exhibited, are now considered a fundamental part of the Armenian and Azerbaijani cultural legacy; mostly, because their work is considered to be more personal, original and innovative than the official art.

With such questions, art historian Dickran Kouymjian opens an article about Armenian Art in Exile.[14] 'Although the artists are Armenian by their ethnic origin, many of them were born outside of Armenia or spent their entire creative life in countries other than Armenia. Is their art individually or collectively Armenian?'[15] As the author writes, when limiting the idea of Armenian art to those artists who live and work in Armenia, we might find a number of common factors. 'But are there such shared qualities among diasporean artists scattered over three continents with little, if any, contact among themselves or with the homeland? What then is Armenian art?'[16] Even if the question is difficult, the author identifies some common lines in Armenian art in exile. For instance, he refers to the family and its unity as a frequent and common theme, 'probably representing an attempt by the artist (Gorky, for example) to unite on canvas that which was dissolved by the Genocide.'[17] Another common characteristic, notes the critic, is the palette: colors tend to be deep, rich, brilliant, like those of the manuscript illuminations or oriental rugs and textiles so habitual in Armenian households. According to Kouymjian, another subtler, but still very frequent theme is the longing to escape from a reality that was not only difficult because of poverty and estrangement, but constantly disturbed by the memory of massacre and loss. 'This tendency is manifested in many ways: the flight to fantasy where nature is intentionally distorted or reordered (Gorky, Tutundjian, Garabedian, Altoon, Carzou) or surrendered to the precision and exactness of geometric abstractions (Tutundjian, Assadour, Vahramian, Mkrtchian), which instantly nullifies the normal unpredictability and messiness of real life.'[18]

Art as a way to reclaim a lost past and memories is an aspect that is actually the axis of the whole artistic output of artist Alakbar Rezaguliyev, especially in the last years of his life. Having been in prison or in exile for twenty-five years, he developed, after his return at home in Baku, a frenetic artistic activity till his death – as an attempt, as he would admit, to reclaim the 'lost time,' his ideas, and memories, all that prison and exile had taken from him.[19] He devoted the last decades of his life to making numerous black and white linoleum prints (since he never painted with colors after his exile), which represent ordinary life, people, and activities. They show a nostalgic view of the Baku of his childhood. But, as Patterson points out, 'his prints glorify work,' although not for the sake of production; rather 'the artist invites us to appreciate the mundane, ordinary and sheer physical process of creating with one's hands and mind.' Rezaguliyev, as another exiled and persecuted artist, places the individual and the system in opposition. Individual feelings, expression and creativity are placed beside the intimate pleasure of enjoyment with one's own work.

Another case of an artist who made part of his work in exile or in prison is the Armenian artist and film director Sergei Parajanov. Most of his screenplays were rejected or censured. One of his most important films, *The Color of Armenian Land* (1967), was censured and remade in Russia and would appear twenty years later in *Parajanov: The Last Spring*. Parajanov was arrested twice with different charges (once of homosexuality), but even in the periods he spent in prison, Parajanov continued to create his art, which helped him survive. Art for Parajanov was both an instrument of expression and a weapon against creative, ideological and personal oppression. He made madly fascinating (surrealist) collages and drawings, and wrote impressive and sometimes delirious letters. Parajanov's films had in his lifetime international recognition. His work reflected themes and scenes from Armenia and Caucasus but his style was always experimental and in the line of the Western avant-garde. Most of this work can be admired in the Sergei Parajanov Museum in Yerevan.[20]

Beauty and the Beast: The artist against the system

Until the Eighties, social-realism was the predominant style in art in the Soviet republics, including Armenia and Azerbaijan. For art critic Dilara Vahabova (closer to the official culture), this was not an impediment for the flowering of brilliant talents who, in the frame of realism, gave to painting a personal and original print. For artist and art critic Taymur Daimi (2002), the dominant socialist ideology, along with the 'neutral' non committal landscape, portrait and still-life genre, and the 'censured' or excluded cultural world of the 'non-conformist' artists, radically separated art of these countries from 'the modern art of more developed countries.' The result, according to Daimi, was the creation of a hermetic art and a certain 'spiritual sterilization' that he calls the *'iron curtain factor.'* 'After the formation of the Soviet Union, there prevailed a common mental-ideological regime, permeating almost all cells of the social and cultural life, and artificially separating soviet culture from the context of contemporary world culture.'[21] Nevertheless, those non-conformist artists – Javad Mirjavadov, Kamal Akhmedow, Rasim Babayev, Mislim Abbasov or Nazim Rahmanow, who were already working in the Sixties and Seventies – 'prepared a hidden "upheaval" in Azerbaijani art after 1985, during the agony of the communistic regime'. For art historian Dilara Vahabova, such artists formed part of a group devoted to expressing their inner world, their emotions and feelings, along with experimenting with expressive possibilities, rather than following the mainstream of official art. The artist looks inside himself and throws in work worries or questions of a philosophical or ontological character, more than social or daily life depictions. Another common tendency is to appeal to national and classic myths, legends and tales, trying to solve stylistic problems in a different way to that of Soviet propaganda.[22]

In the following pages I will focus on one of those non-conformist artists, Javad Mirjavadov, whose work (as I mentioned in the introduction) I had the opportunity of appreciating in the private collection of his wife, the poet and artist Luba Mirjavadova. She is currently busy with promoting his work, since it still does not have 'official' recognition. What I find interesting in his work, besides its strength and its terrible and awful beauty, are the connections he established with western avant-garde and, at the same time, with ancient Caucasian art and also with oriental and African primitive art.

During his studies in Leningrad when he was young, Mirjavadov learned about the West European avant-garde. As he declares in his notes and writings, masters such as Vincent van Gogh (one of his main artistic references), Gauguin, Salvador Dalí or Picasso occupied a privileged place as inspiration for his own art. Indeed the tracks of Impressionism, Expressionism or Fauvism are pretty visible in Mirjavadov's work; on one hand, the themes and techniques (the colors, style, inspiration in primitive and also oriental art, apology of countryside life and people) and on the other hand, the artistic philosophy and position of the artist in life (a critical view to the established system and rejection of burgees art, for instance). Before dying, Javad Mirjavadov wrote an 'autobiographical sketch,' entitled *My Eternal Path*, which is a kind of manifesto of what had been his artistic principles and their creative influences. His ideas about inner nature and his sense of art and of the artists recalls some of the statements of the avant-garde movements of the final years of the nineteenth century and the beginning of the twentieth. As he wrote:

> An artist is clairvoyant. He puts his creative work above life. Art goes ahead of science, it leads to mysterious distances, it helps people to understand themselves and the surrounding life, informs people of the invisible. An artist is a Messiah. The search for the meaning of life embodies vivid artistic forms; penetration into the unknown and the subconscious; prediction of one's own thought – all break loose miraculously in a painting; everything accumulated by you, by your ancestors and perhaps by life and many more things that are inexplicable – all this is creative work.[23]

Some of his statements –mainly, art as a search for the meaning of life – are common in the art world, especially in certain movements as Surrealism, which is partially inspired by Freudian theories, as we know. One of its main principles is, in fact, the penetration into the unknown, both to create 'a new reality' more beautiful, more interesting, special, etc., than the 'real life', and in order to acquire knowledge of the 'visible' reality, through the exploration of the 'invisible.'[24] According to these ideas, the artist acts like a medium, a 'Messiah', as Mirjavadov wrote. This description of painting, as a way to look beyond the surface of things we see, makes a link with the poetic theories by García Lorca, who was very close to some aspects of Surrealism is his later works. Lorca argued that poetry is the hidden soul of all things, and the mission of the poet is to bring it to the surface, through poetic creation.[25] The consideration of the artist as a kind of medium and art as a kind of religion or way to go beyond the surface of reality, connect in a very special way with the ideas of Chilean avant-gardist Vicente Huidobro. 'The poet is a little god', he writes in his poem *Arte Poética*. Huidobro is the creator of an avant-garde movement known as *Creacionismo* (art as creation of a new reality), which found its influence in Hispanic poetry.[26]

In his brief 'Declaration' Mirjavadov had written something similar: 'each of my paintings is not the reflection of the world – it is the world itself. In this world I place the sun, the moon, people, horses, the stars in the sky, patterns of carpets and crystals – the manifestations of abundant life are pulsating from my canvases.'[27] Even if Javad Mirjavadov is not directly influenced by Lorca's and Huidobro's theories – although he probably knew them – he is very close to them, as a result of this learning and communion with European avant-garde movements. This means that, from the beginning of his artistic carrier, he separated his artistic ideas and creation from Soviet socialist art, which would make it almost impossible for him to exhibit his paintings and get recognition throughout his career. In the Sixties, in desperation, he burned all the work he had made until that moment, and a decade later he had to bury all the work he had made –mainly collages and sculptures – in his atelier, 'a dacha which used to belong to a teacher of Marxism and Leninism philosophy,' to avoid it being destroyed, as he was accused of being 'anti-Soviet stuff'. 'One day he saw my 'terrible' works and demanded that I removed all that anti-Soviet stuff otherwise he would annihilate them himself. I had neither a workshop nor money to transport it. The Soviet system was an executioner of my art.'[28]

In 1982 he painted one of his masterpieces, *The last supper*, of which I would like to talk briefly. This impressive and large painting (220x160) is beautiful and terrible at the same time; dramatic and carnavalesque, grotesque and frightening, primitive and modern. The painting shows a table surrounded by Jesus and other characters: a donkey (Judas), a demon (a male-coat), a naked woman represented as a primitive female fertility idol without arms, and some musicians. The composition is quite heterodox for the motive the painting shows. Jesus Christ is not in the center of the table but on the left side of the spectator, between the demon (the male-coat), trying to seduce the female idol, and Judas, represented as half human-half donkey and cheering to Christ with a glass of red wine (which may be blood). The glass in Judas's hand is, actually, the central axis of the whole composition. Only Jesus, the Demon and Judas are seated at the table, the rest of the figures: a woman playing a tambourine (it also resembles a piece of bread), and two other musicians, represented as buffoons, are, at the right side, before the table. Although the style of the painting could be described as figurative Impressionism with a lot of ingredients of primitive art, the composition, the chaos, the strong, desperate and passionate character of it, as well as some details, recall *Guernica* (1937) by Pablo Picasso. Other elements, like the bulb hanging from the sky, the demon, which looks like more like a bull than a male-goat, the female figures, suggest that Mirjavadov had Guernica in mind, due to the symbolic meaning of this painting and also because Picasso was one of his masters. In 1985, Luba Mirjavadova, in an essay about *The Last Supper*, explained how the painting was conceived and its meaning.[29] As she writes, the intention of Mirjavadov was not to make a religious painting but 'it had been getting ripe for a long time as a history of Man,' the 'free, strong and kind Man.' Luba makes a connection here with *The Last Supper* painted by Salvador Dalí, arguing that both recreations speak about the same thing: 'the abyss between the spirit and life. Both, in a different way to Leonardo's Last Supper (argues Luba), recreate a lonely Jesus; a man speaking for nobody.

This 'solitude' of Jesus Christ could be taken here as a metaphor of the artist, speaking for almost nobody other than himself or for a few people close to him, and creating in a context that does not understand him. This was also the case for some of artists mentioned above (like Parajanov or Rezaguliyev). Art, therefore, as the artists' self-confession, becomes not only a instrument of expression of a way of life, but is life itself: the only world where those 'non-conformist' artists – misunderstood, isolated, denied and even punished by the official political (and cultural) system – could experience life. 'Art has made me', wrote Javad; because art, for these artists, was not just a product or a process of creation but rather the creator itself.

As Daimi has pointed out, Javad Mirjavadov influenced some of his contemporaries and also generations of young artists after him. One of them is his wife, Luvob Mirjavadova. She also forms part of those Azerbaijani artists opposed through their ideas and their work to the official culture. Although Luba's colorful palette is more vivid and lighter than that of Javad, Mirjavadov's tracks can be found in the same 'expressionist' mode of painting, the powerful brush, some themes like human passions, ontological and metaphysical questions and, mainly, in her apology of creative individuality. Some of her paintings strongly denounce violence against women and human beings in general; and motherhood and the female body are frequent motifs. Movement, strength, passion, a dance of colors – red, blue, yellow, mainly – and forms characterize her whole work. Luba is a clear defender of individual, mainly of the creative and original personality of an artist, beyond any pressure, ideology, censorship or system. She is a passionate defender of the freedom of speech and is strongly opposed to any form of radicalism (ideological, religious or political).[30] This is her main principle, which she applies to her life and her art.

This land is of all of us: Reality and utopia in South Caucasus in the change of the millennium

Artist and art critic Taymus Daimi (2002) differentiates between four periods in the art of Azerbaijan in the last decades of the twentieth century. In his creation of these divisions, Daimi conscientiously connects those cultural periods with the social and political circumstances of the country. From these periods I will focus mainly on the last one, and on some examples of current artistic activity, connecting it with current Armenian art. The first period is called the 'Pre-perestroika stage' (1980-1985), when along with the inertial domination of social realism there are some non-formal artists whose creative works did not fall into the pattern of official art. In this group Daimi alludes to Javad Mirjavadov as one of the most representative artists. The second period, called the 'Perestroika stage' (1985-1990), is the frame for a dynamical cultural life. The Baku Center of Arts was established in this period, as well as non-formal art-groups. Due to this increasing and cultural dynamism, Daimi calls this period the 'Golden Age of modern Azerbaijani art'. A remarkable date is 1988, the year of Garabagh (Armenian-Azerbaijani) conflict and the beginning of the national liberation movement for the political independence of Azerbaijan. These events turned the public attention to a socio-political level, but regardless of unfavorable conditions the art kept on developing. The declaration of the state of independence had actualized the problem of national self-identification: 'Who are we? Where are our roots?' After the collapse of Soviet cultural and ideological space, the Azerbaijani intellectual elite began to show an interest in revealing their own beginnings. The 'Peyker' art-group was founded in this period (with artists like Sanan Gurbanov, Elchin Aslanov, Adalat Bayramov, Elchin Mamedov and Mazahir Afshar), trying to solve those problems.[31] The third period is a 'stage of postcolonial independency' (1990-2000), in which Daimi includes himself at the beginning of his artistic activity. This decade is characterized by a deep crisis in Azerbaijani art, framed by a 'postcolonial transition period'. Daimi underlines here two main problems: economic collapse and conservatism in the educational system, and stereotypes of perception; these would be the main causes for deficient development in new creative forms (like video-art and new technologies art). Artistic activity in that period was mainly focused around organization of the international symposiums, which made it possible to fight against the information blockade (the result of the cultural isolation of Azerbaijan due to armed conflict with the neighboring country). In 1997, the Center of Modern Culture 'ARTS etc.' was inaugurated in Baku, and in the same year the 'Labyrinth' group was established (Sana Aleskerov, Sabina Shihlinskaya, Ujal Akhverdiyev, Elnur Babayev, Elena Akhverdiyeva, Eliyar Alimirzoyev, Guseyn Akhverdiyev, Ayten Rzakuliyeva, Shahin Shihaliyev, Museyib Amirov, Zakir Guseynov). Actions organized by the Labyrinth group were not so much of artistic and aesthetic meaning, but rather of socio-cultural meaning aimed at 'art-diagnostics of ecosphere of the region we live in'. After the collapse of USSR and the breakdown of economic structures of the society, Baku city and nearby places became ecologically dangerous zones, the so-called 'desolation places': trash dumps, deserted plants, empty hangars, etc.[32] Projects of the Labyrinth group, for instance, being nominally of 'land-art nature', were in fact actualizing exactly those social aspects and canalizing the public attention to the problem of inhabiting the ecologically unfavorable spaces. The lack of both a cultural and artistic frame and an appropriate, healthy and habitable physical space leads Daimi to refer to the 1990s as the period of 'living in non-existing context'.

Finally, Daimi distinguishes a 'stage of relative stabilization/revival' (from 2000 to the present). In spite of all collisions of the 'transition period', by the beginning of the third millennium the situation in Azerbaijani modern art had improved gradually, also due to joining the Council of Europe in 2000. Numerous European (political, social and cultural) organizations have been working in connection with Azerbaijani artists and organizations to help to reconstruct the socio-cultural landscape of the region. In 2000, the Academy of Arts was also created, which became the place for a new generation of young artists, free of Soviet cultural program stereotypes. But, in spite of this, Daimi complains that on a global scale, due to a lack of modern art infrastructure, Azerbaijan is still an 'outsider of world artistic process'. The author's conclusion is that in a time of 'religious and political discrepancies, modern culture appears as almost the only model of international (cultural) collaboration'; and it should be the instrument to allow Azerbaijan (and Caucasus) to realize a mission of unifying West and East (and North and South), establishing a closer dialogue with representatives of Oriental and Asian geocultural mentalities, in order to prevent a 'collision of the civilizations'.[33]

This kind of ideal or recommendation is, in fact, the motor for a great part of the current artistic and cultural activity in Armenia and Azerbaijan. A lot of young artists try, on one side, to reflect and denounce the social, religious and political situation, and ecological and environment problems, and, on the other side, to create a bridge between artists of other Caucasian countries, through artistic collaboration.

One of these artists is the Azeri social-documentary photographer Rena Effendi. Her work focuses on themes of urbanization, post-conflict societies, and the oil industry's effects on people's lives. Her photos show different scenes, people and landscapes of Azerbaijan and other surrounding countries. A good example of this motivation is a six-year study along 1,700 kilometers oil pipeline through Georgia and Turkey, where she has collected stories along the way. Her camera focuses mainly on women and children. In several interviews she has expressed her motivation for the themes she chooses. In the following fragment below, she expresses her need to document the drastic changes in Baku as a result of the political and economic transformations of the last years:

> I began my first social documentary project by walking the streets of the neighborhood I was living in. It was changing every day in front of me with new high-rise buildings replacing the old slums. People were being re-located, the face of the city was changing rapidly, it's bastion of traditional culture collapsing. I decided to document these changes. I took portraits of residents in the slums that were losing their houses to a money-laundering, oil fueled construction boom. These portraits are now a gallery of faces that symbolize my city's urban nightmare. Baku has become an unmanageable city with traffic jams and air thick with pollution and cement dust. This story leaded me to other stories in my way of trying to understand the developments in my country. Yes, you can say that it is a political attitude. People ask: why don't you go and take pictures of beautiful things, mountains, waterfalls and the rural landscape? Why do you always see the bad side of things? Usually I take pictures of things that bother me. There has to be something that kicks me out of bed, and it's usually not beautiful waterfalls that do it. I am not putting together a tourist book of my country. It's a very personal view of things that bite me. I want to bite them back with my photographs.[34]

Another Azerbaijani artist who is concerned with the political and social context in South Caucasus is the writer Ali Akbar. His last novel is a good example of it. *Artush and Zaur*, published in Baku in 2009, is the story of a romance between two, Armenian and Azeri, men. When I met him in Baku in 2007, he told me he was writing a novel about two homosexuals and he was sure its reception would be very polemic. It has been so. As several reviews show, the novel has been controversial, having sold out in some bookshops, but with other vendors having to stop selling it due to the pressure of religious customers. According to Akbar, he has 'started a war against two major stereotypes' in Azerbaijan: Armenians and homosexuals.[35] Akbar's plot is straightforward: Artush, an Armenian, and Zaur, an Azeri, become attracted to one another as schoolboys in Baku, but are separated as violence breaks out between their countries over the disputed territory of Nagorno-Karabakh. Zaur is left wandering the streets of Baku, mourning the loss of Artush to Armenia. *Artush and Zaur* is part of an Azeri tradition of using literature to challenge political reality. For some people the book's title echoes the 1937 Azeri novel *Ali and Nino: a love story*, by Kurban Said, in which an Azerbaijani man falls in love with a Georgian princess.[36] Ali Akbar is one of those artists using his work as an instrument to denounce war and Azerbaijani political and social problems. Since his older brother died in the Karabak war, he argues to be in the right of writing about the absurdity of war.[37] Ali Akbar is a member of the artist and civil organization 'South Caucasus Center for Peace-Making Initiatives,' established in Yerevan and made up of participating artists from Azerbaijan, Armenia, Georgia, South Osetia and Nagorno Karabakh. The chair of the organization, also one of the founders, is the theatre director and writer Georgy Vanyan. The organization brings artists of those countries together by organizing several meetings and cultural activities. They claim an alternative concept of civil dialogue. As Vanyan expresses in an interview: 'our society (Armenia) is tired, exhausted by years, centuries old aiming of claims from its neighbors, exhausted by unnatural opposition of itself to the entire world, exhausted by obsession to its groundless and imaginary messianism.'[38]

Conclusion

This paper has tried to show a (very general) panoramic of some of the (non-official) art in Armenia and Azerbaijan from the last part of the twentieth century until now. In my opinion, what the reviewed artists have in common, along with their own peculiarities, is, on the one side a 'non conformist' attitude with established cultural and artistic production and with the political and social system, and the fact that they directly affront the problems of their respective countries in their works. For these artists, art and culture is not only a way of expressing themselves, even a way of life, but is also the alternative for a political and civil dialogue to call for understanding, collaboration and peace among South Caucasus cultures and also with East and West Europe.

This is the position of the paintings of Javad and Luba Mirjavadov, the photography of Rena, the books of Ali Akbar or the cinema of Sergei Parajanov. The work of these artists goes beyond any physical or political border, showing that free artistic creation is temporary and universal. Engaged and free of any political dictates, an important part of contemporary modern Caucasian art reflect its closest reality at the same time that it tries to connect with the international cultural world, with other artists. Beyond time and space, beyond any ideology and belief and beyond any form of war, conflict, prejudices or frontiers. Uniting, through artistic creation, different cultures, traditions and way of expression, but moved by the same love for life, for people and for art. Under the same moon; under the same sky.

Notes

1   Vahabova, D. (2005). *The known as unknown.* Catalogue. Baku: Yeni Qaleyera.
2   Barthes, R. (1997). *El grado cero de la escritura.* Madrid: Siglo XXI.
3   Sánchez Trigueros, A. ed. (1996). *Sociología de la literatura.* Madrid: Síntesis.
4   Vahabova, op cit., p.7.
5   Vahabova, op cit., p.7.
6   Vahabova, op cit., p.19.
7   Daimi, T. (2002). Azerbaijan contemporary fine art of the end of II and beginning of III millennium. http://www.artdaimi.com/eng/text/esse3.html; Samadoglu, V. (1998). The Sixties: a roadmap to independence. http://azer.com/aiweb/categories/magazine/61_folder/61_articles/61_sixties.html
8   Vahabova, op cit., p.8.
9   Barthes, R. (1997). *El grado cero de la escritura.* Madrid: Siglo XXI.
10 Vahabova, op cit., p.7.
11 Daimi, T. (2002). Azerbaijan contemporary fine art of the end of II and beginning of III millennium. On the artist's site: http://www.artdaimi.com/eng/text/esse3.html

12 Kouymjian, D. (1995). Art in Exile: Armenian Artists of the Ninteenth & Twentieth Century. http://armenianstudies.csufresno.edu/faculty/kouymjian/articles/exile.htm

13 Daimi, T. (2002). Azerbaijan contemporary fine art of the end of II and beginning of III millennium. http://www.artdaimi.com/eng/text/esse3.html

14 This essay was published under the title 'Künstler in der Diaspora,' as part of the book-catalogue: Armenien. Wiederentdeckung einer alten Kulturlandschaft, an exhibit in the Museum Bochum, Bochum, 1995, pp. 363-366.

15 Kouymjian, D. (1995). Art in Exile: Armenian Artists of the Ninteenth & Twentieth Century. http://armenianstudies.csufresno.edu/faculty/kouymjian/articles/exile.htm

16 Ibid.

17 Ibid.

18 Ibid.

19 Patterson, J. (2002). Art As Memory: Alakbar Rezaguliyev's Prints of Azerbaijan.
http://azer.com/aiweb/categories/magazine/ai103_folder/103_articles/103_rezaguiyev.html

20 Sources: Ron Holloway. An Interview With Parajanov. http://www.kinema.uwaterloo.ca/hollo961.htm and also the artist's official site: www.parajanov.com

21 Daimi, op cit.

22 Vahabova, op cit., p. 28-32.

23 Mirjavadova, L. (2002). *Javad*. Baku: Mirjavadova. This book, with a sample of the painter's pictures, writings and notes, as well as some art critics' comments, was edited as a private, non-commercial, publication by the wife of Javad, Luba Mirjavadova, since she is fully dedicated to spreading Mirjavadov's work. She received neither institutional nor economical support to produce this collection. I got one exemplar from the artist herself. There are no pages number in the edition.

24 Breton, A. (1924). *Le Manifeste du Surréalisme*.

25 García Lorca, F. (1918). Prologue to *Impresiones y Paisajes*.

26 Huidobro, V. (1916). 'Arte Poética' and 'Creacionismo'. In Costa, René (ed.). 1996. *Vicente Huidobro. Poesía y Poética, 1911-1948. Antología*. Madrid: Alianza.

27 Mirjavadova, op cit.

28 Mirjavadova, op cit.

29 Mirjavadova, op cit.

30 One of her paintings is dedicated to Dutch filmmaker Theo van Gogh, who was murdered by a Muslim fundamentalist in November 2004. Luba's moti-

vation to make this painting was a strong and clear defense of the freedom of speech. I still remember her excited words: 'Nobody has the right to murder any artist, any person, for saying what they feel. Nobody!'

31 Daimi, op cit.
32 Daimi, op cit.
33 Daimi, op cit.
34 Quilici, R. (2006). Interview de Rena Effendi photojournaliste, *Le Monde*, 25 November 2006. http://noravr.blog.lemonde.fr/2006/11/25/interview-de-rena-effendi-photojournaliste/
35 Khadija, I. (2009). Controversial Azeri Novel Takes On Double Taboos. March 09-2009. http://www.rferl.org/content/Controversial_Azeri_Novel_Takes_On_Double_Taboos/1506890.html
36 Ibid.
37 Kester, Sacha, (2009). 'Liefde tussen twee mannen schokt Kaukasus.' *Volkskrant*, 12 maart 2009
http://www.volkskrant.nl/buitenland/article1163171.ece/Liefde_tussen_twee_mannen_schokt_Kaukasus
38 Kasanov, A. (2009). Interview with Georgi Vanyan. Day. AZ, April 2009. http://day.az/news/armenia/155033.html

List of Contributors

Max Bader is a doctoral candidate at the Department of European Studies of the University of Amsterdam. Bader is an expert on the former Soviet Union and has conducted extensive research on democracy promotion in Georgia and Ukraine.

Françoise Companjen is affiliated to the Vrije Universiteit Amsterdam, Faculty of Social Sciences as a Senior Lecturer. She is specialized in civil society and democracy building in the South Caucasus. She organizes debates for Caucasus Interconnect and comments on the South Caucasus for Dutch radio and TV.

René Does is affiliated to the Department of European Studies of the University of Amsterdam as a scientific editor. He is a specialist on current affairs in the former Soviet Union.

Charlotte Hille is affiliated to the Department of Political Science University of Amsterdam as an Assistant Professor. She is specialized in state building and conflict resolution in the Caucasus. Earlier she worked as policy advisor for the Dutch Ministry of Foreign Affairs and as senior policy advisor to the Deputy Minister of Social Affairs.

Marc Jansen is affiliated to the Department of European Studies at the University of Amsterdam. He is a historian, teaches Russian and East European Studies, and publishes books and articles on Russian and Soviet history and politics, including the history and politics of the Caucasus.

Micha Kemper is Chair of Eastern European Studies at the Department of European Studies at the University of Amsterdam. He is specialized in Islam in Central Asia and the Caucasus.

László Marácz is affiliated to the Department of European Studies at the University of Amsterdam. He is a specialist on Hungarian linguistics, the history of Eastern European and actual political developments in Eastern Europe and coordinates within the same department an MA program on European Union policy.

Eva Navarro Martínez is affiliated to the Department of Audiovisual Communication and Marketing of the University of Valladolid, Campus of Segovia as an Assistant Professor. She is a specialist on Theory of Culture and Interrelations on Literature and Media and is currently working on the Media Literacy in Castilla León project.

Oliver Reisner holds a position as a project manager at the European Union Delegation to Georgia and regularly publishes on Georgia's history and nation building. Before that he worked as a human rights program manager for World Vision in Georgia on a civic integration project and he established an MA program 'Central Asia /Caucasus' at the Department for Central Asian Studies at the Humboldt University in Berlin.

Lia Versteegh is affiliated to the Department of European Studies at the University of Amsterdam as a legal scholar. Her research topics are European law and comparative law on the subjects of civil society, human rights, minorities and equality.

For Product Safety Concerns and Information please contact our EU
representative GPSR@taylorandfrancis.com
Taylor & Francis Verlag GmbH, Kaufingerstraße 24, 80331 München, Germany